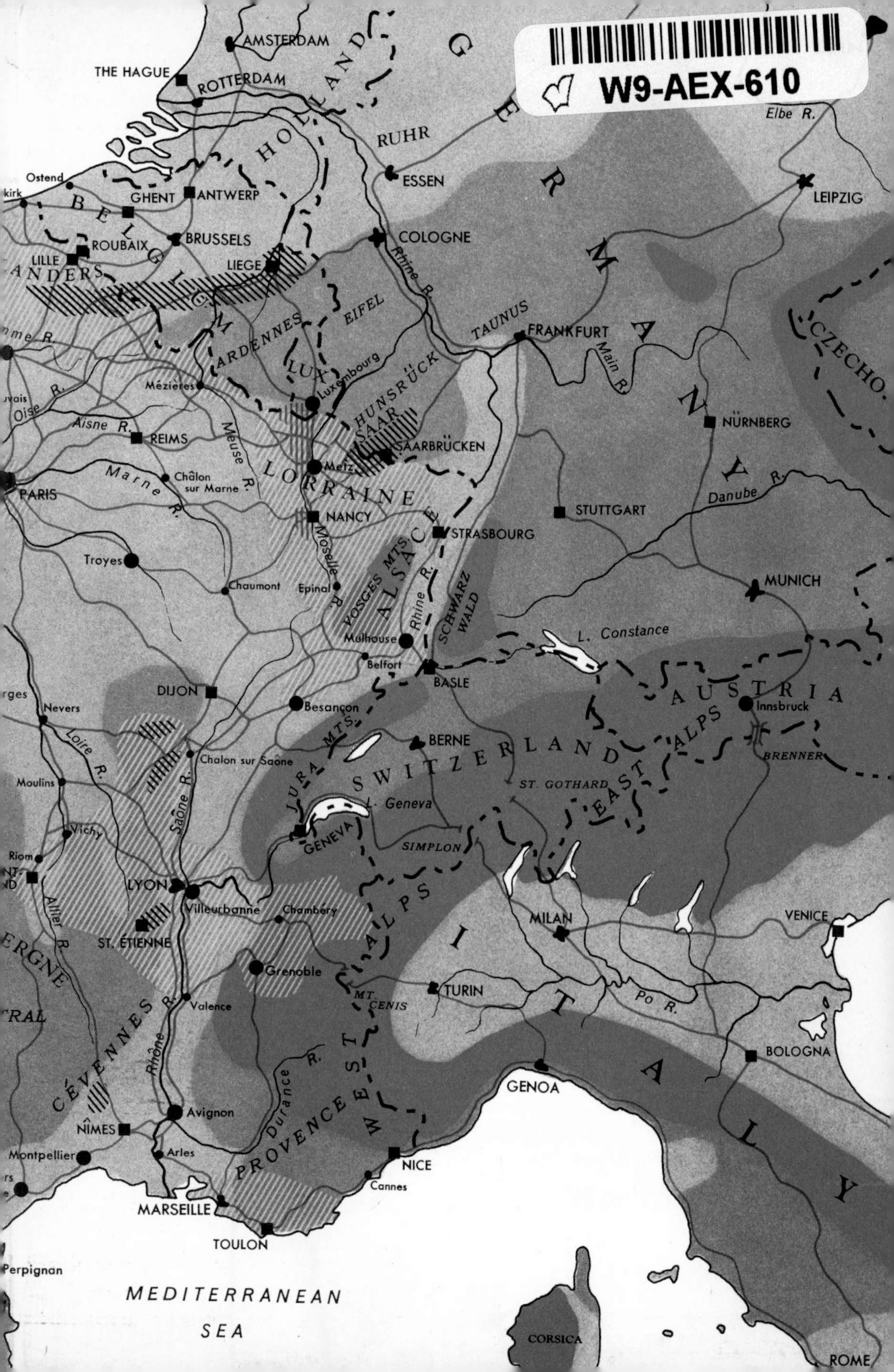
AMSTERDAM
THE HAGUE
ROTTERDAM
HOLLAND
GERMANY
RUHR
ESSEN
Elbe R.
LEIPZIG
Ostend
GHENT
ANTWERP
BELGIUM
ROUBAIX
BRUSSELS
LILLE
LIEGE
COLOGNE
Rhine R.
EIFEL
ARDENNES
TAUNUS
FRANKFURT
Main R.
CZECHO.
LUX.
Luxembourg
HUNSRÜCK
Mézieres
Oise R.
Aisne R.
REIMS
Meuse R.
SAAR
SAARBRÜCKEN
NÜRNBERG
Marne R.
Châlon sur Marne
PARIS
Metz
LORRAINE
NANCY
Moselle R.
STUTTGART
Danube R.
STRASBOURG
ALSACE
VOSGES MTS.
SCHWARZ WALD
Troyes
Chaumont
Epinal
MUNICH
Mulhouse
L. Constance
Belfort
BASLE
AUSTRIA
DIJON
Besançon
Innsbruck
Nevers
JURA MTS.
BERNE
Loire R.
Chalon sur Saône
SWITZERLAND
EAST ALPS
BRENNER
Moulins
Saône R.
ST. GOTHARD
L. Geneva
Vichy
GENEVA
SIMPLON
Riom
LYON
Villeurbanne
ALPS
Allier R.
Chambéry
MILAN
VENICE
ST. ÉTIENNE
Grenoble
TURIN
Po R.
Valence
MT. CENIS
CÉVENNES
Rhône R.
Durance R.
WEST
BOLOGNA
ITALY
GENOA
Avignon
PROVENCE
NÎMES
Arles
Montpellier
NICE
Cannes
MARSEILLE
TOULON
Perpignan
MEDITERRANEAN SEA
CORSICA
ROME

The United States and France

THE AMERICAN FOREIGN POLICY LIBRARY

SUMNER WELLES, EDITOR

DONALD C. MCKAY, ASSOCIATE EDITOR

The United States and Britain
BY CRANE BRINTON

The United States and the Near East
BY E. A. SPEISER

The United States and the Caribbean
BY DEXTER PERKINS

The United States and Russia
BY VERA MICHELES DEAN

The United States and South America
The Northern Republics
BY ARTHUR P. WHITAKER

The United States and China
BY JOHN KING FAIRBANK

The United States and Scandinavia
BY FRANKLIN D. SCOTT

The United States and Japan
BY EDWIN O. REISCHAUER

The United States and France
BY DONALD C. MCKAY

THE UNITED STATES AND *France*

By

Donald C. McKay

HARVARD UNIVERSITY PRESS
Cambridge, Massachusetts
1951

Distributed in Great Britain by
GEOFFREY CUMBERLEGE
OXFORD UNIVERSITY PRESS
LONDON

MAPS PREPARED UNDER THE CARTOGRAPHIC DIRECTION
OF ARTHUR H. ROBINSON

PRINTED IN THE UNITED STATES OF AMERICA

For Ruth

CONTENTS

INTRODUCTION, *by the Honorable Sumner Welles* ix

AUTHOR'S PREFACE xv

1. Common Interests 1

2. The Land 7
   1. Where Is France? 8
   2. How Big Is France? 10
   3. How Coherent Is France? 11
   4. How Rich Is France? 15
   5. How Strong Is France? 18

3. The People 20
   1. The Population as a Whole 20
   2. Class Structure 25
   3. Some Characteristics of the French 35

4. Government 51
   1. Local Government 52
   2. The Central Administration 54
   3. The Government of the Third Republic 58

5. Two Centuries of Franco-American Relations (to 1939) 74
   1. Colonial America and France 76
   2. France and the American Revolution 77
   3. The French Revolution 81
   4. Relations with Napoleon 83
   5. Aftermath of the Napoleonic Wars 85
   6. The Revolutions of the Nineteenth Century 88
   7. Napoleon III and Mexico 89
   8. Relations with the Third Republic 91
   9. Coöperation in World War I 95
   10. Disillusionment of the Twenties 98
   11. Relations in the Thirties 105

6. Defeat, Occupation, Liberation—in Perspective 106
1. The Debacle of 1940 110
2. The Problem of the Armistice 116
3. The United States and Vichy 121
4. The Nature of the Resistance 125
5. The United States and de Gaulle 132

7. Economic Problems 137
1. Agriculture 137
2. Industry 142
3. World War II 148
4. Post-Liberation Problems 150
5. Organized Labor 172

8. Political Problems 179
1. The Third Force 181
2. The Extremes 198

9. France Overseas 217
1. What Overseas France Includes 218
2. French Colonial Policy 222
3. Post-Liberation Problems 228
4. The French in Indochina 231

10. The International Scene: France and the United States 245
1. France in the Postwar World 245
2. The United States in the Postwar World 258
3. Postscript, September 1950 273

APPENDIX I. Some Vital Facts about France. Complied by Aaron Noland 285

APPENDIX II. Suggested Reading 310

INDEX 321

MAPS

France in the Atlantic Community 9
The French Union 220

INTRODUCTION

While I am sure that this volume, *France and the United States*, by Donald C. McKay, will prove to be of enduring value because of its historical significance, because of its convincing demonstration of what France means to Western civilization, and because of its exceptionally perceptive analysis of the relations between the two countries, its initial publication could hardly have taken place at a more opportune time.

In this year of 1951 the free peoples are passing through what may well prove to be the period that will determine whether the world is to have peace or war. The course of aggressive expansion that is being pursued by the Soviet dictatorship, in its manifestations in Europe, in the Near East and in Asia, not only jeopardizes the creation of that effective form of collective security which was one of the major objectives sought by the American people in the last war, but jeopardizes equally the independence and the integrity of all other nations. By the policies they have adopted since 1946, and by the international agreements in which the United States has recently participated, the American people have now made it plain that they recognize that the freedom and security of Western Europe are essential to their own security. The Atlantic Defense Pact is the logical result of this wholly novel development in American foreign policy.

Without the wholehearted coöperation of France in the effort to attain the objectives sought in the Atlantic Defense Pact, Great Britain and the other nations of the Atlantic community could not succeed in saving Western Europe from Soviet domination. For France has long been and is today more than ever before the keystone in the arch of Western European security.

From the standpoint of the highest interests of Western Europe as well as of those of the United States nothing could, consequently, be more deplorable than the series of recurrent misunderstandings which have marred Franco-American relations since the Second World War.

We Americans seem all too prone to forget the tragedies that France has suffered since 1914. We fail to remember that at the close of the First World War one out of every five adult Frenchmen had either died in battle or had been gravely wounded. We are apt to ignore the equally significant fact that as a result of the Second World War and the protracted German occupation not only was France bled white, but the morale of the French people suffered a blow which must inevitably prove to have far-reaching consequences.

Due in part to the assistance rendered them through the Marshall Plan, but due as well to their own tireless efforts, the economy of the French people is now convalescent. The political stability of France has recently become greatly enhanced. But every gain won for French Democracy and for France's rehabilitation has been achieved in the face of the persistent attempt of a strong Communist minority under Moscow's orders to disrupt the entire political, social, and economic structure of the nation.

As former Prime Minister Pleven said not long ago when he visited the United States, it is only natural for peoples with differing historical backgrounds to have occasional differences of view as to the methods by which their common objectives should be sought. But at a moment of supreme crisis such as this, such differences of view between traditionally friendly peoples must necessarily be harmonized in the interest of their common safety.

In recent years the French people have only too frequently had reason to wonder whether their American friends and allies had not in truth forgotten the history of the past forty years and had not overlooked all of the immense sacrifices that the French people had made for the preservation of Western democracy. They have heard many influential Americans engage in bitter recriminations against them and their democratic governments because they were unwilling to subscribe without further ado to an American proposal to rearm Germany before France had received any practical guaranties that she would be safeguarded against future German aggression. They remembered, if their American critics did not, that only five years before, the victorious allies had proclaimed that "Germany must be deprived of the power to rearm."

And although France is now devoting more than 28 per cent of her total budget for defense, is providing for the creation of a continental army which will be considerably larger than that which she possessed in 1939, and is draining her manpower and her resources to the utmost in order to combat the Communist attempt to extend the Red dominion through Indochina over the rest of Southeast Asia, the French have also been obliged to hear other influential Americans complain that France is not doing her share in Korea, that France is making no real attempt to provide for her own self-defense, and urge that no further American assistance be given until and unless the views of these critics as to what France should do are fully met.

It is, of course, true that in the early period after Germany's defeat a large segment of French public opinion maintained that France during the postwar crisis should pursue a policy of "neutralism." It was a very human and a very natural reaction to the bitter memories of what the French people had suffered in 1940 and to the equally bitter memories of what they had undergone during the years of German occupation. It was as fundamentally mistaken a concept as that of our own American isolationists when they delude themselves that the United States can be isolated from war if a new war should break out.

Yet the average Frenchman, outside of the Communist Party, has now abandoned that fallacious political philosophy. We are witnessing not only an economic and a political but also a moral renaissance in France. The Schuman Plan, which is the most constructive initiative that any government has yet proposed in behalf of European peace and of European unity, represented to French public opinion evidence that France was resuming a position of enlightened leadership in international councils. And the implementation of the Atlantic Defense Pact, with the establishment of General Eisenhower's headquarters in Versailles, has given the French new and concrete assurance that American armed support has become a reality, in sharp distinction to the disillusionment that they had suffered in 1920.

Except for the English-speaking countries, no nation since the time of the French Revolution has done more than France to advance the cause of individual liberty and the liberation of the human spirit. These values still remain supreme in the French manner of being.

There was a story current in Paris when I was there a few months ago which purported to relate a conversation between Stalin and the diplomatic representative in Moscow of a small European country, which this diplomat had in turn reported to the French Foreign Office. Stalin was alleged to have said that he could not understand why it was that even after five years of German occupation French culture and French thought had been so little changed. He added grimly that five years of Soviet occupation would bring about very different results. It is not pleasant to conceive of all that which French culture means in Western civilization obliterated under the relentless heel of Soviet regimentation.

I believe that the French are today as aware as we that if the kind of life they wish to live is threatened they must fight to preserve it. If differences and misunderstandings between France and the United States are permitted to drive a real wedge between the two peoples, not only would the effort of the United States to defend herself be gravely impeded, but the attempt of Western Europe to preserve its freedom might well prove hopeless.

It is because the American people are up against these basic realities of international life in the world of today that I believe

Professor McKay's book to be so outstandingly valuable at this time.

He has necessarily written his book as an American for the benefit of American public opinion. But he has written it as an American who truly knows France, and who justly appraises what France represents in the alliance of free peoples. He has written it with peculiar authority and with exceptional factual precision.

I am confident that this book will do much to help the American people better to understand France's problems realistically. I further believe it will remove many of the misconceptions on our part which have so lamentably beclouded Franco-American relations in recent years.

Sumner Welles

AUTHOR'S PREFACE

Every book is a shared enterprise, and no writer can pretend to know the subtle topography of his obligations. The list of readings in Appendix II indicates only a few of the considerable body of printed materials I have used. To name them here would only embarrass the numerous and coöperative American and French officials whom I have consulted. And it would be quite futile to try to identify those who have contributed over the years to my understanding of the French scene, imperfect and challenging as that must always remain. There are those, however, who have been so directly helpful to this task that I should like to express to them a special sense of obligation.

My editor, Sumner Welles, has brought his wide and exact knowledge, both of history and of the diplomacy of the past decades, to the criticism of these chapters. His unfailing courtesy and fundamental tolerance of views that differ with his own have made this coöperation a source of deep satisfaction to me.

Georges Bourgin, former Director of the Archives Nationales, Albert Léon Guérard, and Crane Brinton gave me detailed, expert, and most helpful criticism of the whole manuscript, as did also Howard Mumford Jones, who has enjoyed a special relationship to this series from the beginning. Paul Mus, Professor at the *Collège de France* and one of the most detached French critics of Indochina, gave me extended and candid comments on Chapter 9; Dexter Perkins made most helpful criticisms on Chapter 5; my colleague, Alexander Gerschenkron, on Chapter 7. Richard H. Heindel gave me extensive suggestions when I was preparing Chapter 5. To my colleague, John E. Sawyer, I am indebted both for his criticism of the manuscript, based on an extraordinary knowledge of French developments in recent years, and for the stimulating ideas which he has injected into our numerous conversations and which here appear unblushingly unacknowledged. My collaborator in all problems touching this series, Thomas J. Wilson, the Director of the Harvard University Press, has brought his sure judgment to bear on a variety of problems touching the manuscript. I am sure that if I had accepted more of the suggestions offered by my critics, this would have been a better book. For the text as it stands I am, of course, solely responsible.

Professor Aaron Noland, who was my research assistant for a period of three years, compiled Appendix I, and most skillfully and energetically gathered materials for various aspects of the book. He was succeeded by Alvin D. Coox, who helpfully carried on for the succeeding year. My office staff has been exceedingly patient in the preparation of the manuscript in the midst of more pressing duties—Elizabeth C. MacLeod and her assistants, Janet A. Johnson, Alice Jeghelian, and Mary Louise Carroll.

In the case of this volume, as in that of others in *The American Foreign Policy Library*, I am most happy to acknowledge the understanding and consistent coöperation of the various members of the staff of the Harvard University Press, and in this instance, particularly the care with which Marion L. Hawkes has seen the manuscript through the copy-editing stage.

The Committee on Research in the Social Sciences at Harvard made available to me a research sum remaining from a prewar allocation, and I received also generous grants from the Clark and Milton Funds, particularly in connection with trips to France in 1947, 1949, and 1950.

Finally, my wife, Ruth Capers McKay, has listened patiently

to the discussion of the innumerable problems involved in a book of this kind, some of which I am sure were of peripheral interest to her, has read the manuscript in its variant forms, and has been unusually candid in her dissection of it.

Donald C. McKay

Cambridge
January 29, 1951

1. Common Interests

The strongest single link between the United States and France is their joint possession of free institutions deeply anchored in the traditions of the Christian civilization of the West. Men have been free at few times and for short intervals during the long record of history. When freedom is imperiled as it now is, threatened even with imminent destruction, men sense far more acutely the values of that heritage. The precariousness of possession lends a poignancy to their fears for its loss. And the meaning of that loss is starkly evident to all who scrutinize those societies on which night has already descended.

To the tradition of freedom in the West both French and Americans have richly contributed, in ideas and in experience. This is a broad and complicated story into which we cannot enter here. In a recent statement to a French parliamentary committee, Milton Katz, United States Special Representative in Europe, in charge of the Economic Coöperation Administration, caught the central quality of American democracy and its relation to Europe when he said:

> You have heard of the American dream, the dream that each individual should have the opportunity to realize to the full his potentialities for growth as a human being. In a sense, of course, this is a universal dream. That is, it has been the dream of individual men and women the world over. But America constitutes the first national society in which this universal dream of individuals has been an organic part of the national history and sense of purpose.
>
> The American understands in his bones that this dream is the essence of democracy. He understands that democracy at its core

is a spiritual testament. He feels an obligation to vindicate this testament for all men. He feels this obligation with particular force toward the people of that ancient European civilization in which he finds his moral roots.

Both French and Americans are deeply committed to the preservation of freedom in the West. If freedom were to disappear in Europe, we Americans should find ourselves alone, still perhaps possessed of free institutions, but enjoying a kind of ironical and precarious isolation in the midst of our unfree and hostile neighbors beyond the Atlantic, an isolation that would drive us almost certainly to adopt measures menacing the very institutions we would preserve—far-reaching internal controls, massive taxation, large standing armed forces.

France has a second, and not unconnected, interest for Americans. Over the centuries French civilization has been more completely at the center of the development of the West than that of any other single society. There were long periods—such as the age of Louis XIV—when this predominance was not only clear but universally accepted. There have been other periods, such as the late nineteenth century, when the total impact of France has been somewhat less and when many of her ideas have taken effective form only beyond her borders; but even in these periods the sum of her intellectual influence has been very great.

The special position of Paris is an index of the magnitude of this influence. It has long been the intellectual capital of the world, and one of the surest indications of this is the variety and importance of the work which has been accomplished there by intellectuals from other countries.* As one sits in the Gardens of the Luxembourg—which have themselves figured so often and so variously in French literature—one justly asks whether any other plot of land has contributed so much to the

* Its great importance as a student center since the Middle Ages needs no emphasis. More than 5000 American students a year were visiting Paris in the late twenties—"doubtless the greatest student migration in history . . ." (Francis Miller and Helen Hill, *The Giant of the Western World* [New York, 1930], p. 78).

intellectual capital of the West as that within a three-mile radius of this most characteristic French setting. Paris is an international city in the full sense of the word, a possession not merely of the French but of all men to whom the western tradition is vital. Both the Germans and the Allies spared it during the last war as they did not spare Florence or Munich.

Over the centuries, then, France has been the great fabricator of ideas. We have seen these ideas tightly woven into the pattern of our political heritage. They have left a heavy impress on American culture, as the magistral study of Howard Mumford Jones has shown.* The discoveries of Frenchmen lie in many cases at the base of our great technological and economic advances. French names are there as landmarks of scientific discovery in the past two centuries—Lagrange, Laplace, Leverrier, Poincaré in mathematics and astronomy; Lavoisier, Ampère, the Curies, the Joliot-Curies in chemistry and physics; Cuvier, Lamarck, Claude Bernard, Pasteur in the biological and medical sciences. In late 1947, Dr. Karl Compton, then President of the Massachusetts Institute of Technology, could state that the American wartime achievement in the field of atomic power rested on a rough dozen fundamental ideas, some nine or ten of which came from Europe, including the original discoveries of radioactivity and nuclear fission.

Here again the French have been important contributors. Radioactivity was the discovery of A. H. Becquerel in 1896, and the latter's discoveries were carried further by Pierre and Marie Curie. Frederic Joliot and Irene Curie in 1932 participated in the discoveries leading to our knowledge of the neutron, and in 1934 they discovered "artificial radioactivity." In 1939 Joliot was one of those who did important work on the problem of fission. All of the above were winners of the Nobel Prize.

If France were to pass behind the iron curtain, the blight of totalitarianism would fall upon her intellectual life, and even to such ideas as she did develop we would have precarious ac-

* *America and French Culture, 1750–1848* (Chapel Hill, 1927).

cess. The effect on the future development of the United States of the elimination of France—and western Europe—as a source of general ideas and fundamental discoveries is a subject which deserves our most urgent and probing thought.

France and the United States have long had an important community of economic interest. Since the Great Depression the French have had serious reservations as to the capacity of Americans to manage their economy successfully, and this preoccupation has been a particularly important one since Liberation, when the United States has become an even larger factor in world economic stability. The United States in turn has been deeply interested in the recovery of French industry and trade, because we are exporters and seek reviving markets, because a strong American economy is related to a strong European economy, and because an economically healthy Europe involves a stable France, which in the twenties was fourth among the trading nations of the world. Even in the restricted terms of direct trade with France, we have a substantial interest. In 1938, for instance, France purchased more from the United States, by 60 per cent, than from any other country; 1938 was undoubtedly an abnormal year, but we find that as early as 1854 the United States was second of the suppliers of France, and that in 1909 and again in 1938, she was our fourth best customer. American investments in France have also been substantial: in 1938 "direct investments," that is, those which conferred substantial or complete control of management, totaled about $117,000,000.

On a purely economic level, the United States could do without France, could indeed shut itself within a Chinese tariff wall and build up an independent economy—with tensions, no doubt, and probably with important sacrifices of freedom. But the postwar situation has posed the problem of our economic interest in France on a much wider base. In the Marshall Plan we have proposed to use economic means for a political end: to rob communism of its appeal to men made desperate by want. The core of Secretary Marshall's statement at Harvard in June 1947 states the case: "Our policy is directed not against any country or doctrine but against hunger, poverty, desperation, and chaos. Its purpose should be the revival of a working economy in the world so as to permit the emergence of political and social conditions in which free institutions can exist." This brings us to the common security concerns of the two countries, closely related to the three interests we have been discussing and recently posed in a form of brutal urgency.

Usually, but by no means invariably, independent states pursue their own interests, and coöperate only when these interests are parallel or mergent. The interests of France and the United States have been parallel or mergent at various times in their history: during the American Revolution, when French aid made it possible for us to achieve our freedom; during most, but not all, of the twentieth century, when American aid twice tipped the scales of victory in Europe. But it will do no service to either country to conceal the fact that our relations have also been bad for considerable periods.

The majority of both Americans and Frenchmen believe that our security interests are mergent at the present time, just as they did in World Wars I and II. For Americans the problem is the very old one—the British faced it first in earlier centuries—as to whether we can safely allow Europe to pass under the control of a single hostile power. Most Americans have now resolved that question in a clear negative and are prepared for a vast and accelerated effort to build up such strength in western Europe that the Soviets will hesitate to strike. This is basically a policy of peace. But if it comes to war, the French argue that they must be part of a coalition able to prevent a new occupation and one of so inevitably ruthless a character that their society would be unrecognizably disfigured. And it has been the consistent view of American policy that the loss of Europe would place this country in a position of acute jeopardy.

But these views are by no means shared by all men in either

country. In France the isolationists are represented in particular by that curious group of "neutralists" who appear to believe that in a Soviet-American conflict their country can somehow contrive to stand aside. In the United States the last war had notably quieted isolationism in this country, but the dangerous turn of events in the Far East has precipitated a sharp revival. These neo-isolationists, although naturally varying in view, go so far as to be willing to write off Europe and Asia and to have the United States take a stand alone against a hostile Eurasia.

The great debate between these two groups is well under way as these words are written, and we have no intention of forecasting its further course at this point. This book has been quite frankly written, however, on the assumption that the main lines of American policy toward France—which we have not hesitated to criticize in detail—are sound. This whole question we develop in detail in the final chapter.

2. The Land

Geography is a much maligned subject. To most of us it recalls those dry-as-dust days in elementary school when we were confused and frustrated by statistics on Peruvian imports or lists of the fabrications of Manchester, all thrown at us with utter disregard for their meaning or our interest. World War II revitalized geography. It carried millions of men to strange—and often distasteful—parts of the globe. It awakened the minds of large numbers of Americans to the significance and interest of the foreign scene, an interest essential to the postwar recruitment of new talents in support of our widening responsibilities overseas. It has made millions of Americans aware that even distant and exotic places, like Assam and Accra, can have immediate and compelling interest for us in a world in which there are no longer any "distant" places. The dream world of isolationism—the America surrounded by a broad belt of protecting oceans—succumbed finally to the solvent and direct experience of individual men. And it has of course by no means entirely disappeared.

We are not here concerned with the "geography of France" as the French school children see it: French-centered, almost Ptolemaic, and drenched in the emotions attached to a country of diversified scene and very old culture. This is a frankly American view—France as we see it across the no longer very broad Atlantic and at the western extremity of the Eurasian continent. What is it about France that concerns us? We can frame our interest in a series of direct, and misleadingly simple, questions: Where is it? How large is it? How coherent is it?

How rich is it? And, finally, in this day of unending cold war, how strong is it?

1. WHERE IS FRANCE?

Position is always a question of *relationship*. Not just *where* is France? But where is France in relation to *what?* France is generally described as a part of Europe. It is true that her neighbors are European and that she shares their civilization. But we can easily be misled by the facile assumption that a continent, since it is *one* land mass, has some kind of inner unity and that it is in turn sharply differentiated from other continents because oceans lie between. This confusion has arisen in part from the notion that land masses facilitate travel and that oceans handicap it, although through most of history the contrary has been true—the sea has been a highway more often than a barrier. Thus, the countries of South America have been accessible to us by sea and not by land—and incidentally the countries below the "bulge," an important part of our Western Hemisphere defense responsibility, are more distant from New York than are the countries of western Europe.

France lies at almost the extreme western end of the peninsula of Europe, one of the four great peninsulas which push out from the central land mass of Eurasia. But what does it mean to say that France is part of Eurasia? During most of its history Eurasia has nourished a series of civilizations along its margins —the long periphery extending from Japan, through India, to western Europe. All of these civilizations, save that of Europe, have been alien to the French. All have been remote in space as well. In contrast, the societies which grew up in the Western Hemisphere have been far more accessible in terms of travel distance, and their founders carried to them not only European, but almost exclusively *western* European, civilization. The French themselves settled Canada, islands of the West Indies, and certain other areas. And the United States, although it adapted to its needs institutions which came in large measure

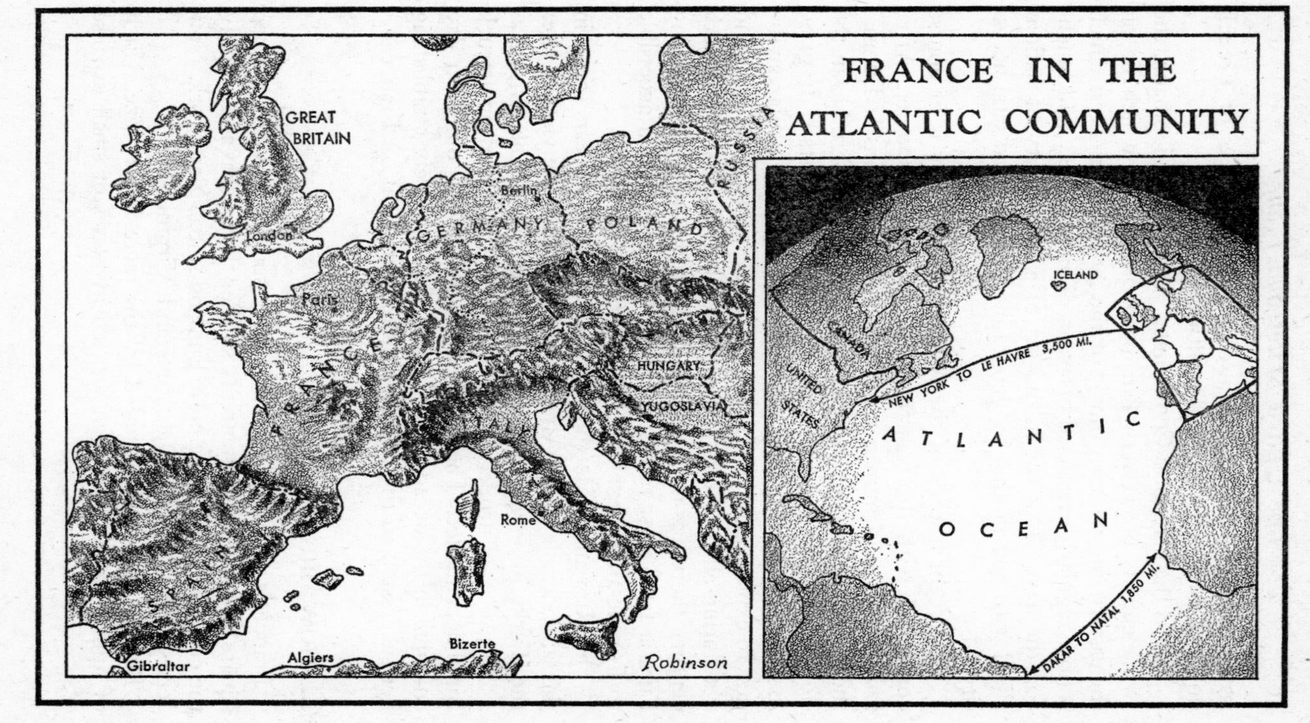
FRANCE IN THE ATLANTIC COMMUNITY
GREAT BRITAIN
London
Paris
FRANCE
GERMANY
Berlin
POLAND
RUSSIA
HUNGARY
YUGOSLAVIA
ITALY
Rome
SPAIN
Gibraltar
Algiers
Bizerte
Robinson
ICELAND
CANADA
UNITED STATES
NEW YORK TO LE HAVRE 3,500 MI.
ATLANTIC
OCEAN
DAKAR TO NATAL 1,850 MI.

from Britain, drew deeply also from the sources of French political thought of the eighteenth century.

This is the "Atlantic Community" of Walter Lippmann, the two elements of western European civilization which lie on the eastern and western shores of the Atlantic, an ocean which is now regularly traversed between dinner one day and luncheon the next. "It is the inland sea of a community of nations allied with one another by geography, history, and vital necessity."

The recent history of the Atlantic Community is of course connected with the transformation of Russian power. After long centuries of human activity along the margins of Eurasia, the center of that great continent stirred, and there began the slow process of the formation of the Russian state. It grew first in Europe and then reached out with spectacular swiftness to explore and lay claim to the vast expanse of Siberia. And yet during all the years down to the opening of the twentieth century there was no rapid and practicable method of crossing Eurasia from west to east, and the Orient remained accessible to Europe almost exclusively by sea.

The Russians made their debut on the European scene in the same decade as the Americans. Only after the victory over the Turks in 1774 did the Russians appear to the British as a "threat" to Europe. In the next year the Americans struck for independence. The two "super-powers" of our own day emerged in the decades when Britain was securely establishing her succession to the power position long held by France.

2. HOW BIG IS FRANCE?

France is a small country by our standards. With 213,000 square miles, she is substantially smaller than Texas and roughly the combined size of the New England states, New York, New Jersey, Pennsylvania, Delaware, and Virginia.

But we must not be misled by the mere fact of size. Much of human history has been written by states of small expanse

—Athens, Sparta, England, Germany, Japan. It is true that modern industrial strength rests on a broad pattern of natural resources, and that states with extensive territory are more likely to possess a wide variety of such resources. Even so, certain small states—Britain, France, Germany—have found themselves rather richly endowed with key resources. France has, for instance, the largest iron field in Europe, second only to the Lake Superior fields in world importance. And Britain and France have both had access to rich resources in their overseas empires.

It is something of a paradox that France, following her defeat by Germany in 1870 and in a period of notable domestic difficulties, acquired most of what is now the world's second-largest overseas empire. The latter has an area of 4,700,000 square miles, to be compared with the 3,750,000 which is the area of the United States. The population of the French empire is 112,000,000, which includes some 68,000,000 natives and 44,000,000 "Frenchmen," only about 2,000,000 of whom live outside metropolitan France.

Again, we must not be misled by the great size of the French overseas empire. With the dislocations of the recent war and the recent progress of nationalism and communism, the French hold on the empire has been seriously shaken, and parts of it, especially Indochina, have become a heavy drain on the Metropole.

3. HOW COHERENT IS FRANCE?

The *distribution* of geographic factors favors or hinders human activity. When the arrangement of these factors is favorable, we say that the country has a high degree of geographic coherence. In the case of the United States, for instance, a good two-fifths of the country—in the West—consists of high mountains and deserts which handicap transportation and contribute only modestly to the total national product. As a westerner deeply attached to the region I knew as a boy, I suggest with some hesitation that our country would have far greater geographic coherence and a notably more efficient economy if it were narrower from east to west, if its western mountains were lower (assuring better distribution of rainfall and a greater acreage of arable land), and perhaps also if its mineral resources were found in the Alleghenies rather than in the Rockies and Sierras. This fanciful picture, alas, takes no account of the tremendous aesthetic loss involved by so drastic a piece of surgery—nor even the economic loss to the vacation industry! But it will in any case serve to make clear our general point about geographic coherence. We could make the point also on the political or strategic plane: Pearl Harbor taught us something of the peril of holding an exposed and distant outpost.

Geographic factors, in the case of France, make for a high degree of economic and political coherence. The country is relatively small. On three sides it faces the sea. Its lowlands are extensive and have easily traversable interconnections. Its highlands can in large measure be avoided by transport routes.

The end-paper map sets all this forth with graphic emphasis. The lowlands extend in a great crescent from Bayonne to Flanders, and secondarily along the narrower north-south corridor of the Rhône and the Saône. The highlands are, first, the ramparts which lie on the southeastern and southwestern frontiers—the Pyrenees, the Alps, the Jura, and, second, the lower ranges and plateaus of the "center," the east and Brittany. The highlands flank the lowlands and divide France into three principal geographic "regions"—the Basin of Aquitaine, the Paris Basin, and the Rhône-Saône Depression. The prevailingly gentle terrain of these basins and the low gaps connecting them form the geographic framework in which man has developed highly articulated road and rail systems. These systems center in Paris and radiate like spider webs in all directions to the frontiers and the sea, their density in general varying inversely with the distance from the capital.

With internal water transport, France is less well endowed, the rivers being generally swift or subject to excessive seasonal variations. But the Seine system and the neighboring rivers in the northeast are not only navigable but extensively intersected by canals, which means that France does have an admirable system of water transport precisely in that part of the country which is most highly industrialized.

At the termini of various of its routes France also has excellent and well-distributed ports, and the sea has played a large role in her history. For centuries the intrepid fisher folk of Brittany and Normandy have left each spring to seek a perilous catch off Iceland or the fog-bound banks of Newfoundland, and their men have traditionally formed the backbone of the merchant marine and the navy. During the period when French power led the world, the sea was an avenue to conquest and expansion abroad. As French power waned during the past century, the role of the sea was reversed and it became a highway over which, in times of crisis, crucial aid could reach France.

The geographic factor again bears close relation to the political coherence of France, although it does not of course "explain" it in any neat, deterministic sense. Had great segments of medieval "France" been able to develop separate traditions and maintain their power against the King—a not at all unthinkable result—modern France might have ended as a federal state. Instead the King—by force, guile, talent, and luck—absorbed one by one additions to his originally frail patrimony and sought steadily to strengthen the state in the interest of further expansion. And so, in the end, the kingdom came to have a highly centralized character, which was further exaggerated by the administrative streamlining of the Napoleonic dictatorship and even more through the new instruments of control fashioned by the industrial revolution.

Here again, however, geography has played its part. Ease of communication has made for the rapid suppression of internal threats to the state and for relatively swift and effective administration in more normal times. The nerve center of this administrative network is Paris. A casual glance at the map reveals the capital in the northern quarter of the country, anything but in the center. It is true that historic, more than geographic, factors explain the location of Paris. And yet there is much geographic logic in its position: it lies on the most usable of the French river systems; it has a central place in the most important of the three great basins with easy access to the other two; and the course of modern industrialization has shifted the French population strongly to the north and east.

When it comes to strategic coherence, France is less favored by geography. The seas offer her protection on three sides, and it is well to remember that the invasions of 1944 were successful only because they were carried out in overwhelming force against an enemy markedly wasted by his efforts in the East. The Alps and the Pyrenees are significant ramparts, but they give protection against states which have been relatively weak in recent centuries. The Achilles heel is in the northeast where geography contributed relatively little to defense or to clarity, where for centuries national frontiers have shifted within a patchwork of peoples and languages. It is this area which has repeatedly invited the invader from the East, whose classic route has lain across the flatlands of the "Flanders Gateway," where the Paris Basin merges with the great northern European plain sweeping across Germany and broadening into Poland and Russia. Through this area Moltke's armies in 1914 wheeled their right wing to surround Paris and were narrowly frustrated at the Marne. Through the same region Hitler's armies struck in 1940, although it is true that their main thrust came through a sector which the French mistakenly felt was almost impenetrable. The northeast of France has not only proved difficult to defend, but it includes the bulk of French coal and heavy industry which falls promptly to an invading enemy, with crippling effect on her economy.

For all its coherence, the face of France, like that of California, presents features of extraordinary diversity—from the stark and ice-carved heights of the Alps to the undulating grain fields about Chartres, from the smoke and clamor of the monotonously flat industrial north to the bare and silent volcanic uplands of Auvergne. These great geographical diversities underlie the striking cultural differences which one finds from region to region—sometimes separated by a matter of only miles. Often these differences reflect the relative cultural isolation of areas for periods of centuries, when transport was indifferent and political authority almost exclusively local. In these instances political, economic, and geographic factors have coalesced to produce diversity.

At the other end of the scale from isolation is accessibility, above all a function of her sea fronts on three sides. The position of France in Europe has made her accessible to foreign ideas, practices, and techniques which have profoundly affected her civilization—grain came to her from the Levant, corn and the potato from America, through Spain, weaving and metallurgical techniques from the Flemings and the Walloons, glass making and silk weaving from Italy, and a whole complex of her new technology from the England which developed the industrial revolution of the eighteenth century. In other instances impulses from abroad have had a more local influence and have tended to accentuate the results of isolation. A Celtic language crossed the sea from ancient Wales to set the Bretons apart from other Frenchmen. From Spain the Basques filtered around the western end of the Pyrenees, bringing a language related to no other the French have known. In a somewhat different category is the Alsace which still speaks a German dialect and whose territory is part of that confused *Zwischenland* where French and German culture mingle. Geographic isolation and geographic accessibility have each played their part in stamping an overlay of cultural diversity on the basic geographic coherence of France.

4. HOW RICH IS FRANCE?

This is a very complex question. It begins with resources: what has nature given France to work with? But then it enters the complicated realm of human geography: to what extent has their culture, in the anthropological sense, enabled the French —or tempted them—to make use of nature's gifts?

France has many, but by no means all, the resources that are required by modern industry. She has iron ore reserves estimated to exceed those of the whole of non-Russian Europe. Of bauxite, the mineral from which aluminum is made, she produced nearly a third of the world's total in 1938. With potash salt, bauxite, iron, and coal (and with phosphate rock in North Africa), she built up the world's fourth most considerable prewar chemical industry. France also has antimony in quantity, but in the other essential minerals—copper, lead, zinc, tin, nickel, chromium, manganese, etc.—she is almost wholly lacking, although she receives important supplies of some of these from her empire.

The textile industries, employing the second largest number of workers in the field of manufacture, import no less than 90 per cent of their raw materials, and the flax mills alone can meet their requirements from domestic production.

But it is in fuels that the French position is weakest. The location and geologic structure of her coal mines are such that France finds it economically feasible to produce only two-thirds of her coal requirements. For the remainder she is largely dependent on Germany and Britain, and pays a price higher than is asked by either in the domestic market. This perennial coal shortage, with its attendant higher cost, has been the greatest single handicap to French industrial progress. Happily the discovery of a new field in Lorraine—near the steel plants—and the postwar development of a process which promises metallurgical coke from previously unusable coals in the Lorraine and other fields, may make an important contribution to the solution of this crucial bottleneck.

In petroleum, the situation is more serious. Metropolitan France produces less than 1 per cent of her requirements, although recent drilling in the south has yielded favorable results. Gasoline costs about two and a half times what it does in the United States, a figure which understates the difficulty which the average Frenchman, with lower real wages than his American counterpart, has in owning a car.

As compensation, France has vast reserves of hydroelectric power, especially in the mountainous areas of the southern half of the country—reserves estimated to be four times as large as those of pre-Hitlerite Germany. Since the Liberation, France has made important strides in the further development of this latent power, but the process is of course a long and very expensive one.

Despite certain critical shortages on the industrial side, the French do possess in their agriculture the basis for a balanced economy. In good prewar years France produced about enough food for her domestic requirements. Forty per cent of her land is arable, and much of this is rich. She produces more wine than any other country. She has large flocks. Before the war her forests supplied three-quarters of her timber, pulp, and paper requirements.

In climate, France also has a rich resource. To be sure, climate is in some degree a subjective matter. The winter climate of Boston is praised by the English for its sunshine and denounced by Californians for its gloom. Even if we discount the panegyrics of French enthusiasts, however, it is clear that France enjoys a climate whose moderation is perhaps unmatched by any other area of the same magnitude. Small regions excepted, the climate is well suited to human activity in general and specifically to a wide variety of industry and to a highly diversified agriculture. It is likewise a healthful climate, although this will no doubt be denied by those Americans who have wintered in the provinces without benefit of central heating.

The moderation of the French climate reflects of course a phenomenon which is common to all of northwestern Europe. The warm seas of the "North Atlantic Drift" (extension of the Gulf Stream) wash the western and northern shores of France, producing a temperature many degrees warmer than the world average for these latitudes (remember that Paris is just south of Winnipeg and well north of Quebec!). The prevailing westerly winds bring a perennial burden of rain. In our own West, the Sierras catch and dissipate the comparable moisture from the Pacific, creating the great inland deserts. France has no coastal mountains, and the rain-laden winds generously water almost the whole of the country—at least in "normal" years.

The French climate, then, is moderate. It is also varied, and its diversity tends further to emphasize the topographic and cultural variety we have earlier described. Brittany, in the extreme northwest, is exposed to the sea on three sides and is bathed in almost interminable showers, its intense greens indistinguishable from those of western England. Paris has much less rain but still has it very frequently. Its climate is milder than that of New York—six degrees warmer in January, nine degrees cooler in July—and even its torrid days are usually followed by a life-giving breeze at sundown. The highlands of Lorraine and Alsace are hot in summer and have substantial amounts of snow in winter. The Mediterranean shore, shut off from the rest of France by the Alps and the Cévennes, has long, dry, hot summers with an almost monotonous succession of fine days (Marseilles and Los Angeles have almost the same July temperature), and generally mild winters, punctuated by short and violent rains and the occasional cold, dry blast from the north—the *mistral*.

5. HOW STRONG IS FRANCE?

This is the core of our interest. In the easygoing and relatively unthreatened days of the late nineteenth century we would certainly have been concerned with the effective peacetime functioning of French society. But now our interest is fixed on French power, on the capacity of France to meet the tests of the cold war—and, if worse comes to worst, the tests of another general conflict. Position, size, coherence, resources

—all these factors are relevant here. But we need to see these basic geographic considerations in the larger frame of human geography—the extent to which the French have been able and willing to use the possibilities which nature has provided. This is the subject of much of the rest of this book, and particularly of the final chapter.

3. The People

1. THE POPULATION AS A WHOLE

With the Pyrenees a barrier of kinds, France lies effectively at the western end of the European peninsula, and successive waves of invasion and immigration over the centuries have generally come to rest there. Iberians, Celts, Romans, Franks, Arabs, Normans, and in modern times Jews, Irish, Italians, Greeks, Poles, and others have contributed to make the French population—anthropologically—the most heterogeneous and interesting in Europe. France, like the United States, has been a "melting pot," but with the very important difference that these "foreign" contributions have been made over a period of many centuries; hence their cultural fusion has been slow and far more complete. The same cannot be said for certain immigrant groups, like the Italians and Poles, which have come in recent decades.

When we reach the question of "race," this fusion is far less complete. The Nordic strains—the long-headed, taller, and fairer French—occupy in general the great "axis of fertility" which extends from Flanders to Bordeaux. The long-headed, brunet Mediterranean stock are found along the southern seacoast and extend northward into the Rhône valley. Finally, the "round heads" (the Alpine stock) are segregated in the economically poorer and less hospitable areas of France: they extend like a scimitar from the borders of Luxembourg through the Vosges, Jura, Alps, Central Plateau, and on into the Pyrenees—with a detached "island" in Brittany.

We must not take all this too literally and see these "racial areas" as containing nothing but men with the characteristics we describe. Modern transportation and the consequent mobility of man have blurred the neater lines of another day and mixed Frenchmen up pretty thoroughly. But the "typical" is still to be found in abundance. The blond and ruddy-faced Norman clearly betrays his northern ancestry and his kinship with the English. The black hair and olive skin of the *Marseillais* speak of the time when "the Province" was an integral part of the Roman Republic. Pierre Laval, the squat, coarse-jowled, swarthy Auvergnat, was an unmistakable example of the men of the high Central Plateau.

The French population, during the past century and a half, has experienced three very significant changes. (1) The industrial revolution tremendously stimulated the growth of the cities. (2) The forces of that same revolution brought about a striking regional redistribution of Frenchmen. (3) The rate of population growth has steadily fallen until during the interwar years the French became a static people, only to see their numbers take a sharp upward turn following the Liberation.

I

The complex of economic and other forces which have remolded the agrarian society of Thomas Jefferson to give us the America we know today have of course recast the face of France as well. There the change has been less striking because France entered the race in the mid-eighteenth century as the leading economic power and then developed far less rapidly in the next century and a half than did her principal rivals.

Even in France, however, the changes in the landscape were sufficiently striking. Old and well-established cities grew with rapidity—Marseilles from 111,000 to 801,000 between 1800 and 1930, Lyons from 110,000 to 580,000 during the same period. "New" cities were forged from overgrown villages: Roubaix had 8000 in 1800 and 117,000 in 1930; Saint Étienne grew in the same period from 16,000 to 191,000 to become the center of a thriving industrial sub-region southwest of Lyons. Paris itself, already the Continent's leading city in 1810 with a population of 600,000, grew as a great commercial center in the early nineteenth century and then, with ample surplus labor supply, attracted industry on a large scale. In the last decade Greater Paris came to have a population of more than five and a half million, and nearly one Frenchman out of seven lived in the capital.

2

It was not merely that individual cities grew, but great clusters of cities appeared in those parts of France which experienced rapid industrial change. Parts of the country which had played a minor or secondary role in the eighteenth century moved to the center of the stage as the new forces of the industrial revolution made themselves felt. Above all, men were rapidly drawn to the coal seams of the north and the iron mines of the east. The Department of the Pas-de-Calais doubled in population, that of the Nord tripled. And this demographic shift—the result largely of internal migration—concentrated six of the thirteen most densely peopled departments, and those containing the most important elements of French heavy industry, along the vulnerable northeastern frontier.

3

For centuries the French population was the largest in Europe, and then about the time of the Great Revolution Russia left France behind. During the next century and a half the *rate* of population increase declined more rapidly in France than was general in Europe, and France was passed by the newly unified Germany, Austria-Hungary, the United Kingdom, and finally by Italy. In 1750 France had 18 per cent of Europe's population, in 1936 less than 8 per cent. As World War I drew near, the French population was increasing by an average of only 70,000 a year, and this meager growth included 50,000 immigrants.

The "reasons" for the decline in the rate of population growth in France and other parts of Europe have been the subject of almost endless speculation. What is involved is a decline in fertility, which is not physiological but which reflects complex changes in the general cultural pattern. In France emphasis can be laid on such factors as urbanization, education, occupational milieu, the level of income, intensification of interclass mobility, Napoleonic laws on equal division of property, and a variety of others. For our immediate purposes the *fact* of decline is perhaps enough.

On this already precarious manpower position, the heavy wastage of World War I fell. The stark statistics tell one side of this story. Dead and missing were 1,345,000, a heavier loss in percentage terms than that suffered by any power save Roumania and Serbia. A comparable loss for the United States in the last war would have been more than four and a half million dead and missing, something over 15 times our actual losses. This figure needs to be kept clearly in mind if we are to understand the psychological reactions of the French and many of their policies during the interwar period. The excess of civilian deaths over births was 1,523,000; this means that disease, malnutrition, the absence of potential fathers in prison camps, and other war causes produced net civilian losses even *higher* than those on the field of battle.

Unfortunately, the war also struck selective blows at the French population. The military classes of 1912 to 1915 suffered permanent losses of 27 to 29 per cent, and these were to be felt most acutely in the "hollow years" of the thirties when the total number of births dropped sharply. Even more serious were losses of the French élite. The *École Normale Supérieure*, nursery of intellectuals and political leaders—Bergson, Jaurès, Giraudoux, Blum—lost in dead alone roughly half the military classes of 1911 to 1913. The meaning of all this for leadership in France today is only too clear. In the post-Liberation period one was constantly reminded: "We have the generation of Blum, distinguished but now too old. We have the younger generation—that of men like Robert Marjolin (the Secretary General of OEEC), who are just now maturing for top positions. But a large proportion of the men in the generation between those two lie on the fields of the Marne and Verdun. This is the tragedy of French leadership since 1930."

The French were of course deeply concerned with the problem of the stagnation of population growth even before 1914. They became even more concerned after the massive losses of the war. The losses of World War II * were significant but not comparable with those of the previous conflict. And then a dramatic, and unexpected, event took place. With the war at an end, the birth rate shot up and the mortality rate dropped. In 1945 the excess of deaths over births was 17,000, a figure comparable with that of prewar years. In 1946 the excess of births over deaths was 294,000, and this figure continued to grow during the succeeding two years, until, in 1948, France had the smallest number of deaths in the history of her records.

This important development can be ascribed in part to the system of family allocations, which puts a definite financial premium on larger families. The tax system leans in the same direction. It has been said that in a world of financial and political insecurity, the average man prizes more highly than ever the family, that the Frenchman is tending to shed his "esprit de rentier" and to assume more readily the financial responsibilities of marriage. Infant mortality has declined with the progress of medical science and the availability of medical services through social security. But the demographers point out that this development is also part of a longer cycle. The depression of the thirties led to the postponement of children, and the lower birth rate was further accentuated by the smaller number of young mothers from the stricken generation of World War I. Then the coming of World War II caused the post-

* See Appendix I, p. 305.

ponement of many marriages. The present postwar upswing in the birth rate reflects in some measure the liquidation of the accumulated effect of these postponed children and postponed marriages. The statistics suggest that we have now reached the top of the curve, and that a few years hence the smaller number of young mothers from the "hollow years" 1935–1945 will again bring about a decline in the birth rate.

Meanwhile the substantial increase in the French population is an encouraging development for a country which is short of workers and has an ambitious plan for industrialization. But for the short term the new trend makes problems rather than solves them: France finds herself with more "dependents"—more old people and more young people—at a moment when the burden of expenditure for social security is already very heavy. With more than twelve million persons under 19 years of age, and six and three-quarters millions 60 or over, nearly half of the total French population falls in these two categories.

2. CLASS STRUCTURE

Society never presents itself in the neat compartments which delight the heart of the social scientist. In this instance, we shall do well not to have too precise ideas on the subject of "class." And yet we do find in society large groups of individuals who have come to have similarities in outlook, mode of life, and forms of behavior, as a result of the fact that they have similar occupations and education and the same general range of wealth—men who meet each other on equal terms and who themselves consider that they belong to the same group. This is perhaps as near as we need come to precision in the matter of "class."

I

France was long a land of peasants. Not far from half of the population still lives in agricultural communities with a center of fewer than 2000 people. And a large number of those now living in cities have migrated in recent decades from the countryside. Even the city dweller tends to retain strong vestiges of his peasant psychology. His attachment to the land is witnessed in the persistence with which the peasant tills his garden long after he has become a city dweller, a miner, a migrant in the colonies. "Cybele," says the Catholic poet, François Mauriac, "has more worshipers in France than Christ."

The typical French farm is small, and it is peasant-owned. The standard of living of the peasant is high, if we compare it for instance with that of the Polish peasant during the inter-war years. It is low compared with that of the Canadian farmer. Houses are often inadequate, with merely a wall between the living room and the stable. Plumbing is almost nonexistent. Fewer than a third of all the communes of France had a regular water supply in 1937, although electricity was available in 96 per cent of them. Even so, lack of mechanization of either the farm or the household is acute and means excessive drudgery and long hours of work. There are few distractions, and a very real sense of isolation. The maid in the house in which I first stayed in Paris had just had her first experience of a railroad—when she came from the center of France to the capital to begin her new life there.

The peasant's psychology reflects his condition and his past. His history has been an age-old struggle for the soil, against both man and nature—a struggle to free himself from the ancient shackles of feudalism, a struggle to enlarge his cherished plot almost inch by inch in a country where land was scarce and where there was no American West into which he could expand. He is almost abnormally suspicious. He is profoundly conservative, despite his political aberrations among the political extremists of the Left. He is frugal—a great saver—and usually prudent, although he sank millions of francs in dubious foreign ventures such as the projected de Lesseps canal in Panama and pre-1914 Tsarist bonds. Despite the spread of literacy —a function of the diffusion of schools and the demands of universal military service—the peasant is often ignorant and superstitious, "more readily seeking the bone-setter than the physician, the sorcerer than the veterinary."

2

The French proletariat numbers somewhat more than five and a half million, naturally a smaller proportion of the population than is found in more highly industrialized countries like Britain and the United States. French industrial workers are concentrated in a few areas and a relatively few cities: with Greater Paris alone having a population of five and a half million, fewer than four million Frenchmen live in other cities of more than 100,000.

This concentration makes for coöperation and effective group action, but there are other factors which oppose it. The French worker, as we have seen, was until recently—sometimes very recently—a peasant, and brings to the city the caution and suspicion of his background (incidentally his peasant connections long continue and often enable him in hard times to return to the farm or to rely on his family for food packages).

Industrial establishments are characteristically small: before World War II fewer than half of all industrial workers were employed in plants numbering more than 100, and about a third of all plants employed fewer than ten workers. The psychology of the average worker has been molded by small plant experience, with quality rather than quantity, objectives. He is less adaptable to large-scale enterprise and the assembly line than is the American worker.

The "anarchist" and Proudhonist strain has contributed further to the independence of the French worker. He has characteristically preferred small and local unions, has been much more difficult to organize than the British or American worker, and has thus contributed to the very loose structure and fluctuating size of the French labor movement. This situation has also been affected by the fact that our worker-peasant has been highly allergic to the payment of union dues.

Perhaps reflecting again his peasant psychology, the worker

has been an opponent of extremism. Prior to World War I the Socialist Party spoke in Marxist strains, and the national confederation of unions, the CGT, awaited "le grand soir" when the general strike would bring down the whole capitalist structure. But when war came, it was clear that the leaders spoke a language to which the rank and file would not respond. Even today, when postwar economic conditions have greatly sharpened the appeal of extremism, Communist Party cards number perhaps no more than 600,000.

In France, as in other industrial societies, the worker is highly vulnerable to the corroding effects of economic crises. He suffers first from unemployment and is caught in the vise of inequitable inflations such as that which followed this last war. It is only in the context of economic deterioration that a phenomenon like the French Communist Party is possible: several million *non-Communist* workers are currently giving political support to the Communist Party, many doubtless sympathetic to Communist doctrine but others voting Communist out of economic desperation. The large Communist vote is a commentary on how difficult conditions have been, since organized labor has a long and explicit tradition of abstention from direct political activity.

3

Intermediate between the proletariat and the lower reaches of the bourgeoisie is the class of artisans. Like the proletariat, they have a manual calling, but, like certain of the middle class, they own and control the means of production: they are entrepreneurs on a modest scale, employing labor, buying their own raw material, and selling directly to the consumer, often on order.

Nothing is more characteristically French than these manual skills which have descended through the centuries and which find their expression in the myriads of tiny shops in the Paris we know—cabinetmakers; workers in gold, in ivory, in iron; painters of glass and of china; makers of musical instruments;

bookbinders; and of course dressmakers of every conceivable description. These artisans—and there are dozens of other categories—work alone, or with one or two members of the family, or with one or two other artisans and perhaps an apprentice learning the trade.

The typical shop of an artisan practicing an ancient trade is itself an education in the French way of life. To give a commission to a bookbinder on the Left Bank is to spend the good part of an afternoon while he goes painstakingly through his samples, consults his assistants, and finally arrives at a decision as to the artistically and historically correct binding for each book. Integrity, craftsmanship, pride in an ancient tradition, unite to produce the result uniquely suited to the purchaser.

This class is large in France. Many of its products have of course been absorbed by large-scale manufacture in the course of the past century; but the interwar years saw an actual growth in the number of larger artisan shops, a result in considerable measure of the increase in relatively new—and less romantic—callings, such as those of mechanics, electricians, and photographers. The statistics give no reliable picture of the size of this class, but it numbered two to two and a half million in the years before the last war.

4

The middle class in France is a large and somewhat hazy conception. When the peasantry, proletariat, and the artisans have been subtracted from the social spectrum, the bourgeoisie includes "everything else." To be sure, bourgeoisie and middle class are no longer equivalent, as they were in the middle ages when the rise of the towns first created a new class between the medieval feudality and the peasant. In present-day French society it will be more useful to discuss together, as composing the middle class, the *petite bourgeoisie* and the *moyenne bourgeoisie*, and leave the *haute bourgeoisie*—that small group with great economic power—for separate consideration.

The middle class is distinguished from the proletariat by the possession of some property, and from both proletariat and artisans by the exercise of a non-manual calling and by the possession of a better education and the enjoyment of a generally easier way of life. But the frontiers are sharp in neither case. Civil servants and secondary school teachers both have a middle-class outlook, but both are unionized. Many artisans have an education and standard of living superior to that of poorer members of the lower middle class.

In the lower middle class one finds characteristically the white-collar worker—the great mass of the civil servants, primary school teachers, and stenographers, for instance. They have sound primary education, generally some savings; they are likely to be Socialist in political outlook (although the Communists have organized large sectors of the primary school teachers). The members of this class have often ascended recently from the peasantry or proletariat—or perhaps successively from both—and have preserved the characteristic energy of the worker in the fields. Their views are apt to be narrow and practical, their outlook skeptical and suspicious. We have to do here with Balzac's Cousin Pons and Cousine Bette.

The upper middle class (*moyenne bourgeoisie*) is precisely the group that the American visitor—as opposed to the mere tourist—knows best. The average member of this class living in Paris has one servant, more rarely two. If he has an automobile, which is the exception, it will be one of the small and less expensive types. Here we find professors, writers, artists, doctors, lawyers, architects, political figures, men who form the backbone of the higher civil administration, businessmen of medium stature.

This is a class which has great variety and which refuses to be imprisoned by *clichés*. Yet those Americans who knew typically bourgeois French families during the interwar period carried away two impressions perhaps above all others—incredible industry and endless saving: the father who has achieved some degree of eminence in the professional world—

and a very modest salary in our terms—after a youth devoted to unremitting study; the mother who repairs her family's clothing unceasingly so that the same things serve for incredible periods, who does a day's work which an average American domestic would refuse to consider, and who is withal the cohesive spiritual force in a family of boundless ambitions; the children, endlessly encouraged to study for the next examination—and the next and the next—in that long procession which leads finally to certification by the state, a career, and "security."

And for all this, money was the essential. In the interwar period no matter how small the salary, something was saved. The French middle class had developed to an exceptional degree that rare capacity—Herbert Feis calls it an art—to sacrifice in the present for security in the future. The son's education, the daughter's dowry, the savings for one's old age—all these were constantly in the mind of our middle-class family. Money unquestionably plays an exceptional role in France. It is very hard to come by; it has a psychological value which responds to the fundamental French preoccupation with security. The very financial and political instability of this postwar world has had a profoundly unsettling effect on the middle-class Frenchman by raising doubts about the validity of his saving habits.

Saving, however, has been only one of numerous middle-class preoccupations with security and order. In the troubled times when the medieval towns were being grafted on a feudal and rural society, the rising middle class won the right to impose order so that it might safely do business. In the eighteenth century, an age of prolific economic growth, the middle class sought to create "order" in the government and administration so that capitalist enterprise could find the "space" in which to grow and flourish—the result was the French Revolution. In the nineteenth century it continued the struggle for "order" and fought off the threat of the reëstablishment of noble power, on one hand, and the vigorous assertion of the power of the rising proletariat, on the other. And yet there is a paradox here: this class, outwardly so devoted to "order," has developed certain revolutionary potentialities since the end of World War I.

The facts are these. A large part of the middle class works for a salary. In times of catastrophic inflation and monetary instability, which have characterized much of the period since 1919, the salaried middle class finds its savings blasted and sees its purchasing power deteriorate. The proletariat possesses the unions and the weapon of the strike with which to seek remedy for the decline in real wages. With some exceptions, the middle class must be content with the slow action of government or "natural" economic forces to redress the balance. Under these conditions, a class which is normally conservative becomes prey to social frustration and is strongly attracted to political extremes. In our time it has provided support for both communism and fascism.

In the mid-thirties the class was riven by the impact of the depression and of the rising tide of fascism abroad. The attrition of a prolonged economic crisis carried important segments into the fascist leagues. Meanwhile the Radical Socialists momentarily carried another, and much larger, group into the Popular Front. But this group was soon disillusioned by the "failures" and "excesses" of the Blum experiment, and its defection made possible both the domestic and foreign appeasement of the French government in the period leading up to the war.

Again in the years since Liberation the middle class has been caught in the frustrations of inflation and the insecurities of political extremism on both Left and Right. Periodically segments of the class have looked to Right or Left for salvation. As the Communist threat mounts, a group is driven into the arms of de Gaulle, and then in turn the fear of de Gaulle drives left-wing members of the class toward coöperation with the Communists. The revolutionary potentialities of this unstable conduct of the middle class are clear. Its instabilities seriously handicap the creation of a viable government from which the extremes are excluded.

5

The sociologist's "top layer" in France is the *haute bourgeoisie*, often snobbishly dubbed *la classe supérieure*. It is a relatively small element in the population but still very much larger than is suggested by the traditional cliché, "the two hundred families."

This is a class characterized by the possession of wealth, and wealth in France is far more concentrated than is sometimes realized: in the mid-thirties 1 per cent of the population possessed perhaps 40 per cent of the accumulated wealth.* It is a class which represents the social and economic merging of the world of Adolphe Thiers—the great bankers and industrialists created by the industrial revolution of the nineteenth century—and the world of Marcel Proust—the decaying remnant of feudalism, grasping at the straws of economic salvation which intermarriage with the leaders of big business offered, whilst the latter were no less pleased to fortify their social position by these bonds of traditional respectability.

In our own time the *haute bourgeoisie* has included the top industrialists, brokers, bankers, lawyers, doctors, army officers in Paris and the same range in the provinces, plus the great landowners and such special groups as the leading shipbuilders of the great port towns. It includes also, of course, the idle rich, that relatively small group of men and women whose profession is pleasure and who are the principal architects of that dizzy and unending dance which is Paris "high life" (a term significantly borrowed from English and characteristically rendered "ee-gleef" by the French). A typical member of this group at the turn of the century was Boni de Castellane who

* As measured by declarations of estates at the time of death, a source obviously subject to a rather wide possibility of error but still useful as a general guide. Paul Beik's study indicates that 7/10 of 1 per cent of the population of Paris in 1930–31 possessed 63 per cent of the total of personal fortunes (*Political Science Quarterly*, September 1941, pp. 371–73).

allied himself with Anna Gould, designed fetes in the tradition of Louis XIV whose cost was worthy of the Sun King himself, and spread money in his wake with more taste, but all the abandon, of a Western copper magnate—at least until the Goulds finally became worried and Anna divorced him.

In the decades prior to World War II this class exercised enormous power in France. Its names were found with monotonous regularity on the Boards of Directors of the most important enterprises. One writer estimates that perhaps 200 corporations and 200 to 300 individual directors dominated the whole French business scene. Big business possessed an admirably organized national federation—similar to our NAM—which functioned, through propaganda, electoral influence, lobbying, and other techniques as a vast pressure group.

Family has played a role in French business much greater than in other leading industrial states. The characteristic business of the mid-nineteenth century was family-owned and directed, and even with the increasing importance of the joint stock company various families have continued to dominate enterprises such as those of the Schneiders and the Rothschilds. Some of these families, like the De Wendels, were prominent already in the early eighteenth century, and a number of the leading banking families had their beginnings at the time of the first Napoleon. Extensive intermarriage has further strengthened the economic relationships within this class. Its members are largely Catholic, but there is notable Protestant and Jewish representation, whose influence in both cases is quite out of proportion to the relatively small numbers of these two groups in the total population.

Like all aristocracies of wealth, this group has lived in considerable isolation from the rest of society, and intermarriage with the nobility has done nothing to weaken this tendency. Many, but by no means all, of its members have shown little real comprehension of the need for social change and of the problems of the welfare of the worker in a society which is prey to the wide swings of the business cycle. The class has done much to expose itself to the justified attacks of the Left and has made its own important contribution to the growth of Communist strength. The arrival of the Popular Front influenced many of its members to become shortsighted appeasers, preferring the interests of their class to the interests of the nation. And the same narrowly conceived class impulses left many tarred by the brush of collaborationism under Vichy.

Despite the post-Liberation wave of nationalization of industry, the French economic scene is still dominated by private enterprise. In fact the latter has tended to come increasingly into its own since the Communists were dropped from the government and since the Queuille regime in 1948–49 achieved important successes through more orthodox economic procedures. With this development and increasingly successful attempts to rehabilitate Vichyite reputations, the influence of the *haute bourgeoisie* in France is once again growing.

3. SOME CHARACTERISTICS OF THE FRENCH

It is perfectly clear even to the most casual traveler that peoples differ, that when one takes a boat at Gdynia in Poland and lands some time later in Stockholm, he has passed from one world to another. And yet many people, including some social scientists, cast doubt on the existence of "national differences," and have had this prejudice strengthened in past years by the unfortunate Nazi distortion of the term "race."

Anthropologists tell us that the pattern of man's action is conditioned by nature and by nurture, or in more elaborate language by his biological make-up and by his "culture." Anthropologists don't know just what "human nature" is, although it is becoming increasingly clear that there are certain elements in man's make-up which are so general as to suggest that they are innate. The differences which people exhibit are apparently due very largely to differences in their culture, the way in which "they have been brought up." Americans of completely Italian descent fought magnificently in Italy in

1943 against the indifferent resistance of their own cousins whose morale had been wasted by the false objectives and the signal failures of the fascist regime.

Now Americans and Frenchmen have been brought up under very dissimilar conditions, and the outlook of the two peoples is vastly different. On the whole, they are not very well suited to understanding each other, as the successive American "invasions" of France–whether of soldiers or tourists–have revealed. And yet it is profoundly important that the two–inhabiting the opposite shores of that much shrunken "inland sea" and linked anew by common purposes and common fears–should understand each other and develop that tolerance of difference which is basic to coöperation.

Much that is French flows from the fact that France is old–old in the sense that China is old. "There is a striking likeness between the Chinese and ourselves," suggests the critic, Paul Morand, "the same passion for economy by making things last by repairing them endlessly, the same genius for cooking, the same caution and old world courtesy; an inveterate but passive hatred of foreigners, conservatism tempered by social gales, lack of public spirit, and the same indestructible vitality of old people who have passed the age of illness. Should not we think that all ancient civilizations have much in common?"

There were centuries when France had a significant role in the development of Western civilization; and other centuries when she occupied the most important place in that development. The monuments of this long history are numerous; many of them are concentrated in or near Paris. No Frenchman can escape his history, for it is displayed on every side. He is subjected to an endless reiteration of it during his school career, and perhaps no people has been more *consciously* caught in the web of its own development.

To the Frenchman of course his history means many things. As a part of the Roman Empire, France shared the Greco-Roman tradition which underlies and penetrates the whole of the development of western society. In the Middle Ages France was the center of the development of Catholic faith and thought, "eldest daughter of the Church"—and her people have remained overwhelmingly Catholic, even though a considerable part of them are Catholic in a very limited sense. The monarchy, culminating in Louis XIV, gave France substantially the territorial make-up and the centralized administrative coherence which has characterized the state from that time until the present. Recent history—and the French generally refer to the period since 1789 as "contemporary"—has seen Frenchmen divided politically by the events of the Great Revolution and its later repercussions, and divided economically and socially by the impact of the industrial revolution. Finally, the disaster of 1940 has obliged the French to reassess their history and painfully to readjust themselves to a world very different from the one they anticipated.

In complete contrast, we Americans have had a short history. Our country is barely a century and three-quarters old; only three centuries if we go back to the beginning of our colonial experience. Our national history has fallen largely within the period of the industrial revolution, and has witnessed the conquest of a continent. It has been characterized by vast and rapid changes, and by an unparalleled geographical and social mobility. The striking and even revolutionary character of these events has riveted the American's attention on the present—and the future—and has often left him indifferent to a past which seemed remote and alien to his concerns. The revolutionary break with Britain seemed to divorce his present from Europe's past, and the nineteenth-century distribution of power in Europe enabled him to enjoy this dream in isolation. He embarked on his national history a "New Man."

For these and other reasons the attitude of the American toward his history has been poles removed from that of the Frenchman. The latter, deeply conscious of the limitations imposed by the past and its lessons for the future, tends to look backward at least twice before he dares move forward. With a short history and one which has offered him almost limitless opportunities, the American has tended to view the future as unshackled by the past, as essentially malleable, ready to receive whatever impress he chose to give it. He has moved ahead fearlessly—and often naïvely—to its conquest.

A long history and a deep awareness of it have made Frenchmen profoundly conservative. The caricature of the Frenchman so dear to the heart of the foreigner gives us an emotional and capricious individual strongly drawn to utopian ideas and by nature a revolutionary. Nothing could be farther from the truth. The majority of Frenchmen have until recently been peasants, intent on maintaining and enlarging their holdings, suspicious of, or alarmed by, any revolutionary movement which threatened their property rights. And a large proportion of urban Frenchmen have either prized order and stability above other things or, like most socialists, have wanted to bring about "revolutionary" change only by legal and pacific means.

This fundamental conservatism has scarcely prepared Frenchmen to deal with our modern world of dynamic change. France emerged, for instance, from the War of 1914 with no desire more widely felt than to return to the world she had known before. In the years following, even serious writers like André Siegfried expressed a touching nostalgia for the lost world of the nineteenth century and called for the preservation of the social and economic balance of French life in an age rapidly giving itself over to the industrialization of the Americans and the Germans. Not only were the French often unequipped to understand the events and thought patterns of the new age, they were condemned at the same time to compete in a world in which the defeated powers—Germany and Russia—were unburdened by any desires to return to the past and were already girding themselves with new ideas for the struggles of the future.

* * *

In many—but by no means all—phases of their activity, the French exhibit an inveterate caution, reflection again of their essential conservatism. The word "caution" is indeed scarcely big enough to express the profound and pervading concern of the French with the uncertainties of the future. Life is an eternal quest for security—security against the enemy abroad, thrice shattered during a long lifetime and now again threatened by the monopolistic power of the Soviets; security against the enemy at home, which is want.

France possesses no national wealth comparable to that of Britain or the United States, yet she maintained an army at or near the top in size and cost during the period between the War of 1870 and that of 1939. And the whole of French life was shot through with anxiety for her future safety in a world of competing powers. At the same time the individual Frenchman is no less concerned about his own future, and to provide for it he has been an inveterate saver.

Caution seeps into almost every corner of French life. It is evident in the market place, where the average businessman is very reluctant to take risks even in the interests of greater profit: he prefers to operate in his cautious and traditional manner for a more modest—and, he believes, a more assured—income. In a world in which the characteristic business is family-owned, the fact that financial operations are closely scrutinized by those immediately interested has contributed further to this attitude of caution. This outlook has tended to inhibit the rapid industrialization of France in an age when she was competing with other countries of more adventurous business spirit.

Again, the French have generally distrusted youth and preferred the experience of age for places of responsibility. The bitter German gibe of the thirties ran that France was governed by men of seventy-five because those of eighty were dead. And the French, despite the magnificent triumphs of their countrymen in the field of pure science, have been slow indeed to apply their own findings—and even more those from abroad—in practical fields. It has *not* been in France that the discoveries of Pasteur have made their greatest impact.

The Frenchman is an individualist. He wants to stand on his own feet. He is psychologically of the stuff from which democrats are made. Intellectually, he holds his own views with great tenacity, and compromises only with real hesitation and suspicion—hence political parties are formed with difficulty (since they necessarily include more than one Frenchman) and, once formed, they almost invariably start on a process of fragmentation.

The Frenchman wants to be no less self-sufficient economically—that is where his saving for the future comes in. His family life is sacred, and is shared with only a few chosen friends—foreigners know how difficult it is to penetrate those hallowed precincts! The average Frenchman is a "little man," fearful (and to a point envious) of the great and powerful, an attitude descending from the days when he knew the dominance of the feudal nobility and one reinforced by the appearance of the new masters of the modern business world. Jacques, the friend of Alain, the theorist of French Radicalism, is a philosophical bootmaker. Jacques expects no one to give him an income; he knows that rich men are inevitable, but "I don't want them to say they are my masters . . . It is not equality in wealth which seems to me the fundamental justice, but equality in attitude and in manners, and freedom of opinion. In short, I want consideration."

The weak side of individualism is the Frenchman's resistance to coöperation and his lamentable lack of civic virtue. Tax evasion has been one of the most serious problems connected with post-Liberation recovery, and it has a long history in France. Coöperation for national ends during the epic days of the Resistance was in many instances superb, but when the cohesion of the crisis had passed, both old and new quarrels found their way to the surface. The contrast is sharp with their neighbors, the British, who have shown once again in this postwar world that they can go to unheard-of, and at times almost ludicrous, lengths in spontaneous self-discipline—a characteristic which detached French observers are not slow to admire.

The Frenchman resists collective action in general, whether it be the discipline of the trade union or that of the assembly line (René Clair's movie, "À Nous la Liberté," states this with graphic and humorous emphasis). "Although the French understand organization as well as anyone, they will coöperate only in an emergency," admits André Siegfried. The Frenchman lends himself neither to the discipline of modern technology nor to that of totalitarian organization—it is well to note that even the French Communist Party has never managed to attract more than a million members and has won its victories through the temporary support of several times that number of non-Communist voters.

This is an energetic people, despite the unintended libels of innocent American soldiers who saw war-stricken groups of the French in an hour of discouragement and lassitude. It is still essentially a peasant people, and the sturdiness of its urban dwellers suggests that it is really not long since they left the fields. The Parisian family that lives on the seventh floor of a Left Bank apartment without an elevator, the professor's wife who treks half way across Paris to the central market three times a week to save a few essential sous, the myriad Parisians who cycle long distances to and from work through incredibly heavy traffic (and the inescapable ritual of *déjeuner* means two round trips a day!), the student endlessly preparing for his competitive examinations—these are mere random evidences of energy one sees on every side.

We have said the French are cautious. There is nothing inconsistent in the fact that they are also courageous and even at times foolhardy. It is an endless source of mystery to the new arrival in Paris why the minuscule French cars which weave in and out through the traffic at high speed are not crushed by the busses, which are also blazing along with a fine disregard for everything, above all the pedestrian. During the Italian campaign of the last war American troops entering an enemy village proceeded against machine gun nests indirectly and with great caution in the interests of saving lives, whereas the French often smothered such objectives in a single charge.

The Resistance movement of the recent war was made for the French. It required courage (without bravado), energy, persistence, and that quality which is so distinctively French —the capacity to "se débrouiller," an untranslatable expression which means "to get out of a fix." When a situation is really *snafu*, it becomes a challenge to the average Frenchman. Rescuing their imprisoned sons and fathers in Germany was such a challenge. They inserted messages in chicken bones or in flat chocolates forwarded as Red Cross packages through Switzerland (it took the Germans about three years to discover this one, it is said). In the same way they sent tiny pieces of men's suits which were then patiently sewn together at the other end to become disguises in which prisoners could safely make their way across Germany (later in the war there were so many French workers in Germany that a French-speaking individual was scarcely noticed). One clever Alsatian, who spoke good German, stole a German officer's uniform and then marched three of his fellow prisoners across the country, nominally on their way to another prison camp but actually back to France. One of my good friends, a young woman of thirty, was professor in a *lycée* at Chartres when the Allied air bombardment in the spring of 1944 began to get hot. The authorities closed the *lycée* and urged that she leave town. With the railroads bombed out, no busses running, and with her only pair of shoes virtually worn through, she put her things in a rucksack, managed to buy a piece of ham, used the grease for her feet, ate the remainder en route, and walked the forty-five miles to Paris in two days, breaking the journey with a night spent with one of her students.

Salvador de Madariaga suggests that the Frenchman is a "man of thought" as contrasted with the Britisher whom he calls a "man of action." The Frenchman, as we have seen, is the product of a mature and very old civilization, which has been one of the great sources of ideas in the West. Those ideas have been made regularly available to a large number of Frenchmen through a superb regime of "general education," the product of the French *lycée*, a state secondary school of very high standards, and until recently reserved to the middle and upper classes through the requirements of tuition payment. The *lycée* has given the Frenchman a fundamental grasp of his own civilization and a certain, though much more limited, understanding of European civilization in general. In its methods, and particularly through the detailed study of his own language, the *lycée* has provided him with an instrument, logic, for dealing with his environment.

There are weaknesses in the logical attack. The environment is complex; the use of logic demands the discovery of premises; hence the argument necessarily begins with limitation and definition. The "limitation of his field of vision leads him to sacrifice certain aspects of active reality," and he often suppresses those elements of the situation that do not fit his theory. This is no academic discussion. The attitude and the method lie deeply embedded in the French mind. The Frenchman built a Maginot Line and created around it a defense he believed impregnable, because he could not envisage a second blood-letting like that of World War I and because the successful defense of Verdun had "proved" the value of fixed fortifications. The premises took no account of the new weapons—the dive bomber, the tank, the parachute, motorization, the fifth column, above all speed and surprise—and so in 1940 the premises and conclusions were swept away together in the debacle.

The average well-educated Frenchman feels that he must have well-ordered ideas on almost every subject, from politics to love and cooking—to be without them would be almost like appearing in public without a shirt. Since the educated Frenchman is often a very able conversationalist with a well-ordered and well-stored intellect, and since he often seems more concerned about airing his own ideas than about knowing yours, he comes as something of an initial shock to the American or Englishman, both less inclined to have fixed and well-buttressed ideas and more given to enter an argument with a stock of information and to let the conclusions emerge.

There is another sharp contrast between our hypothetical American and his French counterpart. The latter is much more concerned about the art of living and less concerned about the problem of making a living. Put another way, the contrast is between a qualitative and a quantitative outlook on life. Americans are a young people; they have been absorbed in the building of a country of heroic proportions. The American is drawn to concrete achievement and to the measurable: in school he is apt to think of grades and letter awards in sports; in mature life in terms of dollar income. He lives in the midst of measurable things—the tallest building, the longest bridge, the biggest dam, and his thoughts are shot through with notions of size. If he takes a long automobile trip, he will tell you how rapidly he covered the route rather than the quality of the landscape or the character of the architecture he saw.

Make no mistake, the Frenchman is very much concerned about money, too, but with a rather different emphasis. He wants to acquire it, not as a symbol of his place in the social hierarchy, but as a means of satisfying his ambition to live well. The Frenchman, for instance, is notoriously given to retiring early in life so that he may devote himself to interests other than those of his vocation. His formal education has awakened a wide range of interests—in literature, painting, architecture, *décor*, history, politics. This formal education has been reinforced by the general setting of his life—from an early age he has heard stimulating conversation on serious subjects, and he has gradually been initiated into the mysteries of the French cuisine and French wines.

I had last summer a not atypical conversation over a long luncheon with a French businessman, head of an important company making and distributing electricity. He discussed his own business problems in the context of French economic recovery and the political situation in France and abroad, and his general understanding of the larger forces revealed a penetration and maturity which one finds only rarely among his confreres in the United States, even when their specialized business competence is of a very high order. More strikingly different was the later turn which the conversation took. My host admitted that he was tremendously interested in the problems which his business raised but made it clear that the most important consideration was that his income made it possible for him to buy the books he wanted. He launched into a long discussion of French literary trends of the past half century and talked with wit and zest of Gide and Proust on a very high amateur level.

If one may generalize, Americans show a higher specialized competence in making a living, the French know better what to do with their leisure once they get it. It is not without importance also that the range of interests which appeals most strongly to the French makes them far less accessible to the blandishments of sports and the movie and more attached to activities which by their very nature center about the home.

The widely differing attitudes of Frenchmen toward the Catholic Church are among the most difficult for the average Anglo-Saxon to understand, accustomed as he is to a variety of competing sects. If the foreign observer relies on that often misleading form of information—statistics—he comes away with the conviction that France is almost universally Catholic in its religious belief. The last census of religious groups in France—that of 1872—reported 581,000 Protestants (four-fifths Calvinists, and most of the rest Lutherans), 49,000 Jews, and almost all the remainder of the population, 35,388,000, Catholic.

France is *not* universally Catholic in the sense that the statistics seem to imply. It is, however, not Protestantism but the "lay spirit" which is the principal opponent of Catholicism. Not since Protestantism was drenched in the blood of the religious wars of the sixteenth century has the religious struggle lain between Protestant and Catholic in France. Protestantism has revealed notable vitality, it is true: from the shattered remnants of the early years of the nineteenth century when Napoleon gave it official status not dissimilar to that of Catholicism, its numbers increased to something less than a million in the late thirties. Four of the six principal sects—Reformed, Evangelical, Free, and Methodist—joined hands in 1938 to give French Protestantism substantial unity in the new Reformed Church of France.* Protestantism has furnished distinguished leadership to the nation and a leaven of liberal thought. But it has had no significant role as an opponent of Catholicism.

The lay spirit entered the lists against Catholicism two centuries ago, and a long and bitter struggle ensued. "Lay" is the English version of the untranslatable French word "laïc," which is untranslatable precisely because we have no factor in our society which corresponds to it. The lay Frenchman inscribes himself as a Catholic when the census asks him his religion, he is regularly baptized in the Church, and often he is buried by it. His other relations to the Church, if any, are of the ritual—even routine—variety. The lay Frenchman is not necessarily antireligious. Against a background of intellectual liberty, skepticism, and a highly developed civilization, comments André Siegfried, "the French mind is trained to throw the clutch out with marvelous ease when religion and politics are to be kept in their respective spheres." The lay Frenchman is prepared to see the proprieties observed, in religion, as else-

* Lutherans and Baptists abstained.

where; but beyond that he wants no intervention by the Church in politics or in any other sphere of life beyond what he conceives to be its proper religious and moral concerns. This positive manifestation of the lay spirit is "anticlericalism." Since the Church has a profound concern with the education of the young, this has been one of the principal battlegrounds between anticlericals and the Church.

French Catholicism is a venerable tree, deeply rooted, adapting itself to the changing seasons, robust before the storm, eternally tapping new sources of strength. It is old, as so much else is old in France: Gaul was painfully Christianized while it was still Roman.

The Church's opponent, the lay spirit, grew in the soil of the eighteenth-century Enlightenment. The thinkers of that age lost faith in the validity of the Church's prescription for salvation. Some of them lost interest in salvation itself. At the same time they developed a perhaps exaggerated faith in the capacity of man's reason. And presently, with reason as an instrument, they were making an attack on a broad front against the Church and its interests, spiritual and temporal.

This attack came at an unhappy time for the Church. It was the possessor of vast lands. It made a disproportionately small contribution to the income of the state. And it was, at least in its upper reaches, allied with the reactionary elements in society which were determined to preserve a regime of privilege, at the very time that the proponents of reason were urging a system in which men should be free, equal, and the beneficiaries of British parliamentarism.

The French Revolution swept away the lands and the privileged position of the Church, notably its control of education, and for a time attempted to uproot Catholicism entirely and to supplant it with a synthetic state religion born of rationalism and the guillotine. But France was more deeply Catholic than many had believed, and persecution only strengthened the Church.

Bonaparte was no believer, but he was a realist, and he

promptly made his peace with the Pope. The Concordat of 1801 recognized Catholicism as "the religion of the great majority of French citizens," and the French state accepted responsibility for payment of the salaries of the clergy, since the Church had lost the income for this purpose from the lands confiscated during the Revolution. In unilateral legislation Bonaparte further limited the powers of the Papacy over the French Church and in general reasserted those "Gallican Liberties" which the French monarchs had long cherished. The arrangement with the Papacy was vague in important respects, and contributed to further misunderstanding and conflict during the following century.

It was the Third Republic which proved the next effective enemy of the Church. Its new leadership, and notably Jules Ferry, were true descendants of the Great Revolution, men devoted to the lay ideal. The Church they associated with conservative and anti-Republican forces in society, and their first concern was to curb its power, above all to place the training of Republican youth in "trustworthy hands." They swept religious teaching from the primary schools and made public elementary education free and compulsory. The Catholics retorted by the founding of numerous private schools, which were permitted under the law. But large numbers of Catholic children were unable to pay the tuition which many of these schools were obliged to ask.

The Dreyfus Affair of the late nineties, in which the lay Republic and the Church were aligned against each other, deeply embittered this struggle and provoked an upsurge of anticlericalism akin to nothing which had been known since the days of the Revolution. When the Republic emerged triumphant from this ordeal, the inevitable result was a frontal assault on the Church. It began with the anticlerical legislation of 1901 (which led to the dissolution of many monastic and other Catholic organizations), and culminated in the law of 1905 which destroyed the Concordat of 1801 and separated the Church and state.

The Separation Law was a shock to the Church, on one hand, since it involved both a certain loss of prestige, arising from the Church's earlier recognition by the state, and a very large loss of revenue, essential to its functions. On the other hand, it gave the Church a new independence. The state no longer had any influence in the appointment of bishops. And many members of the clergy came to welcome the Separation for the new "spiritual independence" which it brought. The high-water mark of anticlericalism had been passed, and a period of improved relations between Church and state set in, leading eventually to the formation of the powerful social Catholic party, the *Mouvement Républicain Populaire.*

There has been in recent decades a great deal of writing on the subject of French "nationalism," some of it pretty unrealistic. The French of the interwar period have been painted as aggressively chauvinistic—a description more appropriate to certain earlier periods of their history—at a time when they wanted above all to be left alone in peace. Even when the Frenchman appeared most nationalistic, he wanted primarily to suppress the German danger—sometimes in crude and unrealistic ways—so that he might be left to the pursuit of his own parochial interests. How deep ran this desire for peace was made evident by the successive sacrifices of *real* French interests in the face of growing German power in the thirties.

Nations, like individuals, have self-esteem. In the case of nations, it is more complex in its character and its manifestations. This "nationalism," like individual self-esteem, is an essential cohesive force, which provides morale for the execution of national purposes. But it has another side, too: by its very nature, it tends to set nations off one against another at the very time when men have been seeking desperately to find a principle transcending this narrower loyalty and leading to the wider ground of international understanding.

The strength of French nationalism is once again rooted in logic and history. For considerable periods France has been the leading military power in Europe, and for long stretches of her history she has been the intellectual center of the Western world. Her military history, which appeals with particular force to a people who react to the aesthetic attraction of "la gloire," has in it many generous chapters—the Crusades, the French Revolution, the liberation of Italy. Out of these and other less defensible military enterprises has evolved a mythology of the uniform beneficence of French power which is much like the folklore in which every people clothes its past.

In the field of the intellect, France has often been the source of new ideas and often the leader in new—and generous—movements. Here again, the French were being rapidly outdistanced in many fields during the past century, but the average Frenchman managed to maintain the picture of French intellectual leadership in its unsullied purity.

This history of past greatness is vividly present in the minds of Frenchmen: for the educated man it is almost as real as his personal experience. This fact is of great importance in the light of the disasters which have befallen France in the past seventy-five years. Her visible decline began with the defeat by the Germans in 1870. It continued silently as she fell behind in the population and industrial race in the following decades. And it became brutally manifest in the disaster of 1940. Since the liberation of 1944, France has reacted pretty much as any normal individual would react under similar circumstances. She is tormented by the great memories of her past and exhibits an acute—and perfectly understandable—sensitivity with reference to her reduced position in the present.

It is a thankless task to attempt to circumscribe any people within such a strait jacket of generalizations as we have suggested above. The problem is at best unscientific and impressionistic. No two observers would agree as to the colors and shading for such a picture. Our picture will probably satisfy neither Frenchmen nor Americans. Perhaps to that extent it may be considered "objective."

4. Government

Americans tend to be highly critical of French political arrangements. They question the vitality of democracy in France and note that the French, through repeated revolutions—the most recent that of 1940—have given themselves all kinds of regimes during the past hundred and sixty years, some of them far from democratic. They point an accusing finger at what they believe to be endemic and uncontrollable instability as witnessed by seemingly unending ministerial crises. And they adduce glaring scandals such as those associated with Panama and Stavisky as typical examples of dishonesty in high places.

Concerning changes in regime, it is well to remember that the French revolted in 1789 against a system which was autocratic and antiquated—deeply arrested as compared with the free institutions which the British and Americans had been slowly evolving over the centuries. The French have sought to achieve democratic institutions over a shorter period of time and often under conditions of exceptional difficulty—as witness the Revolutionary and Napoleonic Wars. That a certain amount of disorder and violence has accompanied this process will surprise no careful student of the origins of democracy in history. And it is scarcely a basis for disparagement on our part: we achieved our own unity and affirmed our institutions only after the domestic war of 1861 which was far more costly in lives than all the civil strife of the French revolutions since 1789.

A very large proportion of the French people emerged from

the recent war quite naturally determined to see their country with a constitution very different from that of the Third Republic, on which they blamed much of their misfortune. But the ironic outcome of bitter debate and compromise was a constitution which differed all too little from its predecessor. Our analysis of French governmental arrangements will have more depth if we center it on the relatively long experience of the Third Republic and then note later certain changes made by its successor.

1. LOCAL GOVERNMENT

We shall do well to begin our study of government at the grass roots. Like the New England states, the whole of the surface of France is divided into townships or "communes"—38,000 of them in all, of which nearly 20,000 have a population of 500 people or fewer. These tiny communes may betray their ancient origin by a span of Roman aqueduct or by the Gothic portal of a church; but their political institutions are thoroughly modern. Every four years, their citizens elect ten * of their own number as a governing body, the communal council, and this group in turn elects a mayor and a deputy mayor. The council debates matters of policy, and the mayor executes its decisions. These communal councils are a significant educational factor in France, the means of bringing some 400,000 citizens, mostly from the ranks of the peasantry, into active participation in political life.

At first blush this system appears a good deal like our own local government. But when we look more closely, we see that the council is dealing with rather unexciting problems, like the upkeep of roads or the repair of municipal buildings; that even here its latitude is restricted by law; and that a great many of its decisions need the approval of higher authority—for instance, it cannot even eliminate a street or grant a franchise to a bus company of its own will. The mayor, too, can act in some

* The number increases with the size of the commune.

cases on his own authority or on that of the council, but in many of the most important questions he needs authorization from above or is simply ordered to do things by someone higher up.

All this etches out for us the fundamental difference between our own system, which is federal, with a great deal of power reserved to state and local authorities, and the French, which is unitary and centralized, with authority concentrated in the government and bureaucracy in Paris and with mere driblets of it allowed to reach the provinces. Here is a brain in Paris with a nervous system extending to every corner of the realm, bearing impulses to the capital and decisions from it.

As we ascend from the commune, we pass in turn two other administrative divisions, the canton and the *arrondissement*, but these are of only marginal importance. Our interest centers in the primary subdivision of France, the department. In their passion to be rid of the old regime in 1789, the revolutionary fathers swept away all the provincial boundaries, hoping to make men forget their local patriotism. And then they erected new divisions which took their politically colorless but geographically poetic names from local features—the *Hautes Alpes*, the *Seine Inférieure*, the *Côtes du Nord*. The founders intended these new divisions to have a great deal of local authority, but the organizing genius of Bonaparte seized upon them as ideally suited to be units in his highly centralized administrative system. With changes adapting it to different political regimes—and very notable alterations of a democratic nature under the Third Republic—France has maintained this Napoleonic administrative system from that day to this.

The department is really the commune writ large. Here again we have a representative body, the "council general," its members elected one from each canton. Its semiannual sessions are open to the public, but if we enter the prefecture on one of these occasions we shall see that the range of its discussions is not much wider than that of the communal council: departmental highways and buildings, welfare and relief services—these are the stuff of its deliberations. The council's decisions are carried out by its executive officer, the prefect, and the latter is appointed by the central government.

Like the mayor, the prefect has a bipolar personality. He executes the decisions of the departmental council, but, more important, he is the representative of the central government. He carries out its orders, he is subject to its discipline, he can be removed at will, and periodically he is transferred to another department so that his responsiveness to the central government will not be undermined by local attachments. During the interwar years the prefect's "local" powers were further impaired as new Paris agencies, reflecting the growth of the state's economic and social responsibilities, tended to by-pass him and to deal directly with their own representatives in the provinces.

2. THE CENTRAL ADMINISTRATION

It is difficult to explain to an American the really predominant position which Paris occupies in the French scene. It has a virtual monopoly of importance among French cities. It is the center of educational, professional, and artistic life. It is the hub of the communication system, and has the heaviest concentration of industry of any region in France. It is the leader in fashion and taste. It is the envy of the provinces, and men of ambition almost invariably make residence in Paris their eventual objective. It is the center and source of political power. It includes, as we have seen, nearly one-seventh of the total population of France, and has in fact no real competitors: Marseilles has fewer than a million people, greater Lyons something more than 800,000, but neither has a cultural importance which would correspond at all to that of our cities which follow New York in size—and beyond Lyons we have Toulouse and Bordeaux, with a quarter of a million each. We can state the relation of Paris to the rest of France by resorting to a statistical fantasy: a single American city containing the same *proportion* of our population—and in general representing the diversity of activity which is found in Paris—would mean the amalgamation of New York, Chicago, Detroit, Boston, and Washington, which have, within their "greater," rather than their corporate limits, something more than 20 million people.

The very nature of her centralized regime means that France has always concentrated far more of her governmental machinery in Paris than have we in Washington. In recent decades the Paris administration has been further swollen by the same forces which have been at work with us: the old "police state," concerned primarily with the maintenance of order, has gradually given way to the modern "welfare state," deeply involved in social policy and reaching out to touch the life of the average citizen at a hundred different points.

In place of our Washington "Departments," France has Ministries. The latter grow and contract in number with changing governments, and they generally embrace functions performed both by our Departments and by various other extradepartmental Washington agencies.

The responsible head of each of the Ministries is of course the Minister. Although the Minister occupies an *administrative* position, he is a *political* official and a member of the government currently in power. He may know something—perhaps quite a little—about the business of the Ministry, but he is in no sense an expert. He may exercise his new function for only a week or a month; he is very unlikely to do so continuously for more than a year. On the other hand, there has been more ministerial continuity in France than some people have believed: of 1026 cabinet positions (1871–1930), 482 were held by 60 individuals, serving from 5 to 20 times.* Poincaré served as Premier for a total of six and a half years, on three different occasions. Briand was continuously Foreign Minister from 1925 to 1932 in a dozen different cabinets.

To his new position the Minister brings a small group of personal secretaries and experts (the *Cabinet du Ministre*)—

* Carl J. Friedrich, *Constitutional Government and Democracy* (Boston, 1946), pp. 366–367.

bright young men like those so characteristic a feature of the official *décor* in Washington these past two decades. But the Minister depends for the most part on that large and permanent group of officials who provide continuity and professional skill for each of the French Ministries—the bureaucracy.

The French have no separate civil service such as ours. But over the years they have developed recruitment systems within the different ministries and a highly articulated system of severe competitive examinations. The result is that the higher reaches of the bureaucracy have long been staffed by an "aristocracy of brains," drawn in more recent years increasingly from all ranks of society. Even so, the French bureaucracy is less interested in efficiency, as such, than in honesty. In operating efficiency it does not compare too favorably with the British administration nor with the better managed of our own agencies, in the opinion of the American who has made the closest study of the French bureaucracy. But our authority emphasizes the deep concern of the French official to be fair with the "little man," and he concludes that, even in the light of such apparent exceptions as the Stavisky scandal, the state bureaucracy is by and large "honestly run." *

In this country, where civil servants are appointed by no fewer than 48 states, as well as by the federal government, it is difficult for us to appreciate the cohesiveness of the French bureaucracy, product as it is of a unitary state. There are at present about 1,500,000 employees of the national and local governments. In the mid-thirties it was estimated that three-quarters of this whole number belonged to the political parties of the Left. A very large part of the bureaucracy was unionized—locally and then in four national organizations. And the problem of strikes has for decades raised the question as to

* Walter Rice Sharp: *The Government of the French Republic* (New York, 1938), pp. 162–163. A. L. Lowell reached much the same conclusion many years ago: "The level of integrity among French officials appears to be extremely high, and though wedded to routine, their efficiency is great . . ." (*Governments and Parties in Continental Europe* [2 vols., Boston and New York: Houghton Mifflin, 1897], I, 132).

where the line should be drawn between proper and improper behavior on the part of state employees.

For anyone who has known the crisscrossing of jurisdictions and the fantastic subdivision and distribution of function in Washington, especially in wartime, the French administrative scene is again familiar country. Immigration in the interwar period, to take only one example, was the business of no one Ministry but of five: Labor, in matters of employment, health, and sanitation; Agriculture, for the recruitment of immigrant farm labor; Foreign Affairs, for the negotiation of immigration treaties; Interior, for policing; and Justice, for naturalization. One writer cites the case of compartmentalism at its most watertight: the Ministry of Finance occupied a wing of the Louvre which was under the jurisdiction of the Division of Fine Arts of the Ministry of Education—and so the Ministry of Finance washed the *inside* of the windows and the Ministry of Education, the *outside*.

Coördination of function has been more difficult in France than in the United States. Here the President has an assured tenure of office and correspondingly greater power. In France, the Premier has often had to step warily: to remove surgically a bureau from the control of a given Minister—even in the recognized interest of amalgamation and increased efficiency—might offend some part of the Premier's precarious majority and precipitate his downfall. Moreover, the French Premier normally assumes the heavy administrative burden involved in the personal direction of one of the Ministries. Léon Blum has long inveighed against this practice and has urged that the Premier remain without portfolio and keep his hands unfettered for the subtle and time-consuming tasks of coördinating his team of ministers. Blum followed precisely this practice when he became head of the Popular Front government in 1936—and again in 1938 and 1946. So also did Pleven in the case of the government formed in July 1950.

3. THE GOVERNMENT OF THE THIRD REPUBLIC

The Third Republic originated in the so-called Constitution of 1875. Constitutions, like men, are the product of both inheritance and environment. Much that one finds in this curious document can be traced to earlier French constitutions, but it was to a very important degree the child of circumstances.

I

The disastrous and unexpected defeat of the French armies in 1870 cast Napoleon III from his throne and opened the road to power for the Republicans of Paris. Even after the grisly siege of the capital, the Republicans wanted to fight on to the bitter end—in the Pyrenees if necessary. In 1871, as in 1940, it was the conservatives who led the campaign for peace with the enemy. Quite naturally, therefore, when elections were called for a National Assembly to decide the great question of peace or war, the country as a whole, weary of the struggle, voted for the conservatives—and the new Assembly found itself with a monarchist majority. Instead of returning home, once it had arranged the peace, the Assembly seized this unexpected opportunity to give France a king and a constitution. We need not follow here the juvenile scruples and unrealistic rigidities of the heir to the throne, who had incidentally a competitor in the younger, Orleanist, branch. The upshot of this comedy was that by the winter of 1875 the monarchists still had a majority but they had no candidate for king. And they were becoming increasingly alarmed by the rising tide of Republicanism and the resurgence of Bonapartism.

Under these conditions, the Assembly grudgingly and hesitatingly voted a series of constitutional laws, and the first of them, which used the word "Republic" in a kind of cautious aside, was accepted by a majority of only one vote. Those monarchists who finally voted for the laws were determined to give the new regime a strongly conservative cast, and they hoped of course that it might prove a "waiting room" for the return of the King.

The Constitution of 1875 was, then, no single articulated document, like our own or the French Constitutions of 1791 and 1848. It consisted instead of three different sets of laws, voted at separate times and beaten out on the anvil of angry compromise. One leading French historian was fond of saying that there was really no Constitution of 1875—merely a collection of laws on different subjects united by the fact that they could be amended by the same process.

The Constitution is not only formless. It is incomplete and ambiguous. It says nothing about taxation, the courts, or the Napoleonic administrative system. It provides no rules for the creation of a Ministry, nor does it even mention the Premier. There is no definition of the rights of Parliament nor reference to the crucial problem of the control of the executive. It leaves particularly unclear the position of the Senate, and irritation with the pretensions of that body was the background for one of the few important innovations in the Constitution of 1946. Nor does it include any reference to civil liberties, although it is true that public law clearly recognized them and the Third Republic was further to legislate on freedom of the press, associations, and teaching. Says one French jurist: "The documents of 1875 are, in fact, merely a sketch, a table of contents." The papal Encyclical of 1864 had condemned liberal principles and institutions in general. One wit remarked of the Constitution of 1875 that it was "the only one to escape the Encyclical, because it rests on no principle."

2

The nominal executive of the Third Republic was the President. He was in fact endowed by the Constitution with powers similar in breadth to those of our own chief executive: he was Commander-in-Chief of the armed forces, had control of foreign relations, and possessed significant powers of appointment.

But what the Constitution gave with one hand, it took away with the other: every act of the President required the countersignature of a Minister. The words of the Constitution clearly enough describe a head of state with functions somewhat like those of the British King—President Félix Faure good-naturedly confessed as much when he said to Poincaré: "I am the Queen of England."

The President of the Third Republic was in fact, both more and less than the British monarch. He lacked the great prestige of the Crown and its potent symbolism as a cohesive force in the Empire. He was, on the other hand, in a position to exercise more influence on the course of affairs. The presidency was not quite, as one writer has caustically suggested, an "honorable retreat for veterans worn out by political battles," its incumbent a "mute idol in a pagoda," his function "to hunt rabbits and not to govern." It is nonetheless true that the ideal —and usual—president was a man with an unspectacular career who had offended the fewest possible people, the "above-party" figure who was neutral in attitude and personality and who had rather broad political experience—presidents of the Senate or the Chamber were favorites. A strong and shrewd figure, like Poincaré, could make a success of the presidency, but Marshal MacMahon and Alexandre Millerand, who blatantly sought inflation of the presidential powers, were both forced out of office.

Our tactful, experienced, mediocre president could make himself felt in two ways. When a ministry fell, it was his function to choose the next premier. Given the multiplicity of parties, hence of possible combinations leading to a new majority, the president sometimes had considerable latitude in choosing the head of the government, and could in this way place a personal impress on the direction of events. In the second place, the president regularly presided over the more important meetings of the cabinet. With his accumulated experience over the years, he was often better informed than members of the government and could again bring tactful influence to bear on decisions. This was notably true in the realm of foreign affairs, where continuity and a good deal of interparty unity were usual. In domestic politics, however, anything like a direct intervention of the president was always viewed with profound suspicion.

The president was elected for a term of seven years, not by direct, popular vote, but by a majority of the "National Assembly"—the Senate and the Chamber sitting together. The fathers of the Constitution had had recent experience of the direct election and subsequent dictatorship of Napoleon III, and they were distinctly allergic to plebiscites and demagogues.

3

The real executive under the Third Republic was the premier and his cabinet—the French call it the "Council of Ministers." "The legislature and the executive live in a state of penetration, of reciprocal dependence," says Léon Blum, "and the very law of our governmental activity is their continuous collaboration." It is indeed precisely the relationship of these two elements—and more specifically of the Chamber of Deputies and the Council of Ministers—that is at the heart of the functioning of the whole French parliamentary system. The Constitution of 1875 could have been interpreted to provide a useful balance between the powers of these two organs. Unfortunately, history shifted the balance dangerously in the direction of the Chamber. And the constitution makers of 1946 did nothing significant to correct this tendency.

An American scanning the French political terrain for the first time is struck by the fact that there are not two parties but many. This multiplicity reflects old political divisions reaching back to the Great Revolution—authoritarian and republican, clerical and anticlerical. It reflects the impact of the industrial revolution, with the rise of socialism and more recently of communism—movements which have frightened much of bourgeois France and driven parts of it far to the Right. Multiplicity is also a reflection of the preoccupation of the average Frenchman with politics and his profound addiction to what he personally believes to be political "truth." Many years ago Mr. Lowell cogently observed that "the Frenchman is theoretical rather than practical in politics. He is inclined to pursue an ideal, striving to realize his conception of a perfect form of society, and is reluctant to give up any part of it for the sake of attaining so much as lies within his reach." * It is in any case not from the soil we have been describing that one produces large and cohesive parties built on compromise. The Communists are an exception, and the source of their cohesion is imported.

The fact of numerous parties is intimately connected with political instability. It has meant that each new premier has had to seek a majority, not in one party, as is normal in Britain, but in at least three and usually several. If the allegiance of one of the tiny fractions of his support—perhaps only a handful of deputies—dissolved, the premier was overturned.

There was another source of ministerial instability. It derived from the security of tenure which the deputies enjoyed. In a parliamentary system such as that of Britain, a revolt against the government and an adverse vote in the House of Commons regularly means a new government or a new election to determine the will of the people on the issues at stake. In France, the Chamber of Deputies became, to use the apt phrase of one writer, a "closed arena." The Constitution provided, to be sure, a clumsy system for dissolution of the Chamber, with the consent of the Senate, but the "improper" use of this instrument by President MacMahon in 1877 discredited it completely. Ever thereafter talk of dissolution at once summoned up the specter of "dictatorship." The result was that the deputies, once elected, knew that they could enjoy an uninterrupted period of four years without the expensive and unpleasant danger of facing the voters. Under these conditions they were quite naturally inclined to forget the platforms on which they

* A. Lawrence Lowell, *Governments and Parties in Continental Europe*, I, 105.

had been elected, and to devote themselves to their own political advancement. One penetrating journalist has accused the deputies of a kind of corporate conspiracy to further their individual political interests in this "Republic of Comrades." "When two deputies of irreconcilable opinion meet for the first time, they call each other 'my dear colleague.' At the next meeting, they are on a first name basis." The new deputy should show himself discreet, talk very little in the corridors of the Chamber, never in the tribune, and concern himself exclusively with making advantageous connections. "After a short time," our critic continues, "he will definitely have lost contact with public opinion and with the taste for a fight. Then he has become a genuine deputy." * This position of security meant that a deputy sometimes took an almost frivolous attitude toward the overturn of a government. If he were in opposition, he had nothing to lose, and he might have something substantial to gain—perhaps even a place in the new government!

There were other reasons why the deputy did not give his attention unreservedly to the national interest. As soon as he announced his candidacy, he was overwhelmed by the pressure of special interests—local, political, economic, personal—which converted him into "a multiplier of abuses." Once in Paris he was subjected to a stream of requests from his constituents, some of them ludicrous: would he do some crucial shopping (in a capital obviously more attractively stocked than the provinces)? Would he consult a physician in his constituent's behalf? Would he be good enough to find a wet nurse for the family?

Arrived in parliament, he was at once subject to economic pressures—if he was from the South, he must "swear by the gospel of wine," if from the North, "by the gospel of beet sugar." André Tardieu, an unfriendly critic of the system, pictures the deputies divided in the mid-thirties along multiple

* Robert de Jouvenel: *La République des Camarades* (Paris, 1914), pp. 15, 28.

lines in the defense of special interests—275 in support of the automobile industry, 200 concerned with the lot of the peasant, 160 interested in the cattle-breeder, 320 in the artisan, 220 in the rights of traveling salesmen, 185 in the aged without pensions—and so on endlessly.

In the legislative setting we have described, the new premier faced a formidable task indeed. He had first to choose a team of ministers representing the different groups which were to constitute his majority—some from the Senate as a rule, but most of them from the Chamber. This task was a most delicate one—each party had to receive ministerial "weight" consonant with its own conception of its importance, no individual of outstanding importance could be neglected. Thus, there came into being a typical coalition cabinet, with widely divergent interests among its members. Formulation of policy and the drafting of bills for Parliament entailed endless debate and compromise.

Here we have touched the nerve center of the problem of governmental instability. The prime fact is not that governments were overturned with some frequency; it is rather the fact that the premier, in order to reach any fundamental policy decisions, had constantly to compromise—frequently on narrowly political grounds—and often seriously to dilute his original intent. If he failed in cabinet sessions to get wholehearted support from the ministers representing any given political group among his supporters, he was sure to be in for serious trouble in the Chamber. The premier could not hope to have that solid one-party support which a British Prime Minister—at least one with a very substantial majority—regularly enjoys and which enables him to design and carry through a pretty consistent policy even over a period of years. The premier tended, therefore, to move cautiously from day to day, avoiding ambitions and long-range views and warily seeking to extract the "possible" from each given situation.

Unfortunately, once the government had agreed on a given policy and embodied it in a bill for the Parliament, its troubles had only begun. When the bill reached the Chamber, it was referred to one of the "Grand (Permanent) Committees." Here a group of partisans, exercising great power, but at the same time escaping governmental and party control, arrogated to themselves the right to alter or even remake the government's bill and to reduce the minister in question to the role of a mere suppliant. The President of the Committee was often an ex-minister or a deputy who aspired to become a minister. The Rapporteur, who presented the Committee's results to the Chamber, was frequently a younger man "on the make," who, like Bonaparte at Toulon, sought to concentrate all eyes on himself, and who not only lent himself to a deformation of the government's bill but to the inflation of a report of incredible dimensions. Sometimes there followed an epic debate in the Chamber between the minister and the rapporteur in which the latter had on occasion to be reminded that he was *not* himself a minister. Enough has been said to indicate that the Grand Committees had not only undermined the powers of the executive but had usurped to a degree the deliberative functions of the Chamber itself.

A final weakness of the executive lay in the lack of effective control over the budget. The government did introduce a budget, but that budget was usually drastically revised by the all-powerful Finance Committee, and could then be subjected to any number of further changes proposed by individual deputies. Viviani once stigmatized this unfortunate process: "The budget might be compared to a caravan traveling through a wild region . . . repeatedly forced to pay ransom to marauding gangs." It is clear that under these conditions governmental responsibility for income and expenditure was illusory.

The French themselves have been very much aware of the weaknesses of their parliamentary system, and there is a whole literature on the subject of reform. Repeatedly, it has been proposed to initiate an effective dissolution procedure which would enable the premier to turn to the country in the event of a struggle with Parliament. Effective power of dissolution in the hands of the premier would, it has been argued, cause individual deputies to think twice before overturning a government and precipitating what might be for them an expensive election of uncertain outcome. The result would be a much more coöperative and better disciplined majority. At the same time the deputy would become more responsive to public opinion, keeping an ear to the grass roots at other times than in election years. And again elections precipitated by a dissolution of the Chamber would tend to be fought on national issues; and since there are more likely to be only two views of questions of this magnitude, there might emerge, clearly not a two-party system, but something nearer that situation than anything that France has had in the past.

Among the most arresting reform proposals were those of Léon Blum, who consistently urged that much could be effected by nothing more than changes in the rules and that no drastic innovations were necessary. We have noted Blum's very sensible proposal that the premier should hold no portfolio. Toward the end of World War I he went further and urged that the premier create a small inner group—its inspiration was Lloyd George's War Cabinet—but again of ministers without portfolio who would meet frequently and devote themselves to the creation and coördination of policy at a high level. This inner cabinet would be assisted in turn by a secretariat of technical experts, men of broad culture and training, who would penetrate the national implications of policies of individual ministries and aid in bringing these measures into some kind of harmony. This technical secretariat would also afford an important minimum of continuity from government to government.

To restore further the authority of the premier and to expedite the business of the Chamber, Blum would refer most bills to special, *ad hoc* committees of deputies chosen for their knowledge of the subject (the practice of the early days of the Republic), insist on brief reports, and retain only the most important of the Grand Committees. Or, better still, he would have bills brought directly before the Chamber and then referred, between the first and second debates, to an Editorial Committee to be put in "proper form." Why, in all conscience, asks Blum, should a bill be drawn by the government, mutilated by a committee, and then altered again by the Chamber—which often restores much that the committee has removed?

Blum would also expedite the business of the Chamber by having the premier, now relieved of ministerial duties, always present to give the debate that expert guidance which his wide knowledge of the issues can afford; and by increasing the authority of the president of the chamber, so that the latter through a more useful division of labor with the vice presidents, might more effectively intervene to keep discussion in channels and move business along more rapidly.

4

We need finally to say a word about the Senate of the Third Republic, although it has now yielded to an anodyne successor, the Council of the Republic. From the beginning, the Senate was resented by good Republicans because it had been fabricated by the Monarchists to act as a brake on the Chamber. With the passing decades the Senate became considerably less conservative but still remained "a somewhat distorted mirror of the political visage of France."

This is easy to understand. Senators hold office for nine years, which meant that in our rapidly moving world they had often lost touch with the wishes of the electorate toward the end of their term. They were, moreover, chosen by a complicated, indirect method which gave the rural areas an altogether disproportionate influence in the election of what Léon Gambetta termed the "Grand Council of the Communes." Over the years the normal senator tended to be a rather conservative member of the provincial middle class whose sound Republicanism, as evidenced by his hostility to the Church, was matched by a highly developed distaste for social and economic reform.

Of greater significance was the fact that the Senate regularly modified the annual budget in a conservative sense, and from time to time (twice in the case of Léon Blum's Popular Front) overturned the government—although its constitutional right to do either has been vigorously challenged by students of the Constitution.

With the swing to the left under the Resistance it was inevitable that there should be widespread agreement that the Senate must go. It was eliminated entirely in the first draft constitution, and reappeared only in a drastically altered form in the second.

5

There is a paradox in the political history of the post-Liberation period. In the fall of 1945, 96 per cent of the electorate voted against the return of the Third Republic. In the autumn of 1946 a majority of those who went to the polls acquiesced in a political system closely resembling that of 1875. The explanation is to be found in the kaleidoscopic changes in the political scene during the two years following Liberation.

From the hardships and frustrations of the occupation period, the vast majority of the French people emerged with a determination to set their feet on a new path. There was a "wave of enthusiasm on the morrow of liberation," notes Gordon Wright; "Frenchmen turned their eyes from the past to the future, and caught the vision of a new, vigorous, rejuvenated *patrie*. The Fourth Republic would be constructed by a people purged of its past errors, unified and tempered by the resistance, guided by the public good alone." *

This honeymoon was subjected almost at once to the solvents of political conflict and economic difficulty. The first "new" fact in the political scene was the Communist Party which

* Gordon Wright, *The Reshaping of French Democracy* (New York, 1948), p. 3.

had emerged from the Resistance period with greatly enhanced —and almost universally recognized—prestige, and with a vastly increased following. The second "new" fact was de Gaulle himself, symbol of the national resistance, who, following his triumphal return to Paris, enjoyed for fourteen months almost unlimited power in what was essentially a "dictatorship by consent."

In the "Republican tradition" of 1793 and 1848, the Communists sought the creation of a single chamber system in which the legislature would hold the executive in firm control. De Gaulle, on the other hand, wanted to strengthen the hand of the executive and thus repair manifold weaknesses in the old regime which we have earlier described. The views of the General appealed, among others, to a wide group of thoughtful men who recognized that the Republican regime badly needed a controlled infusion of authority. But the Communists could play on the traditional fears of the millions of Frenchmen that an executive with real power would shortly become a dictator.

The constituent assembly elected in October 1945 had a political complexion notably different from the chamber of the prewar period. Influences of the Resistance period, reinforced by a curious version of proportional representation handed down by de Gaulle,* resulted in the return of three parties of roughly equal size and occupying more than three-quarters of the total seats. These were the Communists, the Socialists, and the new Social Catholic party, the *Mouvement Républicain Populaire* (MRP), whose origins and growth will be the subject of later discussion. Between the MRP, which sought in general to strengthen the executive, and the Com-

* Instead of totaling party votes on a national basis and giving each party its exact ration of seats ("pure proportional representation"), proportionalism was to be used in each electoral district, normally the Department. This system, which is still in use, favors parties with strong local influence and the formation of coalition tickets; it tends to slow a trend toward either a two-party system or an increase in the number of parties—in short, it favors a few strong party machines.

munists, who wanted a powerful single house, the Socialists held the balance of power. It was an influential position but, as the Socialists have discovered repeatedly since, it was a perilous one—even temporary alignment with either side meant sacrifice of principles and power, and heightened tensions within the party. This frustrating dilemma of the Socialists was to be one of the most unsettling factors in postwar French politics.

In the end, the Socialists voted with the Communists to make the legislature unicameral, to have the premier elected by the assembly, and to strip the president of the republic of all effective power. On the other hand, the Socialists voted with the MRP to create a new "automatic" dissolution procedure and to limit the assembly's legislative powers in various directions. This wavering came temporarily to an end in January 1946, when the Socialists, under heavy pressure for their "cohabitation" with the "clerical" MRP, formed a *comité d'entente* with the Communists and agreed to work more closely with the "brother party." One product of this understanding was a lengthy Declaration of Rights reflecting the tradition of the Declaration of 1789 but stating also a set of principles of social justice in terms of collectivism and a planned economy. Whatever its merits in principle, the Declaration invited wide dissent in certain quarters in the constitutional referendum of May 1946.

In the end the MRP broke with the allied Socialists and Communists over the demand of the MRP that a second chamber, with very limited powers, be created as a modest check on the exorbitant powers of the assembly. When their demands were refused, the MRP came out against the constitutional draft. In the ensuing campaign, the Communists were not content to demand acceptance of the constitution; they boldly suggested that it was high time that a Communist-headed government come to power. Many Frenchmen took fright: a vote for the constitution appeared to be a vote for the Communists. There were several hundred thousand Socialist desertions. And finally, to the acute surprise of most observers, the constitution was defeated in May 1946 by 53 per cent of those voting.

Fresh elections now yielded a new constituent assembly in which the Communists and Socialists lost their small majority and polled only 47 per cent of the vote and in which the MRP, with the largest percentage of the vote polled in any modern French election (28.5), became the country's largest party. The Socialists had seen the handwriting on the wall even before the election and hastened to express willingness to accept a second house with a suspensive veto over legislation.

In the interests of saving debate and time, the new constituent decided to revise, and not discard, the earlier constitution. It threw out the controversial Declaration of Rights, and put in its place a more general and modest Declaration of Principles. It approved a second chamber with the understanding that it was not to be in any sense an image of the old Senate: specifically it had only suspensive control of legislation and it was denied the right to overturn the government. The members of the new Council of the Republic have since come to be called "Senators," and they have in fact made a very real effort to exercise an influence analogous to that of the old Senate. Finally, the constituent restored to the president his right to name the premier, who in the earlier draft was to have been elected by the assembly.

The president enjoys one new power as presiding officer of the *Conseil supérieur de la magistrature*, which has wide powers over the appointment of judges and the administration of the courts. But the executive still remains weak. Where the MRP had wanted to give the premier full and effective powers of dissolution, it was obliged to accept a much weaker version, which in practice–and admittedly under abnormal political conditions–has added nothing to the stature or influence of the cabinet.

De Gaulle, who had dramatically resigned as president in January, now issued a tremendous blast against the new draft

(August 27). The General's action alienated the MRP ("party of fidelity") and rallied the MRP along with the Socialists and Communists to support of the constitution. The French were by now deeply weary of debate, conflict, and delay, and in November 1946—in an atmosphere of political fatigue, apathy, and frustration—the country finally voted to accept the constitution. They accepted it only by a margin of a million votes (nine million to eight) with another eight million abstaining. Said one observer: "All Gaul is still divided into three parts: those who say reluctantly yes, those who say unconditionally no, and those who simply don't give a damn."

The earlier hopes for a brave new world were now largely dissipated, and the constitution itself resembled all too closely its repudiated predecessor of 1875. The partisans of a strong executive and the supporters of an all-powerful legislature had sunk their differences and found themselves pretty much back where they had started. The most radical changes in the new constitution were the elimination of the Senate and the substitution of the Council of the Republic, a mere "chamber of reflection," and the reorganization of the overseas possessions in the French Union, a development which we shall consider at length later. The President of the Republic possesses much the same powers as before, although he may return for reconsideration bills already accepted by the legislature. Despite the introduction of a new, although carefully safeguarded, dissolution procedure, successive premiers have been unwilling to use this threat to discipline their majorities or to turn to the country to find fresh support, doubtless fearing among other things that Gaullist strength in the assembly would be greatly increased by an appeal to the electorate at this time. And so the new constitution has not increased governmental stability. As in the past, deputies feel secure to attack the government, often in most irresponsible ways. The constitution has done nothing to modify the old system of committees, and the latter continue to measure strength with, and even to browbeat, governments.

Even the notion that larger parties would conduce to stability and tend to compensate for weaknesses in the constitution has proved illusory. The very fact that a party is large means that there is more space for faction and dissension. Both Socialists and the MRP have been rent by internal struggles, have for years been in the process of disintegration, and have offered anything but consistent and dependable support to the coalition governments of the so-called "Third Force."

5. Two Centuries of Franco-American Relations (to 1939)

The "relations" between two countries are enormously complex. They run the rich and varied gamut from the casual contacts of individuals, through the sustained relations of scholars and students and the involved association of business houses, to the perennial relations of two governments. They are in short individual, cultural, economic, official—to say nothing of the increasingly important role of public opinion. Here we shall be largely, though by no means exclusively, concerned with official relations, what the French and American governments did and said to each other.

The official relations of two countries are deeply anchored in their respective interests, and interests change—sometimes with alarming rapidity in a dynamic world like ours. Such relations also reflect less rational considerations, like national attitudes, which have to do with the extent to which one people is capable of understanding another. In rather fundamental ways, the French and Americans are almost poles apart in their outlook on life, but their common respect for the dignity of man and for institutions which will permit him to defend it, have given the two peoples a basis for much more effective communication and understanding than has been possible, let us say, between Americans and Russians.

There is a traditional view of Franco-American relations which became general during the War of 1914. It is the gospel of many American expatriates in Paris, pictures our relations as those of almost uniform friendship during the past two centuries, and is based on the two central facts that French intervention in the American Revolution made our victory possible and that American intervention in 1917 tipped the scales for the French. It overlooks the fact that the relations of the two countries have ranged from indifferent to bad during much of the remainder of the period. Skeptics also point out that intervention in these two instances reflected self-interest. This is true, but irrelevant. Nations normally act in their own interest. The important fact is that the interests of the two countries have at various times—and actually for considerable periods—run parallel to each other. This parallelism was never of greater importance than at the present hour.

We shall better understand the relations of France and the United States if we note for a moment the profound differences in the development of the two countries during the past two centuries. The story of the United States is that of dramatic growth—in terms of power—from the time when it was still only a relatively feeble group of British colonies lying along the western fringe of the Atlantic to the position of unique power which it assumed after World War II.

American policy during the period since independence divides rather naturally into three parts. During the long initial period, when we were relatively weak, we took advantage of Europe's absorption in her own quarrels to pursue a policy of isolation that would enable us to conquer and develop the vast and empty parts of our own continent. Rather abruptly at the end of the nineteenth century and following the participation in the war with Spain, the United States emerged as a nation with world responsibilities, increasingly aware of the dangers that could issue from a Europe dominated by a single power. Finally, World War II initiated a third period: that conflict destroyed the old European balance, created a new and essentially extra-European balance with Soviet Russia and the United States the prime factors, and made necessary the complete reformulation of American policy.

The story of France during these two centuries is no less dramatic, but here the drama is one of decline—again in terms of power—and here we intend no implication respecting the extent of French influence in other directions. In sharp antithesis to the American colonies of the mid-eighteenth century, France was the most powerful and most populous state in Europe. The great Revolution swept aside the social and administrative debris of the Old Regime, and nationalist fervor galvanized Frenchmen in the face of attacks from beyond their borders. Napoleon exploited this new national cohesion to conquer and organize large parts of Europe, but, as we look back with more perspective, we recognize now that France was living her last great period of independent national power. For, in the industrial race of the nineteenth century, France, already bested by Britain, was passed by Germany and the United States. Her consequent decline in military potential was reflected in the tragic events of 1870, when the armies of a rejuvenated Germany swept over her borders and inflicted rapid defeat upon her. And in the War of 1914, victory against a still more powerful Germany proved possible only with extra-Continental aid. Finally, the catastrophe of 1940 left France a power factor primarily in the larger context of the integration of the West to meet the threat of Soviet Russia.

1. COLONIAL AMERICA AND FRANCE

During almost the entire period of his colonial existence, the American viewed the Frenchman as an enemy. Indeed the seventeenth and eighteenth centuries witnessed an epic struggle between these two deeply contrasting civilizations—Anglo-American and French—a struggle which, in the somber colors of Parkman's prose, moves on to its conclusion with the seeming inevitability of Greek tragedy. The French had readier access to the North American interior through the St. Lawrence and the Great Lakes than had the British, whom the Appalachians pinned along the narrow fringes of the Atlantic for decades. But France sent few colonists to the New World and took only passing interest in that Canada which Voltaire contemptuously described as a "few acres of snow." The British, on the other hand, sent substantial numbers, and when the vanguard did push westward across the mountains, it met resistance from only a thin chain of French military posts.

In the end, greater manpower and resources, sustained by the firm command of the seas and the very real advantages of the British insular position with consequent freedom from invasion, won out against a population of more military character and an army with more skillful officers. Victory came, says Parkman, to the untrammeled and expansive energies of a free society in contest with a "brave, unthinking people . . . stamped with a soldier's virtues and a soldier's faults," crushed "under the exactions of a grasping hierarch" and stifled "under the curbs and trappings of a feudal monarchy."

The expulsion of the French from the whole area east of the Mississippi had unexpected effects. Directly, the French defeat, which entailed the loss of India as well, laid the basis for the modern power of imperial Britain. But indirectly it led to the independence of the "eldest and greatest of her offspring." For, once freed of the French menace, the colonists "with astonishing audacity . . . affronted the wrath of England in the hour of her triumph." French defeat and French intervention were capital factors in the achievement of American independence.

2. FRANCE AND THE AMERICAN REVOLUTION

It was only natural that the French government, smarting from the humiliation of the Seven Years' War and the loss of the greater part of the overseas empire, should welcome an opportunity to humble Britain and to obtain political and economic advantage from the independence of her American colonies. Even so, the French government was very slow to move after Vergennes, the Foreign Minister, influenced by the reports from America by Beaumarchais, sent secret aid to the Americans before a single American agent had set foot in France. Beyond that, he watched cautiously for a sign of American victory during the years 1776–1778. Meanwhile the outlook and opinion of the French population continued to be in general Anglophile rather than pro-American or libertarian.

After the persuasive American success at Saratoga in 1778, however, the wily Franklin, colonial representative in Paris, proceeded to alarm Vergennes by entering into negotiations with the British, and thus precipitated the alliance between France and the colonies. This alliance provided that the two would fight on until American independence was assured, that neither was to conclude a separate peace, and that each was to guarantee the possessions of the other in America "forever."

The alliance quickly worked a fundamental change in French opinion. Henceforth the majority of the French people were sincerely friendly to America, and official opinion was at least outwardly well disposed toward us. The French government was, of course, pursuing its own interests just as were the colonies. And it is well to remember that the American Revolutionary War was once again part of a world-wide conflict in which the colonies were a distinctly secondary theater, that in only one instance did General Washington command more than 16,000 men (at Yorktown, where nearly half of his troops were French), and that France maneuvered the Spanish and the Dutch into the war and organized almost every other important European state in the league of "armed neutrality" against England. In short, we fought the Revolutionary War as a very secondary element in a conflict on a world scale and with extensive foreign aid, without which our independence would not have been won at that time.

Not only did the French influence the course of our Revolution in a fundamental way, but the American Revolution reacted in turn on France. The war to which the French government had committed itself cost an immense sum and piled up a huge national debt which was directly responsible for the calling of the Estates General in 1789 and the precipitation of the French Revolution. This eighteenth-century Military Aid Program proved disastrous to the French monarchy. In ironic terms, this was a fair exchange: the French had made our revolution a success, and we in turn precipitated theirs.

But the American Revolution exercised an influence in France in various other directions. Participation of numerous Frenchmen in the American Revolutionary War developed and widened their sympathies for a Republican regime, and writings on America consistently perforated the censorship in France. Even an edition of American state constitutions appeared under the royal imprimatur. The stream of reports of French agents and travelers in America, like Crèvecoeur, painted a roseate view of the new country. The French *philosophes*, popularizers of political ideas, who had talked so much of the advantages of a revolution, were now given a concrete example of what a revolution was and indeed how it might be managed. Finally, there were the soldiers, and above all Lafayette.

For France, Lafayette is a subject of controversy. For America, he is a symbol and a myth. Since the time of his participation in the American Revolutionary War, Lafayette has symbolized Franco-American friendship, and his name has contributed steadily to the vitality of the ties between the two countries. Franklin Roosevelt's words to the Congress on May 20, 1934, celebrating the centenary of the death of Lafayette, are quite characteristic:

> In this three-fold role of friendship we, the people of this Nation, have enshrined him in our hearts, and today we cherish his memory more than that of any citizen of a foreign country . . .
>
> Many generations later, more than two million American boys, backed by the solidarity of a great nation, went to France. Those soldiers and sailors were repaying a debt of gratitude to preserve those fundamentals of liberty and democracy to which in a previous age he had dedicated his life.

In the Lafayette story, legend has long obscured fact, as Louis Gottschalk, the leading student of the great Frenchman, has so well shown. He came to America originally not because of his passion for liberty but because he was frustrated, ambitious, and because he hated the British. "More sophisticated men played on these feelings," continues Mr. Gottschalk, "and he was gradually and deliberately set up as a symbol." It was only in America that he became "a crusader for freedom and the rights of man."

And, yet, as a result of his experience in the Revolutionary War, Lafayette became the great link between France and the United States, the "hero of two worlds." He was the "adopted son of Washington," and "the most popular man in France." Enraptured school children listened to masters who spoke as often "of Washington and of Lafayette as of the odes of Horace and the orations of Cicero." Lafayette had learned the lessons of revolution in America from Washington and his other friends, and he became the channel of their influence in France. Through him more than through any other, the spirit of the American Revolution penetrated the potentially revolutionary situation in the France of the seventeen eighties.

The negotiation of the final treaty of peace in 1783 revealed once again the separateness of the interests of the two allies. When John Jay became suspicious—and rightly so—that the French intended to compensate the Spanish for losses in the war by certain territories east of the Mississippi River, he entered into separate negotiations with the British—actually encouraged by Vergennes. When we went further and signed preliminary articles, we violated at least the spirit of the treaty, but we explained this away by noting that these preliminaries were not to take effect until France had also come to terms with the British. As a matter of fact, Vergennes was not unhappy to see the position of Britain strengthened so that he would be able to let the Spanish down more plausibly at Gibraltar (which France had earlier promised to restore to Spain).

The Treaty of 1783 marked both the triumph of the allies and the beginning of their discords. The American colonies had been delighted to accept French aid in their hour of weakness, but they understood only too well the importance of not dissipating their incipient strength in European struggles. Once freed from the domination of Britain, they entered on a long period of isolationism under conditions where the balance of power in Europe permitted them to follow such a policy with relative success. In our own day there are some indications of a reversal of this situation: with a world balance of power created between the Soviets and the United States, an articulate minority in France talks of the possibility of "neutrality" for their country in a future war.

3. THE FRENCH REVOLUTION

During the decade when events were shaping the Revolution of 1789, the American Revolution was the most talked of subject in France. Frenchmen created for themselves "a sentimental and philosophic America," and the people had a "mystic desire to imitate the Americans." As the Estates General began its sessions, the house of Thomas Jefferson, the American Minister in France, became the headquarters of the patriotic party.

When the revolutionaries formulated a new constitution for France, they quite naturally preceded it with a "Declaration of the Rights of Man and Citizen." For this document, which states in classic form the democratic faith of Western man, the most diverse origins have been claimed by various writers. In a recent analysis, Sherman Kent, with characteristic insight and a great deal of common sense, suggests that the Frenchmen who were using these ideas did not discriminate like scholars among the abstruse systems of the thinkers, that representatives of the most diverse views participated in drawing up this document, and that "if ever there was a political philosophy that fell like condensed moisture out of an over-loaded atmosphere, it was that of the Declaration of the Rights of Man and Citizen." In any event, one of the numerous and significant contributions to this *mélange* was American, and the latter came particularly from the various state constitutions.

Having recently passed through their own Revolution, the people of the United States were naturally in a highly receptive mood for the news of French successes. Word of the fall of the Bastille caused a veritable tidal wave of rejoicing, a kind of "Bastille fever." When the autocratic powers to the east invaded France in 1792 and were turned back at the Battle of Valmy, Americans were still stirred with enthusiasm. But when the Terror descended on France, it caused a sharp division among Americans: the Federalists and Conservatives generally believed this movement of violence threatened private property and religion, whereas the Republicans, although regretting its excesses, painted them as the essential price for the achievement of liberty.

When France became involved in war with Britain in 1793, the United States found itself bound to assist her ally in the defense of her possessions in the West Indies under the Treaty of 1778. Happily, the French preferred to have the United States supply her needy West Indian colonies as a friendly neutral, rather than have her as an active participant in the war. It was on this occasion that Washington issued the famous Neutrality Proclamation, which formulated our policy toward Europe for many decades to come, stating that we would be "friendly and impartial toward the belligerent powers." With Washington's Proclamation of Neutrality—which incidentally did not include the word "neutrality"—the relations between the two countries rapidly entered a period of difficulties, more or less acute, which was to last for decades.

Following the outbreak of the war between France and Britain, Citizen Genêt arrived in this country as the first Minister of the new French government. Francophiles gave him a tremendous reception upon his arrival, but Washington and his colleagues received him with far more circumspection and hesitation. In any event, his popular reception encouraged

Genêt to flout American neutrality, to fit out privateers, and in the end to threaten to appeal to the people of the United States over the head of its government. The upshot was official demand for his recall.

In the succeeding years, the countries rapidly moved even farther apart, and in 1796 France announced that it would renew the seizure of American ships (a practice which it had initiated some time earlier) and would treat neutrals as the latter allowed the British to treat them. The United States sent to Paris three commissioners to reach an agreement on this question, and when these gentlemen were subject to solicitation for bribes in the famous XYZ affair, the lid blew off in this country: Congress declared the treaties with France void and authorized the capture of armed French ships. There followed a period of two years of undeclared war, in the course of which the Americans captured more than eighty armed French vessels, largely privateers operating in the waters of the West Indies. Happily, neither side wanted this undeclared war to become war in the full sense of the word, and the courageous action of John Adams in reopening negotiations in the face of opposition from his own party saved the peace in 1800 but brought his own public career to an end.

4. RELATIONS WITH NAPOLEON

Napoleon was the architect of one of the most significant events in our entire history. The territory of Louisiana embraced an immense area between the Mississippi and the Rockies. It offered to the imperial adventurer unplumbed possibilities of extending his influence on the North American continent. But its possession was fraught also with great perils for his power—the possibility, for instance, that it might precipitate an alliance between the United States and Britain. He decided, therefore, to cut his losses, and ceded Louisiana to the United States for what we should now consider a pittance.

The cession of Louisiana was a fact of almost incalculable

importance for our future. It removed the twin dangers of war with France and alliance with Britain. It permitted us instead to develop our strength in peace and isolation. At the same time, it opened a vast territory to our expansion and determined in the last analysis that the United States was eventually to span the continent. Said the late Archibald Cary Coolidge of this event:

> On two occasions in American history the action of the French government has been of so momentous consequence that one can hardly conceive what the destiny of the Union would have been if that action had been different. Without French aid it is very doubtful whether the revolted thirteen colonies could have achieved their independence when they did. Without the Louisiana Purchase, the movement of Westward Expansion would have produced other results. Had France held Louisiana long enough to plant there a considerable French population, two rival nationalities might be struggling today for supremacy in the Southwest. Had she lost the territory to England, and had England joined it to her Canadian possessions, what would have been the future of the United States? *

Our relations with Napoleon, however, were destined to take an acrid turn. In the course of the bitter economic war between France and Britain, associated with the establishment of the so-called Continental System,† the French proceeded to extensive seizures of American vessels—in fact they seized a larger number than did the British—and on occasions they brutally imprisoned the crews. The result of these practices was that in the last years before 1812 American policy was almost schizophrenic in its vacillation: which power was the more offensive and which did we wish more to fight? The upshot was that the United States Senate finally refused to include France in the declaration of war on Britain by a vote of only 18 to 14, so that we fought the War of 1812 against the British alone. This was one instance when we were unable

* Archibald Cary Coolidge, *The United States as a World Power* (New York, 1908), p. 184.

† A Napoleonic policy aiming to ruin Britain by closing Continental European markets to her.

to profit by Europe's divisions: our two enemies were *united* in one thing—their interest in preying on American commerce in the furtherance of their war aims.

5. AFTERMATH OF THE NAPOLEONIC WARS

During the quarter century of general war in Europe ushered in by the French Revolution, we had twice been drawn into the conflict, in 1798 and again in 1812. We had been able to survive because the European powers were locked in a struggle of world proportions. Meanwhile, however, our dignity, and often our interests, received short shrift indeed.

Our hatred of Napoleon and our annoyance with his policies were so profound that when the Bourbon Monarchy was returned to France in 1814, American opinion welcomed this act with enthusiasm. This reaction was general, although quite naturally it was warmest in the case of the Federalists. The toast of a Federalist dinner in New York ran to "Louis, the 18th, King of France and Navarre, heir-at-law to American gratitude." But whatever the initial reactions may have been, the policies of the Bourbon government soon altered our outlook.

As in the case of the Louisiana Purchase, France once again played a capital role, albeit indirectly, in the formulation of the classic American isolationist faith in the Monroe Doctrine of 1823. In 1822, the conservative powers of Europe made a Bourbon France, rapidly adopting more reactionary policies at home and abroad, its agent to crush the Spanish constitutional movement and to restore the Spanish king to his absolute rule. The French government dispatched troops to Spain and effected this happy result, and in the summer of 1823 it looked as though the conservative powers would call a Congress on Latin America to consider the desirability of European intervention to restore Spanish power in the revolted colonies of the Western hemisphere. It was under these conditions that the British Foreign Minister, Canning, proposed to the United

States joint action, but instead, on the advice of the Secretary of State, John Quincy Adams, President Monroe decided to move independently. The result was the President's historic statement to the Congress in December 1823.

The Monroe Doctrine, warning European powers against the danger of intervention in the Western Hemisphere, was an evidence of our profound suspicions of the French. When Lafayette visited the United States for the last time in 1824–25, he was entertained as the nation's guest and his welcome was "unique in its warmth, its unanimity, and its sustained enthusiasm." But the visit of the hero of two worlds was far from being a celebration of Franco-American unity, and served rather to emphasize the lack of harmony and ideals between the two countries and the divergence between the ideals of Lafayette himself and those of a reactionary French government.

It is an unfortunate and ironical fact that a relatively secondary issue poisoned Franco-American relations for more than twenty years after the final defeat of Napoleon, and at one point even brought war on the horizon. The question at issue was the so-called "Spoliation Claims," and in the end these involved something less than six million dollars.

The Spoliation Claims had two sources. The Louisiana Treaty of 1803 provided for the payment of most of "the accumulated claims of either state by citizens of the other." In a second category, we made claims against the French for American ships and cargoes which they had seized during the operation of the Continental System.

We attached substantial importance to the settlement of this question, and accordingly sent Albert Gallatin as Minister to Paris in 1816. In spite of his distinction, Gallatin was permitted to cool his heels in the anterooms of various ministers over a period of seven years, and at the end of that time returned to the United States disgusted and having accomplished nothing. The discussions dragged on through the rest of the reigns of Louis XVIII and Charles X, and, when it finally seemed that concrete results were in the making, the negotiations were overtaken by the events of the Revolution of 1830.

It was characteristic that Andrew Jackson, when he discovered that the new government of Louis-Philippe continued to vacillate over the spoliation issue, decided to take a much stronger line with the French. The government of France finally moved to make a settlement, and we accepted in July 1831 a compromise offer of about five million dollars, which incidentally Gallatin had earlier considered a fair settlement. In return, the United States agreed to pay claims by French citizens amounting to three hundred thousand dollars.

Rarely in the history of diplomacy had a great nation interposed such galling delays on a small one over so trivial a question. But this was not the end. Having agreed to a formal settlement, the French government now dragged its feet over the question of the final ratification by Parliament. Jackson was annoyed, and when the first payment fell due a year from the date of the exchange of ratifications of the treaty, the United States Secretary of the Treasury drew a draft on the French Minister of Finance in February 1833. The French refused to honor the draft, and pointed out that the Treaty had still to be ratified by Parliament. When the Treaty was actually introduced into Parliament in 1834, it went down to defeat.

By now even "Jackson's bitterest political adversaries had spoken to him of a war to preserve the national honor." Jackson himself was furious, and in his annual message to Congress in December 1834 he suggested that, if the French Parliament failed to make the necessary appropriation at the next session, the United States should "make reprisals" on French property in this country. The comedy continued, and in 1835 the French Parliament passed the appropriation bill but with an amendment to the effect that, before payment would be made, the United States should give satisfactory explanations of the President's statement concerning reprisals. The situation had now grown so serious that John Quincy Adams, doubtless with a characteristically pessimistic note of exaggeration, confided to his diary: "If the two countries be saved from war, it seems as if it would only be by a special interposition of Providence."

Happily it did not come to war. In his message to Congress of December 1835, the President made a statement, but not an apology, designed to satisfy the French. The British offered their mediation, and finally the French accepted the Presidential statement as satisfying their honor in 1836.

Once again, on the Texas question, the French took an unfriendly line toward the United States. When Texas won its independence, France, along with Britain, recognized the new Republic in the hope that its independence could be prolonged as a means of weakening the too rapidly growing Yankee power in North America. But when the cards were down in 1845 and events were moving rapidly toward the annexation of Texas by the United States, France hesitated to play as bold a game as Britain and join in a diplomatic act guaranteeing the independence and boundaries of that state. The French government was unwilling to offend the United States at a time when its own problems at home and abroad were considerable and when the general policy of the government of Louis-Philippe was essentially pacific.

6. THE REVOLUTIONS OF THE NINETEENTH CENTURY

It was only natural that the opinion of Americans, who had so recently created democratic institutions themselves, should be favorable to the Revolutions of 1830, 1848, and 1870 in France. In general the masses were enthusiastic in this country, particularly in the case of the first two revolutions. But American approval was by no means unanimous. In 1848 the South in general, and pro-Southern sympathizers in the North, denounced the strong movement for "socialism" in France and the act which freed the slaves in the French colonies. In 1870, the South was favorable to Napoleon, reflecting, as we shall see, his policy during the Civil War. It is worth noting also that the three revolutions were received with diminishing public interest, reflecting a certain feeling of skepticism concerning the usefulness of repeated revolutions and a certain growing sophistication in this country, which in some quarters was even willing to admit that monarchic rule might be a good thing under certain conditions. We recognized each of the three new governments very promptly, and indeed were in every case the first state to take this step.

7. NAPOLEON III AND MEXICO

American opinion viewed the election of Louis Napoleon to the presidency of France in 1848 as a retrograde move toward the reëstablishment of monarchy, and the *coup d'état* of 1851 seemed to bear out the popular belief that the French character was not suited to democratic institutions. The *National Intelligencer* expressed a rather general point of view when it said: "We have ourselves, in a life not very long, already witnessed three French Revolutions, and now witness a fourth. They do not appear to us to improve in quality as they increase in number, but the fifth may be better."

The decade of the fifties witnessed no dangerous antagonisms, although there were sharp differences over Cuba, which the French suspected us of wanting to annex eventually; in the Mexican state of Sonora, where a French adventurer precipitated an abortive revolution and declared the area annexed to France; over the recurring activities of the Emperor relating to an American interoceanic canal; and in connection with the French interest in extending their influence from recently acquired Tahiti to the Hawaiian Islands. But the central problem in Franco-American relations during the reign of Napoleon III was Mexico.

Living in the shadow of his uncle, Napoleon III consistently sought to emulate the brilliant, though disastrous, foreign policy of his predecessor. With declining prestige at home in the early sixties, Napoleon III strongly felt the need to achieve fresh prestige abroad, and so took advantage of our involvement in civil war to create a French puppet state in Mexico, converting an original joint intervention with Britain and Spain (following the suspension of interest payments on Mexican government obligations) into a unilateral French military action. In June 1863, French troops marched into Mexico City, and some time thereafter the Hapsburg, Maximilian, ascended the throne as Emperor of Mexico, supported until 1867 by French troops.

In this "Deepest Thought of the Reign," Napoleon sought not only fresh prestige, but aimed to create a Latin and Catholic monarchy as a bulwark against the growing and aggressive power of the Anglo-Saxon republic to the north. He hoped for a dependable cotton supply with the achievement of the independence of the Confederacy and at a time when the Northern blockade had dealt the French textile business a heavy blow. And, finally, he sought fresh domestic support through the rescue of the Mexican church from the anticlericals at a moment when his Italian policy had deeply alienated French Catholics. This bold and adventurous policy depended for its success on Confederate victory. When that failed, both Maximilian and Napoleon stood in a very exposed position indeed.

The United States deeply resented Napoleon's intervention during their hour of crisis, particularly his proffered mediation of January 1863, after the sharp Northern reversal at Fredericksburg. The Northern press denounced the Maximilian venture from the outset, but naturally Secretary of State Seward had to tread warily at a time when we were in no position to offer effective resistance to French policy. After Appomattox, however, with Northern troops freed for possible action in Mexico, Seward stepped up his demands until they reached almost the pitch of an ultimatum. Finally, in April 1866 the French government publicly announced the withdrawal of its troops from Mexico; in 1867 Maximilian's government collapsed and the Emperor met a firing squad.

Napoleon's withdrawal reflected various pressures. The Mexican venture had imposed a heavy financial burden on

France at a time when the budget could ill accommodate it. The French public had opposed the venture from the beginning, and had given it some support only when French honor became seriously involved. The successful opposition of the Mexicans under the talented political leader, Juárez, made it evident that the difficulties of a complete military reduction of Mexico would be very great. War clouds were settling on the Prussian horizon, although this factor was not prominent in Napoleon's mind at the time of his decision. Finally, there was the specter of American military power, significant even in our hour of exhaustion. Napoleon's retreat was clearly a triumph for the Monroe Doctrine, as its leading student, Dexter Perkins, says: ". . . the final downfall of Maximilian's regime was connected with the acceptance by the American people, to a degree never before realized, of the principles of 1823; and, after the eighteen-sixties, it is fair to say that the Monroe Doctrine was never challenged by any European power." *

It was only natural that the collapse of Napoleonic policy in Mexico should be followed by hostility in the French press, and that later France should deeply resent the message of President Grant, congratulating Prussia on her victory. Meanwhile, among Northerners in the United States, the hatred of Napoleon continued. Says Thomas A. Bailey, a leading authority on American diplomatic history: "The Maximilian affair produced a definite rift in the somewhat illusory traditional Franco-American friendship—illusory because from 1798 to 1867 the Paris government was probably as unfriendly to the United States as that of any other Power." †

8. RELATIONS WITH THE THIRD REPUBLIC

The two decades following the Franco-Prussian War were unmarked by sharp reactions on either side. With the defeat

* *The Evolution of American Foreign Policy* (New York, 1948), p. 52.

† *A Diplomatic History of the American People* (4th ed., New York, 1950), p. 390.

of France and especially with the annexation of Alsace-Lorraine, American opinion in the North rapidly altered in favor of the French, but the violence of the Paris *Commune* tended once again to reverse this trend and to raise serious doubts in many American minds that France would ever be capable of becoming a great power again. This ambivalent attitude—and it has characterized the American outlook from that day to this—is evident in the distinctly patronizing observations of James Russell Lowell, who spent the winter and spring of 1872–73 in France:

> . . . the French are the most wonderful creatures for talking wisely and acting foolishly that I ever saw . . . I feel . . . that they are a different breed for whom I am in no way responsible . . . I don't believe they will make their *République* (a very different thing from a republic, by the way) march, for every one of them wants to squat on the upper bar and to snatch the nuts from their fellows. *Esprit* is their ruin, and an epigram has twice the force of an argument. However, I have learned to like them which is a great comfort, and to see that they have some qualities we might borrow to advantage.*

The continued growth and assertion of German militarism again awakened American sympathy for France, and even the launching of the Panama Canal scheme by the dynamic builder of Suez, Ferdinand de Lesseps, was greeted with definite apathy on the part of the public, although President Hayes took a strong stand against the canal. De Lesseps worked with a liberal hand in the United States, as he did in France, and managed to enlist extensive American support by creating among other things an American Advisory Board with the Secretary of the Navy, Thompson, as its head (the latter resigning to assume his new duties).

Relations on the ceremonial level also improved during this period. It will not do to overemphasize the importance of such manifestations, but it is worth noting that they do not take

* Quoted by Elizabeth B. White, *American Opinion of France* (New York, 1927), pp. 211–212.

place when relations are bad. An important French delegation came for the celebration of the centenary of the Battle of Yorktown, and Secretary of State Evarts, responding to a toast to the "French Alliance," said the friendship of the United States with France was closer than with England. Here was an alliance of "two Republics united against the world. . . Nothing can limit it; nothing can disturb it; nothing shall disparage it."

Discussion of a joint memorial to the War of Independence went back some years. It was finally decided that the French should provide a statue and the Americans a site and pedestal—this decision forming the basis for Robert Sherwood's recent musical comedy, "Miss Liberty." For a period of years, activities on both sides of the water and particularly the raising of a popular subscription in France focused attention on Franco-American relations. And the Statue of Liberty was finally unveiled in 1886 with President Cleveland and the French Premier present and with of course the ubiquitous de Lesseps speaking for France. For weeks the press was full of hands-across-the-sea sentiment, and three years later the American colony in Paris presented that city with a reduced-sized replica of the statue.

The decade of the nineties brought sharp reactions in America, as elsewhere, to events in France. There was much criticism when the French tied their fate to that of Russia in the Franco-Russian alliance, which the American press attacked as a revival of militarism in Europe. Quite naturally the Panama Scandal, linked as it was to the name of de Lesseps, who had enjoyed so wide and respectable a reputation, precipitated a blast of criticism in the American press, much of it lacking in real understanding of the French scene. The *Review of Reviews* was more or less typical: "It is impossible to conceal from the world that a large portion of French society. . . has for years been wallowing in a cesspool of corruption." Finally, the Dreyfus Affair drew denunciations of the French Army and French judicial procedure, and was at the same time the occasion for a generous outpouring of personal letters from Americans to Captain and Madame Dreyfus.

The turn of the century was unquestionably a great pivot in international politics. The ceremonial evidences are there again. In 1900 American school children presented to France a statue of Lafayette, which was unveiled in Paris. In 1902, France presented to the American people a statue of Rochambeau, given a place of honor opposite the White House. Shortly thereafter the body of John Paul Jones was returned to America from France, and in 1912 the French sent a distinguished delegation and a sculptured figure of "La France" by Rodin for the celebration of the tercentenary of Champlain's explorations. But these were only outward indications of a much more fundamental change in the configuration of Franco-American relations.

With the Spanish-American War, the United States became a world power. After 1898, says Dexter Perkins, our country looked "outward" instead of "inward," and in the succeeding years President Roosevelt played a bold and energetic role in the international scene. Archibald Cary Coolidge expresses this in striking words when he says:

> Early in the year 1901, a foreign ambassador at Washington remarked in the course of a conversation that, although he had been in America only a short time, he had seen two different countries—the United States before the war with Spain and the United States since the war with Spain.*

The European imperialist surge of the nineties was central in this fundamental shift. The overseas expansion of France and Britain had brought these two countries face to face at Fashoda in 1898, and the threat of war was so serious that it cleared the air for the general settlement between them which came in the years following. Belatedly, too, the imperialist policy of the Germans led them to the building of a navy in competition with the British, and this in turn impelled the lat-

* *The United States as a World Power,* p. 121.

ter to settle their differences with the French in the same Entente Cordiale of 1904.

As a consequence of these developments, Britain became consistently accommodating in its policy with us in the succeeding years, just at a time when we, too, were becoming increasingly aware of the possible dangers of German militarism and power. And the French, whose press had viciously attacked us during the Spanish-American War, also saw that it was in their interest to solidify the links in the Atlantic community. This new coöperation was symbolized at Algeciras in 1906 when President Roosevelt's actions, although started in motion by the Germans, finally resulted favorably for the French in Morocco. During the prewar years the personality of the French ambassador to Washington, Jules Jusserand, a distinguished historian and very able diplomat, was an important force for unity.

9. COÖPERATION IN WORLD WAR I

So far as American opinion was concerned, France had certain definite advantages over various of the other belligerent powers in World War I. France did not outrage the American public by her actions on the high seas, as did both the Germans and the British, although in different ways. France was an invaded country, and to the man on the street that seemed to mean that the responsibility for the war was clearly on the other side. We have noted the rising suspicion in America of Germany and her objectives during the years preceding the war, although the implications of this were obviously much less clearly seen than in the case of Hitler. In the background were the improving Franco-American relations of the previous years, and of course the ubiquitous Lafayette, whose saga we now revived and embellished. Finally, there was a vigorous and effective group of Francophiles in the United States, led by men of the stature of Charles W. Eliot of Harvard, who gave very effective leadership to this movement for French support.

André Siegfried has put his finger on the nature of this reaction:

> During the War this sympathy increased to enthusiasm—enthusiasm in fact, scarcely expresses the passion of the Americans for France and her cause. This admiration, which even the French found excessive, did not last long, but it is a good illustration of the way in which Franco-American relations are always extreme and insecure.*

In any event, this American sympathy was the setting for both American volunteer action prior to our entry into the war and later for our official coöperation with the French.

The American volunteer effort was impressive. It began at once with a shipment of surgical dressings which arrived in the month of August 1914. Americans in Paris placed the hospital in Neuilly at the disposition of the French government and promptly organized two other hospitals. Soon American aid was arriving in such quantities that an American Clearing House was necessary in the autumn of 1914 to distribute it. André Tardieu lists no fewer than forty unofficial American organizations engaged in sending relief of varying kinds. Richard Harding Davis, Irvin Cobb, and a whole group of American writers created a literature in support of the Allies. The Lafayette Squadron and the American Field Service enlisted Americans in aid of France, and American doctors, engineers, and others offered their services. Nor did this effort end with the war: it made an important contribution during the period of reconstruction, particularly along social lines.

When the United States entered the war, the nature of this coöperation changed overnight. The French government despatched Tardieu himself as High Commissioner for France to the United States for the purpose of coördinating the joint effort. There is no reason to describe in detail that effort, but again it was impressive. The United States sent France some two million tons of steel in various forms, including 170 million shells for their 75's; five million tons of foodstuffs, rep-

* *America Comes of Age* (New York, 1927), pp. 318–319.

resenting a ration for nearly twelve million Frenchmen for eighteen months, roughly the period when we were in the war. France in turn supplied all the 75's and 155's, all the tanks, 81 per cent of the planes, and 57 per cent of the heavy artillery, as well as 65 million shells for the United States Army in France.

Victory can impose more difficult problems upon the victors than upon the vanquished. The latter have at least the advantage of being told what to do. But the victors must compromise their divergent national interests under conditions where the public in each country is emotionally committed to the notion that the unity of war will endure. Wilson seemed to the peoples of the West to symbolize this unity in the weeks following the end of the war, and he was received in Europe with extraordinary evidences of popular support.

In the making of the peace, the divergencies in view of French and Americans rapidly became evident. They were crystallized in the differences of temperament and outlook of Wilson and Clemenceau. Wilson, an idealist and a man whose thinking reflected a strongly academic background, looked upon Europe with that characteristically American optimism which has so often suggested easy and sweeping solutions for very complex and ancient problems; and he brought to the discussion of these problems a no less characteristically American annoyance with the resistance and "recalcitrance" of unbelieving Europeans. Clearly Wilson saw a vision, and one which we have painfully carried one stage farther in the past five years. But the road to the fulfillment of that vision—either in Europe or in the United States—Wilson saw far less clearly. And with a stubbornness rooted in Scotch Presbyterianism, he sought to brush aside all obstacles and to achieve his full objectives almost at once.

Wilson met in Clemenceau a man who had spent his life in the rough and tumble of political controversy and in direct contact with the complex problems of Franco-German relations. Clemenceau had ideals, too, including a deep and sustaining faith in France. But in international relations he trusted only instruments he knew, notably the security deriving from a soundly contrived system of alliances. He was completely skeptical of big and untried solutions like the League of Nations. Perhaps it would be fair to say that Clemenceau looked too resolutely to the past, Wilson too trustingly to the future—and that neither quite understood what he saw in these two unreal lands.

In any event, the clash of these two giants was inevitable. The central problem involved territorial arrangements in western Germany. The French sought to occupy Germany up to the Rhine or to create a buffer state in the Rhineland. Wilson set his face firmly against any such solution as being contrary to the principle of self-determination, and the French finally agreed to occupy the Rhineland and the Saar for a period of fifteen years, with a terminal plebiscite in the latter territory to determine its future. This concession they made in return for a treaty of mutual assistance with the British and Americans. Naturally, the latter required the ratification of the United States Senate.

Clemenceau had an embarrassing time inducing his entourage to accept the treaty of mutual assistance at all, in place of a military frontier in Germany. Moreover, the French public was naïvely convinced that there would be no problem in connection with the ratification by the United States Senate, and official French influence was brought to bear on the French press to have it deal very circumspectly with this question. Hence, when the treaty finally failed to pass the Senate, the disillusionment of the man on the street in France was profound.

10. DISILLUSIONMENT OF THE TWENTIES

In their postwar attitude toward France, Americans faced the most difficult of all psychological readjustments, that of the unrequited lover. We felt that we had offered everything in a generous spirit and in a cause which was not directly ours, and that the French had repaid us by consulting their own parochial and nationalistic interests. Our soldiers returned disgusted with barrack life in war-stricken French towns and with the extortionate prices charged by their hosts. We felt that we had fought a war for idealistic and clear-cut purposes, and that these had been betrayed by actions such as those of the French at the peace table.

Clearly both the thoughts and emotions of the American people were sadly confused at this time. But the result, in any case, was that we resolutely turned our back on Europe and attempted to return to something like the isolationism of the period before 1898. We were fortified in our desire to return to isolationism by a lack of direct experience of European problems and by our reviving prosperity. The latter has proved on more than one occasion a kind of national opiate that quiets the average man's interest in problems which are troublesome but "remote."

Under Warren Harding, and despite the double talk of the President when he was a candidate, the issue of the League of Nations soon became, in the words of one prominent diplomatic historian, "as dead as slavery." Paradoxically, at the very time that we were organizing our political non-coöperation with the new Europe, we were vigorously acquiring colossal private interests in Europe which had profound political and economic consequences later. And while Europe was doing some at least of its diplomatic business around a table by open diplomacy as Wilson had urged, we continued to operate in the grooves of the old "European" tradition: Mr. Hoover characteristically slipped away with Prime Minister MacDonald to settle things in the seclusion of his Rapidan fishing camp.

The American tourist added another complicating factor in this scene. Just at the time when we were growing highly critical of the French, our postwar prosperity sent great waves of Americans to France as visitors. Most of them arrived with little knowledge of France or of the French language, and their contacts with the French people came at a time when the latter were profoundly irritated about our isolationist and debt policies. Comment Miss Hill and Mr. Miller:*

> American return is the return of Europe's Puritan son. The story of the Puritan son is exactly the reverse of the story of the Prodigal Son. During a long sojourn in a far country the Puritan son, instead of wasting his substance in riotous living, has, by a combination of thrift and good fortune, acquired such colossal wealth, that on his return home he wishes to buy up the old place and reorganize it along the lines of his new possessions. The sequel to the story does not disclose the preparation of a feast or the killing of a fatted calf to give him welcome.

The French outlook in this period contributed the other side to the profound misunderstanding which grew up between our two countries. That attitude, too, had its unreasoning elements and its strongly emotional overtones.

Our attempt to return to something like the old isolationism in the years 1920 to 1930 came just when France was emerging from a profoundly traumatic experience of war, when she felt that she had borne the brunt of what was essentially a common cause and had paid a tremendous price in men where we had paid largely in cash and materiel. These losses had induced a profound psychology of pacifism on the part of the French, a determination that it must never happen again, which issued in an almost frenetic search for security—often mistaken in those days for an excessive chauvinism. In the face of this determination to make good their losses in war by preventing its recurrence, the French felt frustrated—first by the desertion of the United States, which failed to ratify the Treaty of Guarantee and refused to come into the League of Nations, and presently by the defection of Britain, attempting to return some distance toward its classic isolationist position, or at least to resume its position as arbiter in the European balance. France saw herself left alone in a Europe in which the defeated powers

* Francis Miller and Helen Hill, *The Giant of the Western World*, p. 151.

—Germany and Russia—were already drawing together and creating a threat to France's last hope of security, an alliance system in the East.

The French tourist did not come to America in any numbers after the war, any more than he came before the war, but there was of course the perennial French visitor. The latter often brought back an uncomplimentary, distorted, and even jaundiced picture of America, in which mechanization and the assembly line were destroying the creativity of the artisan, and American civilization (not really European but something unfortunately different) was sinking into a morass of bad taste.

A somewhat extreme case—and there were examples on the other side—is that of Georges Duhamel, who published his reflections of the early thirties in his *Scènes de la Vie future*, in which the American scene is represented as what Europe will come to eventually. M. Duhamel selects almost random elements of American culture, caricatures them, and compares them with an idealized version of French civilization. He finds the people besotted by the "epidermic pleasures" of the Hollywood product, without recalling that nothing more bitter has ever been said on that subject than what issues regularly from the pens of American critics, without recognizing that the movie is produced for a hierarchy of consumers (with some superbly artistic productions at the top), and without mentioning the fact that French legislators have been obliged most carefully to regulate the inflow of American movies which are in tremendous and highly competitive demand by a great body of Frenchmen, who apparently also enjoy "epidermic pleasures." He finds signs of decay in our professionalized and overtrained athletes, without noting how large a proportion of our people play games for pleasure and relaxation or suggesting that one can exaggerate the "discipline" of the mind as well as of the body, an imbalance in the French educational scene which has been bitterly attacked by the French themselves. This is a book which is only too characteristic of a great deal of the best French writing. It has brilliant *aperçus*, but alas an all too insouciant disregard for supporting evidence.

André Siegfried has given us, in his *America Comes of Age*, a much more responsible and understanding picture, but even he fails to penetrate many aspects of American life and to appraise them at their real value. Siegfried makes bitter and ironic attacks on Rotarianism and "service," a word which he always puts in quotation marks, failing to realize that behind this activity, much of which is undoubtedly silly, lies a highly developed sense of civic responsibility, the lack of which is perhaps the most serious weakness of the French. America, Siegfried finds, is "a materialistic society, organized to produce things rather than people, with output set up as a god." He forgets again that on the basis of this accumulation of wealth has been created an élite in this country, as in France, which has in turn produced superb achievements in the realm of the intellect.

These attitudes speak of the deepening disillusionment of the two peoples with each other. The security problem continued to plague their relations, notably at the Washington Conference of 1922, where the French resisted attempts to reduce their ground forces and would permit no limitation in the categories of cruisers, destroyers, and submarines. The French felt isolated and annoyed when they invaded the Ruhr in the face of stiff official opposition from the Americans and the British—although the American public rallied to the French cause, and the man on the street apparently took the view that the occupation "might not be wise . . . but it was plucky." And then there was the question of the war debts.

When the problem of what should be done about the war debts was raised with President Coolidge, he made the famous reply: "They hired the money, didn't they?" This was unquestionably a response perfectly appropriate in the financial confines of Plymouth, Vermont, and even in those of Boston, but it was clearly too parochial to fit the complicated requirements of the postwar international scene.

Americans were free to view the debts problem either from a moral or an economic point of view. Viewed from either, our policy was a mistake.

The United States entered the war to defend its own interests, not those of France, just as the latter had originally gone into the war to defend its interests and not those of the United States. But these interests were not neatly separable; for the most part they were parallel or merging. It would in any case require the wisdom of a Solomon to assign a relative interest to each of the powers and then to determine, on that basis and the basis of its overall strength, what its contribution should be. The fact is that the United States obviously had a large enough interest in the war to make an all-out effort seem to its people to be justified. What then should be its contribution, in men and in materiel? If the war had lasted another two years and involved large American casualties, we would presumably have accepted these without excessive grumbling. When the war ended much sooner than the best observers expected, so that we were spared a contribution in lives at all comparable to that of the French, we might reasonably be expected to make our contribution in money. The attitude we took on the debts question was morally indefensible.

Even if we neglect the moral side of the picture and put the question on purely economic grounds, however, our policy is still indefensible. For we insisted on the payment of the debts on economic terms that made it impossible for our debtors to comply. And it is questionable whether, even if we had been able to arrange for their compliance, it would have been wise in terms of the economic rehabilitation of the world so necessary to our own economic progress.

We loaned about seven billion dollars to the countries of Europe prior to the Armistice (nine-tenths of this sum was spent in the United States), and we loaned more than three billion to these countries after the war for rehabilitation and relief and for such enterprises as the sustenance of the new Succession States. From the beginning, the European states insisted that reparations and debts were connected, and that in general they could only be expected to pay these debts to the extent that the Germans met their reparations payments. On our side, we refused to grant this connection, although the Hoover moratorium of 1931 came close to it. We did, however, lend weight to its validity when we sent the unofficial Dawes and Young missions to Germany, which sought to save the reparation—hence the debt—structure.

After long negotiations and a great deal of recrimination in the press on both sides of the water, we reached an agreement on the debts with the French in 1926, in which we actually scaled down the interest rate from 5 to 1⁶⁄₁₀ per cent, which meant in effect the elimination of some 60 per cent of the entire debt. But we steadily refused to see that the French could only accomplish the transfer of these huge sums through trade, services, or shipments of gold. Large and continuing exports of gold to the United States would have placed the French currency and economy in jeopardy. Adequate increases in French trade with the United States would have involved some downward revision of our tariff. Instead of this, we pushed our policy to the outer limits of inconsistency by lifting tariff barriers to a new high in the Smoot-Hawley Act of 1930. The depression had already begun and presently it gave the *coup de grâce* to the whole structure of reparations and debts. Perhaps the most telling critique of our debts policy was the fact that the "next time" we resorted to Lend-Lease and the Marshall Plan to achieve the same objectives—and it is not out of the way to point out that President Truman has confessed that the abrupt and premature ending of Lend-Lease just after V–J Day was also a mistake.

The debts problem had precipitated extreme language on both sides of the Atlantic. The French referred persistently to the United States as "Shylock," and Americans were inclined to look on the French as "dishonest ingrates" and to retire further within the carapace of their isolationist sentiment.

11. RELATIONS IN THE THIRTIES

Two events within a few weeks of each other altered Franco-American relations fundamentally. In December 1932 the French settled the debts problem by default, despite the superhuman efforts of Premier Edouard Herriot to obtain at least a token payment. In January 1933 Hitler came to power in Germany. War debts and the other bases for recrimination tended now to move into the background, while the growing Nazi threat came increasingly nearer the center of the stage.

The remainder of the thirties was filled with the growing menace of war. The Ethiopian crisis of 1935 destroyed the lingering belief of many Americans in the efficacy of the League of Nations. As the French moved from one appeasement to another, Americans were lavish in their advice on the virtues of firmness and the dangers of weakness, although we were prey at this very time to our most virulent attack of "ostrichism" and were wholly unwilling to make any meaningful contribution to strengthening the spine of the British and the French.

The perils of the thirties had a twofold and inconsistent effect on the American people. They strengthened American determination to stay out of any second European war, hence lured them into the unreal attempt to legislate isolationism into existence by way of the "neutrality" acts. At the same time, the public opinion polls revealed that an increasing number of Americans were convinced that we would eventually be drawn into any general war which broke out in Europe. Only a strong and resistant France could reconcile these inconsistencies and prevent the dangers of a future war from reaching us across the Atlantic. Hence both interest and belief induced Americans to speak in consistent praise of the Maginot Line and French military power, even when we were most critical of her political frailties and her economic difficulties. World War II descended with the American mind in a state of confusion on the international scene even exceeding that of the French.

6. Defeat, Occupation, Liberation—in Perspective

It is still far too early to write a history of the impact of the recent war on France. This is not mere pedantry. We know too much and too little. The record, although incomplete, is still far too voluminous to master as a whole. At the same time we lack the special studies to canalize it for the writer who would generalize. The period is still drenched with emotion for the French themselves, and the Vichy-de Gaulle controversy has by no means left us Americans untouched. For our present purposes we shall give our story severe limits: a description of the general trends which are of importance for understanding post-Liberation France, and a statement of the nature of certain baffling problems to which the historian has still to give "final" answers—the Armistice of 1940, our Vichy connection, the character of the Resistance, our policy toward de Gaulle.

It goes without saying that we must view the war and the Vichy interlude in the wider setting of French—and European—history of the preceding decades, indeed centuries. In the case of France, unlike certain of the other countries with which the American Foreign Policy Library deals, this story is available to the public in various forms and its detail need not detain us here. Let us simply recall once again the main outlines.

France of the eighteenth century was the leading power on the Continent, and she was probably also the most productive intellectual force in the West. The institutions and outlook of the monarchy, however, were unsuited to express the forces of rapid economic growth and the consequent development of an able and assertive middle class. The series of events which we term loosely the "French Revolution" initially provided a rough solution for this disequilibrium by creating political institutions that gave a strongly controlling voice to the middle class, whose political and economic views were not very different from those of the same class in the American colonies in the pre-Revolutionary period. Political control then passed into successively more radical hands, until the "Terror" became the symbol of political extremism and fixed a deep social and political cleavage, which has remained in France from that day to this.

The normal swing of the political pendulum presently brought to power a dazzling young adventurer, who offered the country, in place of liberty, political and administrative order and a brilliant foreign policy. As in the case of certain other dictators, Napoleon's prestige and popularity spanned the period of his foreign successes, and he was eventually overturned by military defeat.

The moderate monarchists and the upper middle class once again achieved political control when a parliamentary regime in the responsible (British) tradition came briefly on the scene under Louis XVIII, after 1815. But when Louis's successor, Charles X, whose mind had never really migrated from the eighteenth century, attempted to restore symbols of the Old Regime and finally the personal power of the King, elements of the middle class raised the barricades of 1830 and enjoyed for the moment the anomalous support of the inchoate working class of Paris.

The so-called Revolution of 1830 was essentially a "day of dupes." The middle class chose as King the cousin of Charles X, Louis Philippe, in the belief that he would be the willing prisoner of the parliamentary institutions which they reasserted in the revised Charter. The workers believed that the new regime would turn to the solution of the hardships incident to the industrial revolution, now really making itself felt for the first time in France. When the middle class disappointed the workers by taking an almost savagely insular view of their own prerogatives in this new industrial world and when Louis Philippe disappointed the middle class by a cleverly indirect but dangerous assertion of his personal power, the two groups again resisted, the barricades went up, and the monarchy was overturned.

These two groups had radically different views of the meaning of the Revolution of 1848, however, and only the sanguinary June Days in Paris finally arbitrated this deep divergence. Large parts of the population recoiled before this assertion of violence by the rising proletariat, and there was a widespread demand for the restoration of social "order." In this setting Louis Napoleon appeared, with the program of his famous uncle suitably refurbished to accommodate the great economic changes of his age. The conservative forces of the country—with the peasantry numerically far the most important—gave him an overwhelming vote as President of the new Republic, which he shortly converted by force into a dictatorship.

Prosperity, in the setting of economic expansion, and a dazzling, if questionable, foreign policy built Louis Napoleon's prestige high in the fifties. But in the sixties a series of desperate failures in the foreign field alienated his domestic support and opened the way to the attacks of the workers and a dissatisfied middle class. As a result, the dictatorship had dissolved and something close to a parliamentary regime had appeared in France on the eve of the military defeat of 1870, which inevitably precipitated the overturn of the Emperor.

The successful resistance to Napoleon III by the middle class and workers in the sixties was an appropriate precursor to a new republic. And yet the Third Republic, as we have seen, was born under equivocal conditions and lived a harassed existence for a quarter of a century. One domestic crisis after another placed in more or less serious question the validity of the new regime, until the tremendous upheaval of the Dreyfus Affair produced a solution which promised the country a period of internal peace. Then, with the turn of the century, domestic difficulties yielded to a series of drastic international crises and the final precipitation of war in 1914. And yet it is easy to exaggerate the instability, the crisis character, of French political development in these decades. Behind this somewhat misleading façade lay a society fundamentally stable, with a hardy and conservative peasant class, forming about half the population; a city proletariat which was growing at a distinctly slower tempo than that of a number of other industrial countries, with Socialist and labor movements which spoke the language of extremism but acted quite otherwise. With the separation of Church and State in 1905, it appeared to many observers that France was finally destined for a considerable period of orderly and satisfactory domestic development.

The war changed all this. It left the vast physical destruction and losses of men which we have described elsewhere, but the weakening effects of the war were masked by the fact that France was one of the victors. And so she embarked on the formidable tasks of the postwar period in an ambivalent frame of mind: she wanted to recover her earlier economic and military preëminence and play once again the first role in Continental Europe; at the same time her tremendous losses had induced a lack of self-confidence, actually a deep pacifism, an outlook quite unsuited to the boldness and risks demanded by the crises of the thirties.

France passed through four phases during the interwar period, each involving its own disillusionment. During the first, from the end of the war to 1926, France was disillusioned by the failure of reparations, her own connected monetary disorders, the general slowness of postwar economic recovery, and the profound doubts and anxieties which color so much of her literature in the twenties. The second, 1926–1930, witnessed a new and vigorous prosperity, a kind of return to the old pre-1914 world for which the French were so nostalgic, but again disillusioning in its very brevity. With the third came the Great Depression which the French fought with deflation and which, unlike that in most other parts of the world, never really lifted its blight from the country prior to the outbreak of war in 1939. The fourth, ushered in by Hitler's seizure of power, was characterized by deepening anxiety and confusion in response to repeated international crises (sharply contrasting with the confidence and energy which the French—and British—brought to a similar situation prior to 1914). Well before the final outbreak of the conflict, international alarms, coupled with the persisting complications of the depression, had caused deep doubts and divisions within the country and impaired the French will to resist in war.

1. THE DEBACLE OF 1940

The catastrophe of 1940 is the fact of overwhelming importance in the war period, and indeed for the last decade. From it came the German occupation, the Vichy regime, de Gaulle, and practically everything of importance in these years. This vast and unexpected debacle shattered French confidence, and was the beginning of a train of events that redefined the power position of France in the world. These developments have induced a fundamental psychological reorientation, reaching deeply into virtually every phase of French life. We are not suggesting that power and intellectual leadership necessarily go hand in hand, though they often have in history; we are simply saying that a great national tragedy inevitably leaves a heavy impress on a people's culture pattern. France is destined to pass through a long and painful period of readjustment and reassessment of values.

The defeat of 1940 is par excellence the problem of this crowded period which most needs the analysis of the historian. The latter has only begun the complicated problem of sorting and assessing the facts, and it will be long before we can anticipate anything like convincing interpretations. Even so, it is inevitable that a problem of this magnitude should be the subject of endless speculation in the future and presumably never of anything like substantial agreement even among men of good will and "objectivity." Here we shall be content to indicate merely some of the categories of "causes" in the interests of some further clarification of the problem. In the end, the defeat itself was military, but like other military events of this magnitude, it was deeply embedded in social, political, economic, psychological, and other conditions.

France lacked war potential. This is a relative matter: we mean that she lacked the developed potential necessary to hold the Germans north of the Maginot Line until such time as British and American economic strength could be brought to bear. She was seriously deficient in air strength—in number of planes available, and in productive capacity. On the other hand, a recent study finds that she had attained a rough equality in tanks and armored vehicles, and suggests once again that her primary weakness here was the failure to develop a theory of warfare and an *élan* which would fully exploit the effectiveness of these instruments.*

These deficiencies in potential reflected in part the failure of the economy to recover from the depression, the fact that France in 1939 was producing about as much as in 1913. One leading student of this problem, Raymond Aron, has suggested that this stagnation may have been due largely to a mistake in judgment—a refusal to devalue the franc until it was perhaps already too late, and then the simultaneous institution of the forty-hour week by Blum, which limited industrial expansion in a country short of labor (even in the depression years, France never had widespread unemployment as it was known for instance in the United States).

The French High Command lacked imagination. France, suggests Hamilton Fish Armstrong, had "a Maginot Line in the mind." The very fact of victory in 1918 committed her leaders

* Richard D. Challener: "The Military Defeat of 1940 in Retrospect," *Modern France* (Princeton, 1951).

to the methods they had already successfully used. Almost before the ink was dry on the Armistice of November 11, German military thinkers turned to an analysis of their defeat and to the development of new weapons and new tactics. These things were there for the French to see in the German military journals, but the High Command refused to learn either from the enemy or from the forward-looking younger officers in France such as de Gaulle, who developed a very modern doctrine of war. The French adhered to the scattered and defensive use of tanks and the notion of the continuous line of fire when the Germans were developing the new dynamics of the blitzkrieg. The tragedy is that they declined to learn even from the defeat of the Poles, when the Germans literally presented them with a dress rehearsal of the subsequent invasion of France. French leadership, both political and military, lacked that adventurous flexibility of intellect which would have enabled France to cope with dynamic opponents in a new age. Instead, in the field of ideas, France chose to live "on the stockpiles of the past." Pertinax has laid an acid finger on the failure of Gamelin when he says:

> In piercing through to the central cause we are forced to indict the straitened military universe he gradually imprisoned himself in, like a turtle in its shell. It was a world of three dimensions, whereas the German world had four or five. Extreme mobility, the saving of human effort by means of machinery, the stunning surprise effect of new weapons, the political and psychological tricks discovered in the course of civil disturbances in Germany . . . all these weapons were as astounding to the French commander and found him as unprepared as if he had been faced with warriors from Mars.*

France lacked cohesion and unity. Here the traditional cleavage of Right and Left was widened and altered by the inflation, the depression, the rise of Hitler, and the new position of Bolshevik Russia, with its anomalous relation to the Communist Party in France. Where the inflation of the twenties struck

* *The Gravediggers of France* (New York, 1944), p. 82.

at the middle class, the deflation of the thirties was a blow to the workers and opened the way for the Communists. The depression produced wide dissatisfaction in big and little business alike and among the white-collar class. Fascist leagues appeared to arraign the Republic for its failures, and when the response of the Left was the formation of the Popular Front, with the inclusion of the Moscow-dominated Communists, important elements of the Right took alarm. At a time when French security against Hitler's Germany logically demanded a close military arrangement with the traditional ally, Russia, France was prevented from implementing the new alliance with the Soviets by the widespread fears of communism. In fact, the Right, which had for decades supported a vigorous foreign policy, now dramatically reversed itself, and many of its leaders became abject appeasers of the fascist enemy. By 1939 there was in France a group of men—Laval was only one—psychologically prepared to become the willing and even enthusiastic pallbearers of the Republic. The final blow to French unity was struck by the Soviet-German Pact of August 1939, which ranged the French Communists against the war policy of the country. France entered the conflict a deeply divided nation.

During the "Twilight War" and after an official decree had dissolved the Party itself, the Communists went underground and contributed notably to the weakening of French morale. Certain Communist deputies transmitted to Soviet authorities secret details on French defense that had been discussed in secret sessions of Parliamentary committees. Both the Daladier and Reynaud cabinets viewed the activities of French Communist deputies as a grave menace to the security of France. A clandestine version of *Humanité* appeared about once a week all during the months from October 1939 until the Armistice, and this was only one of a number of such publications. Insinuating tracts appeared on every hand and were stuffed surreptitiously into the coat pockets of factory workers. In innumerable ways, the Communists brought significant support to the fifth column of their new-found friends, the Nazis, and their defeatist propaganda unfortunately found an all too general response in a country which was deeply pacifist.

France was pacifist. Her tragic experience in the War of 1914 and her huge manpower losses made Frenchmen profoundly reluctant to be drawn into another war. This was only too evident in the almost universal relief following the Munich crisis, which reached even clear-sighted men like Léon Blum. The Left had been traditionally pacifist and most of the Right had become so when faced in the mid-thirties with the unwelcome choice between coöperation with Communists or Fascists abroad. This aversion to war meant that French foreign policy lacked effective sanctions and that in the end France would be maneuvered into war at a moment of the enemy's choosing.

French will had been sapped by domestic difficulties, internal divisions, aversion for war, and the profound conviction that France could fight a defensive war behind the secure defenses of the Maginot Line. The French proposed to "sit this one out," a psychological attitude which was widespread in Britain and the United States as well. Hitler's psychological offensive, both before and after September 1939, was designed to further this weakening of the French will.

France lacked leadership. The great figures who had guided her to, and through, the first war had passed from the scene —Clemenceau, Poincaré, Briand, Barthou. Far too many men who would have reached the age of leadership in the thirties lay on the battlefields of the first war. France had in high place in the difficult and crucial decade of the thirties too many men whose twisted consciences had been steeped in the virus of defeatism—Laval, Bonnet—or who wished the Republic well but who lacked the competence and will to force unwelcome programs down the throats of their defeatist colleagues—Daladier, Reynaud. On the military side, the story was the same: there were the loyal but incompetent, like Gamelin, and the defeatist and antirepublican, like Pétain. The latter explained the debacle: "Two few children, too few arms, too few allies.

These are the causes of our defeat." And he should have added: "Too few leaders."

French foreign policy was inadequately coördinated with her military policy and with other aspects of her material life. The object of foreign policy, properly understood, is to assure the security and interests of the state abroad. The military is simply one of the arms of foreign policy: it lends the state prestige and strength at the council table in peacetime; it provides it with force in war.

Since the military is an arm of foreign policy, it goes without saying that the closest coördination between the two is essential. It is no less true, however, that a country's economic and other activities should be rationally ordered to give support to its foreign policy, or at the very least the latter should not be more ambitious than the nation's "war potential" justifies. In totalitarian states foreign policy is primary, and the rest of the nation's activities are organized in a more or less monolithic form in support of that policy. In democracies the reverse is likely to be true, with foreign policy tending to conform to domestic, or, what is worse, allowed to extend its ambitions well beyond the state's realized potential. The state is then living beyond its means—as were both France and the United States in the late thirties—and it runs the danger of bankruptcy, which was the fate of France in 1940.

In the field of the coördination of foreign and military policy, French performance was thoroughly inconsistent. If the Czech alliance was to function effectively, France required the continued exclusion of the German Army from the Rhineland, so that she might strike at the heart of Germany and bring prompt aid to her ally. Having sacrificed the Rhineland in 1936, France was then in still greater need of the Russians to give effect to both her Polish and Czech alliances, which she continued to maintain. Instead, France was by that time so divided by the Right's fears of communism, that she refused to put military teeth into the Russian alliance of 1936, and then turned her back in panic on the Soviets at Munich. The German absorption of Czechoslovakia the following spring lost 40 odd Czech divisions to the French, as well as the superb Czech system of defenses.

It was clear now that the British and French must win the Russians against the dynamic Nazi menace, or find themselves isolated and perilously exposed. Both proceeded first, however, to guarantee the boundaries of Poland and Roumania, a slap in the face to the Soviets who had what they considered justifiable territorial ambitions in both countries. Whether the Soviets ever took these negotiations seriously or not, this eleventh-hour diplomatic effort to win their support fell flat when the Russians signed the August pact with the Germans. When France entered the war ten days later, she faced what proved to be a disastrous diplomatic and military situation which her failure to correlate foreign and military policies had done much to create. All of which makes strange reading in the light of the magnitude of the Soviet menace of the present time. But in 1939 the power of Nazi Germany was still the most immediate and potent threat to French security. The anarchic policies of Britain and the United States had further weakened the international position of the French. The British met the brutal menace of Hitler with appeasement, and France felt obliged to follow the line of her only powerful ally, virtually abdicating her independence in foreign policy after the mid-thirties. The United States, which had returned sulking to its hemisphere after the "disillusionments" of the first war, sought safety from European contamination in the neutrality legislation of the thirties. Again France had lost a powerful ally, and her policy was correspondingly unsteadied.

2. THE PROBLEM OF THE ARMISTICE

The second problem which will be studied and fought over for decades is that of the Armistice. And the central question here is: Should the French leaders have made an armistice with Hitler or should they have retired to French North Africa and carried on the struggle from there? This is no academic question. It is often impossible for the historian to understand the meaning of events except in the light of controlled speculation as to what might have been.

First, the setting. After the initial German break-through and drive to the northern coast, General Weygand, who had succeeded Gamelin, attempted a stand along the line of the Somme and the Aisne Rivers. Attacking on June 5, the Germans broke the "Weygand Line" in forty-eight hours and presently were streaming about Paris on two sides, forcing the government to flee to Tours and thence to Bordeaux.

Hundreds of thousands of refugees now choked the roads to the south and the west. They came from as far as Holland and Belgium. They came on foot, in primitive two-wheel carts, by automobile, and by every conceivable form of transport. Paris disgorged its tremendous quota to join this exhausted, frightened, hunted mass of humanity which pressed slowly southward along the main roads, sometimes several lines of vehicles abreast. In these stifling and dust-filled days, the full knowledge of defeat, kept from the public by a misguided French censorship, settled heavily on these agonized columns. It was more than defeat; it was a society in dissolution. For by this time the French army itself was breaking into pieces, and the German panzer claws were striking out in every direction in their plan to encircle great hordes of dazed and directionless men.

It has been argued that in the immense confusion of defeat, there was no other course than to attempt to prevent further losses by the rapid conclusion of an armistice. Yet there were vigorous voices in the government raised against this view, and the final vote was apparently close. Men of the temper of Mandel and Herriot, then President of the Chamber, were ready for the African venture in the now well-established tradition of the other governments in exile, already settled in England. They firmly believed that the advantages of this momentous step far outweighed its liabilities. In the final analysis, the personal equation was of fundamental importance. France lacked a Churchill or a Clemenceau. De Gaulle saw the war in its bigger dimensions, and even his direct experience of the debacle did not taint him with defeatism. He had the faith to believe in eventual victory and the courage to be labeled a traitor, but he did not occupy a position of sufficient importance to influence events in France.

On the other side were ranged the voices of weakness, defeatism, antirepublicanism. Reynaud came to the premiership in March 1940, with a reputation for courage and freshness of view. But he failed to choose a cabinet of outstanding men, and in June added a group of defeatists under the saturnine, sexuo-political influence of his mistress, Madame de Portes. Although Reynaud was by no means the weakest of the governmental team, the accumulating disasters left him a broken man, and the relentless influence of Madame de Portes deprived him of his will. Under these conditions the road was open to men who were convinced that both France and Britain had reached the end of their strength and who were more than willing to exploit this tragedy to strike at institutions in which they had never believed. We shall get nowhere in penetrating a crisis of this magnitude if we fail to see that Pétain and Laval were men completely unable to comprehend the moral grandeur of a man like Churchill and the latter's capacity to extract victory from a situation which could only appear hopeless to men of lesser mold.

The move to Africa offered France and the Allies important advantages. It would have meant the coöperation of the French fleet, second largest in Europe, with those of the Allies. The French fleet, with a large complement of cruisers and destroyers, was well suited to playing an important role in the Atlantic convoy, and Captain Morison has shown graphically and conclusively our desperate need in that crucial operation.* Anglo-French control of the Mediterranean, a tremendously important strategic asset, was another possible result, although it as-

* Samuel Eliot Morison, *The Battle of the Atlantic* (Boston, 1950).

sumes that the Germans did not succeed in taking French North Africa, an eventuality we shall come to in a moment. The Allies would also have been spared the further growth of Anglophobia in France resulting above all from the unfortunate British attack on the French fleet at Mers-el-Kebir.

The removal of the legal French government to Africa would have avoided the fundamental and damaging confusion concerning the nature of the Pétain government and the theory of the "double game"—that the Marshal and de Gaulle were really working together. If a second government had then been set up in France, even with Pétain as its head, it would have been recognized as clearly Quisling. Such a clear-cut solution would have spared France deep social hatreds and distrusts and would have stimulated an early and vigorous growth of the Resistance, responding to the direction of a French government recognized as legal. The arguments that individual French families would have been punished by the Germans for the activities of their members abroad has only the validity it had for the Norwegians, the Dutch, and others who had the courage to take the path of freedom and peril.

By going to Africa, the French would have avoided the deep sense of guilt in defeat and in "desertion" of Britain. They would not have been obliged to seek an outlet for the frustration of defeat in that "dénigration rétrospective" which was widespread during the Vichy period. Instead of analyzing the reasons for the French defeat, we should have been seeking reasons why the French, even in adversity, fight on to the last (this was the pattern of our attitude toward Britain despite the fact that her forces, too, were defeated in France).

Finally, the removal of the government to Africa would have made the whole of the French overseas possessions available at once to the Allies. The implications here are considerable, notably with reference to the increased difficulties which the Japanese would have faced in the conquest of Indochina.

The principal argument against the removal of the government to North Africa has been that the Germans would have followed, conquered North Africa, and deprived us of a subsequent beachhead. Here we need to keep steadily in mind Hitler's fundamental objectives, the destruction of British and Russian power. In this context, his interest in North Africa was necessarily marginal, and the Fuehrer was never willing, for instance, to give Rommel the forces which would have permitted him to overcome the British in Cyrenaica and Egypt. Moreover, the tactical problems of an attack on French North Africa presented very real difficulties. An over-water crossing, even from Spain, would have required a heavy concentration of air power (and also landing craft which the Germans did not possess) against a much superior naval power, and it must be assumed that the Germans could not have undertaken this campaign simultaneously with the blitz against Britain.* Moreover, the conquest of Britain would presumably have meant the crumbling of British power in North Africa. After the failure of the British blitz, the Germans were free to turn elsewhere. But is it conceivable that they would have given the conquest of North Africa higher priority than Russia? And if they had invested a substantial number of divisions in Africa before the Russian campaign, how would this diminution in German striking power have affected the latter?

The French and British did possess certain advantages in North Africa. The French had 60,000 men in Syria, a large number of whom could have been transferred to North Africa. They had four divisions in Tunisia and some hundreds of planes in Morocco. And the French and British fleets—intact, coöperating, and having available to them superb naval bases at Bizerte and Oran—would have been available on a flexible basis to offer the same kind of threat to the Germans in the Mediterranean that the British navy offered to them in the Channel. Naval experts have commented on the great difficulties which the

* It is to be noted that Hitler had no luck in enlisting Spanish coöperation late in 1940 for a move against North Africa even under military conditions much more appealing than they would have been had the French and British been mounting an all-out defense of that area.

Germans would have faced in attempting an over-water crossing in the face of such formidable naval power. Since such a campaign would have required months to mount, the British and French could have moved stores and built up their air power (notably with planes from the United States) in anticipation of such an attack. Mr. Churchill was, to be sure, a deeply interested party in these events, but in looking back he has seen no reason to change his view that the French and British could successfully have resisted from North Africa.

> We should certainly have welcomed in the autumn and winter of 1940 a vehement campaign in or from a friendly French Northwest Africa.
>
> Surveying the whole scene in the afterlight, it seems unlikely that Hitler's main decision and the major events of the war, namely, the Battle of Britain and the German surge to the East, would have been changed by the retirement of the French Government to North Africa. After the fall of Paris, when Hitler danced his jig of joy, he naturally dealt with very large propositions. Once France was prostrate, he must if possible conquer or destroy Great Britain. His only other choice was Russia. A major operation through Spain into Northwest Africa would have prejudiced both these tremendous adventures, or at least have prevented his attack on the Balkans. I have no doubt that it would have been better for all the Allies if the French Government had gone to North Africa. And that this would have remained true whether Hitler followed them and us thither or not.*

We have raised this question in this hypothetical detail, not because we believe it can be answered without much more research and reflection, but because a better answer could in the last analysis serve to illuminate the actual course of events.

3. THE UNITED STATES AND VICHY

Following the armistice with Hitler, Pétain and Laval proceeded to the destruction of republican forms and the creation of the Vichy regime, a curious amalgam of peculiarly French

* Winston S. Churchill: *Their Finest Hour* (Boston, 1949), p. 223.

institutions dredged up from the past and contemporary national socialist conceptions borrowed from the enemy. It is clear that, the armistice once accepted, they had to do something of the kind, since the Germans would not have tolerated the free institutions and the loose police control for which the Republic had inevitably stood. When the British attacked the French fleet at Mers-el-Kebir in early July 1940 in the interests of preventing its possible use by the enemy, the Vichy government broke off relations with Britain. The United States elected to maintain relations with Vichy and did so right down to the invasion of North Africa. That decision has been the subject of long and acrid controversy, which has by no means completely subsided. Our purpose here is simply to comment on certain aspects of this thorny problem, again without attempting anything so ambitious as a solution.

It has always seemed to us that the most telling argument of the defenders of the Vichy connection has been that it furnished the Allied cause intelligence—on France, on other crucial countries with which Vichy maintained relations (this is a significant and sometimes neglected aspect), and finally, and most importantly, on North Africa during the critical period of the preparation of the invasion. In the end it may well appear that, on balance, the intelligence factor alone was enough to justify our Vichy policy. It is to be noted, however, that even the quality of this intelligence has been overstated by some proponents of the Vichy policy. General Eisenhower, shortly after his arrival in North Africa and in connection with the installation of Darlan, declared flatly that "Existing French sentiment here [in North Africa] does not remotely agree with prior calculations." *

With respect to the danger that the Vichy government might under certain conditions hand over the French navy to the Germans, there is an important difference of opinion among the best-informed observers. The central point, however, is that American officials were in no position to rely on the prom-

* *Crusade in Europe* (New York, 1948), p. 109.

ises of the Vichy French, were clearly obliged to take a pessimistic view, and naturally considered that they must do everything possible to keep this still significant force from use by the Germans and Italians. This again is an argument of great importance in favor of the Vichy connection.

Defenders of the Vichy policy have usually emphasized the extent to which we were able to mitigate French collaboration with the Germans. Admiral Leahy's rather frustrated account indicates once again that this influence can easily be overstated, that our approach lay largely through Pétain, and that the latter's authority was severely limited. Pétain "was a dictator in name only, having neither the will nor the stamina to resist the pressure of the conquerors of his people or to put an end to the intriguing of his own palace guard of ministers," states Leahy. "Although I was convinced that Pétain believed that the preservation of friendship between the United States and France was the best course for his country, he had no power to resist repeated demands for concessions to the Axis." *

The problem of the North African invasion again emphasizes the usefulness of the Vichy connection. It is difficult to see how we could have executed this complicated and dangerous operation without the essential groundwork accomplished by American consular offices and others, whose presence was made possible by the North African supply program. There again the intelligence factor is the most important aspect of the supply program, and the influence of the latter in restraining the Germans from moving on Africa appears distinctly secondary. Despite all the alarms concerning Nazi seizure of bases in North Africa, their failure to do so was, as we have already suggested, probably due more to larger considerations of Axis strategy than to American efforts. On the other hand, it is clear that if conditions in North Africa had been allowed to degenerate beyond a certain point, Vichy might then have been obliged to turn to the Germans for help and in that connection to make

* Fleet Admiral William D. Leahy: *I Was There* (New York, 1950), p. 74.

fresh concessions. It was clearly in our interest to prevent such an increase in German influence.

On the negative side, our support of Pétain clearly served to add further to the confusion of the French people—and of our other European friends—and to slow the development of the Resistance. The policy, too, divided Americans at a time when national unity was important. They could not be told some of the weightiest reasons for the pursuit of the policy, and many were deeply disturbed by the ideological implications of our being in business with fascists—as were also many Europeans. No one could agree more than the present writer that there are times when we must work with nations whose principles we neither like nor trust. But we need always to remember that ideas, too, are weapons, and that the ideological factor for that reason is one always deserving careful consideration. Our prolonged unwillingness to give aid to Franco Spain and to return our Ambassador to Madrid reflected a weighing of the importance of certain ideological factors at home and abroad against strategic factors. And ideological considerations still seem to be dominant in our policy toward Spain.

In any final assessment of this problem, we shall need to restudy the course of the development of the Gaullist movement. There is increasing evidence to show that the substantial growth of de Gaulle's influence in France began earlier than our wartime policy suggested (and there were various well-informed observers who were convinced of it even then). As early as March 1942, for instance, the Kremlin agreed to order the French Communists in the Resistance to support de Gaulle. Apparently the Russians were convinced that the General had become the unquestioned rallying point of the now rapidly growing Resistance. Even though we were justified in maintaining the Vichy connection, it is at least questionable whether, even in this early period, we should not have given more positive support to de Gaulle. Later as we shall note presently, this became increasingly desirable.

Again, to these and other questions centering about our

Vichy policy, we propose no final answers. These are questions of large importance which deserve further study and analysis. One direction that study should take is the Resistance, a subject peculiarly difficult to assess because much of the evidence is personal and oral (hence should be gathered soon), because individual and group emotions are strongly involved, because ideological and political considerations tend to distort the evidence, and because individuals are inclined to exaggerate the importance of what they did or even to invent a relationship to the movement which never existed.

4. THE NATURE OF THE RESISTANCE

"Of all the regimes under which France has lived during the past two centuries, Vichy proved to be the most ephemeral, the least capable of putting down roots in the country," states Gordon Wright. "It could hardly have been otherwise, since the regime rested on the faulty premise that Germany would win the war." * During the confusion of the first weeks and months large numbers of Frenchmen rallied to the hero of Verdun as the sole center of cohesion and security in France. Some saw through the sham of this clerico-fascist regime at once—with its suppression of labor unions, farmers' organizations, political parties, and its attempt to introduce fascist patterns in all these fields. Then, as the profoundly antirepublican nature of the new regime gradually became more evident, as it moved sharply in the direction of collaboration with the occupier, and above all as it lent itself to the harshness of the labor draft, large numbers joined the "resistants of the first hour." In the end there were never more than some thousands of Frenchmen who collaborated with the Germans, and only a few men who had had prominent place under the Republic ever played important political roles in the Vichy government—the average reader will have difficulty recalling names beyond those of Pétain and Laval. Even so we shall need to see the

* *The Reshaping of French Democracy* (New York, 1948), p. 27.

Resistance as reflecting primarily the initiative and daring of a relatively small number, supported in one way or another by a much larger segment of the people—a situation normal in all societies, where a minority will take great risks but where most men are suited by temperament to give only limited or passive support.

The French responded to the lure of the Resistance because they hated domination on principle, because the Nazi system affronted both their emotions and their intellects, and because the risks and difficulties of the Resistance and the opportunity to "do the Germans in" appealed to their ingenuity—to their capacity "de se débrouiller." A. J. Liebling has caught the authentic ethos of the Resistance in the bitter introduction to his admirable collection of writings on the movement:

> One of the most dangerous stories in the French language is *La Chèvre de Monsieur Seguin*, by Alphonse Daudet. It is intrinsically dangerous because of its moral implications. It is dangerous to France because of its effect on world opinion. *La Chèvre* of the story is a young white nanny goat who refuses to stay tethered. She wishes to go up on a mountain which she can see from the yard of Monsieur Seguin's house, in order to fulfill her destiny. Monsieur Seguin adjures her to play it safe, which he calls being reasonable. "There is a bad wolf on the mountain who will eat you if you go up there," he says, talking as Marshal Pétain used to. "But if you will be a spineless unimaginative nanny goat and demonstrate a will to co-operate I will even lengthen your tether. There is plenty of grass here if you will just learn to adjust yourself to conditions." But the nanny goat slipped her tether and went up on the mountain, and the wolf ate her, which proved Monsieur Seguin had been right. The Messieurs Seguin-Pétain-Daudet and the counterparts they have in every country are always right, if you accept the stories they make up themselves.
>
> In real life, the men of the French Resistance were like the white nanny goat. They refused to listen to Marshal Seguin-Pétain, even though in real life one story-book attribute had been transposed and the Marshal had the quavering voice of the goat. The Resistance men went up on the mountain and met the wolf. But there real life and the story diverged. Because the Resistance men beat the tar out of the wolf, who only has power over those who fear him. Walt Disney wrote a healthier wolf parable than Alphonse Daudet. The

Daudet story is particularly dangerous because it ascribes benevolent characteristics to the counselor of caution . . . the [present] book is the story of the refusal of the French to accept a lengthened tether in exchange for a destiny.*

De Gaulle was the "first resistant." He made his resounding call to victory, in a war which he saw to be bigger than French defeat, only a few hours after Pétain's apologia for the armistice and at a time of such dissolution and confusion that few men could see beyond the compromises of the next day. No man concerned with the preservation of freedom in the West can afford to forget that, at a seemingly hopeless juncture, when few men believed the British could survive the German onslaught, de Gaulle rallied the remnants of the French army and navy to the Allied cause, prepared the way for the "defection" of important parts of the overseas empire, and emerged himself as the symbol of leadership of the soon to be born Resistance within France. From that day forth increasing thousands of Frenchmen listened regularly to his broadcasts from London and drew courage from his predictions that France would eventually win through to victory.

The Resistance began almost at once: trade union leaders went underground in July 1940 as their movement was suppressed. Of the rapidity of the growth of the movement, we know far less than we need to know, and it is clear that the confusion which Pétain's presence induced in many French minds inhibited its speedier development. Only with the Allied invasion of North Africa, when Vichy accepted the German occupation of all France, did it become clear to thousands of "attentistes" (the fence-sitters) that the regime was thoroughly collaborationist and that the hope of France lay in support of Allied arms.

Meanwhile the Resistance had grown significantly. By the spring of 1941, the Socialist Party had begun to reform its departmental branches. Hitler's invasion of Russia precipitated

* A. J. Liebling, *The Republic of Silence* (New York: Harcourt, Brace & Co., 1947), pp. 3–4.

a *volte-face* of the Communists, and they eventually became the spearhead of the Resistance in many parts of France, the forefront of the risk-takers, the "parti des fusillés." Intellectuals —teachers, students, journalists, politicians—swelled the movement. In fact, it is usually said that the Resistance included very largely intellectuals and workers. The underground press, which began with one or two hand-printed sheets in 1940–41, had more than a hundred papers by 1944, some of them with local editions and with circulations of tens of thousands. Paramilitary and sabotage groups came into existence, grew rapidly in importance after the African invasion, and were eventually organized as the FFI (*Forces Françaises de l'Intérieur*). The latter finally became part of the French Army under the communications and command of de Gaulle and in strained cooperation with General Eisenhower through General Koenig. The guerrillas of the FFI, possessed of no heavy weapons, played an important role in the invasion, providing intelligence, protecting the flanks of mechanized armies, mopping up German pockets, ensuring Allied communications and interrupting those of the enemy. There may have been as many as 250,000 guerrillas operating in the FFI in September 1944.

The Resistance, however, was concerned not merely with driving the Germans from the country; its members wanted also to create a better and stronger France to follow, one which would avoid the weaknesses of the Third Republic whose parliament had capitulated so weakly to Pétain. Strengthening the executive was the order of the day, and various leaders toyed with the idea of a president in the American tradition. More significant, a clandestine *Comité Général d'Études* drew a constitutional draft which greatly strengthened the hand of the executive (the premier was given unrestricted right of dissolution), and sought to correct various abuses in the Constitution of 1875. The Communists promptly torpedoed the CGE hopes that this might become the official constitutional proposal of all the Resistance by asserting that the Third Republic had suffered from an insufficiency of democracy and that the deputies needed to be given more, not less, control over the premier. This view foreshadowed the Communist stand on the final constitutional proposals of 1946.

In May 1943, the National Council of Resistance came into existence to coördinate political and military action throughout the diverse groups which it represented. In March 1944, the Council agreed on a minimum program in the Resistance Charter, which provided both a short-term plan for correlated insurrection at the time of national liberation and a series of broader measures for the reconstitution of democratic society thereafter. The latter we shall have occasion to examine in a later chapter.

For the French themselves the Resistance had a significant role. It gave them an opportunity for that "national introspection" so necessary to the explanation of the disaster of 1940 and the plotting of a surer course for the future. In perilous enterprise, it gave them a sense of participating once more in the war and of contributing in an important way to their own liberation. Its costs, too, were high. By its very nature the Resistance operated in the realm of illegality. It was patriotic to fit out a young worker destined for forced labor in Germany with a new set of papers, a new personality, and a new job in another part of France. It was patriotic for a farmer to direct his produce into the black market so that the Germans could not requisition it, a step incidentally which was often profitable to the farmer as well. But this flouting of legality, so necessary to the frustration of the enemy, unfortunately became a habit difficult to lay aside in peacetime and one which remained to embarrass the post-Liberation life of the French in many directions.

The cost in lives was high as well. There were nearly a thousand killed and almost four thousand wounded in the five-day liberation of Paris alone, and the total number lost during the Resistance is estimated to have been more than 25,000.

It needs to be emphasized, too, that the Resistance took place in a setting of physical difficulty and even very real physical hardship. Consumer goods were short everywhere in a country subject to the perennial legal pillage of the Germans. The great cities shivered all through the war in the midst of a continuing fuel shortage. Food the peasant had in adequate amounts, but he was reluctant to sell it for a franc of uncertain future, and so the larger cities suffered severely from shortages, malnutrition, and disease. From an average of some 2750 calories per day in the prewar years, the wartime figure in the big cities dropped (1941–1944) to about 1800—something more than 1000 provided by rations and the rest coming from the free market, relatives in the country, family gardens, and the black market. This food situation sharply contrasts with that in the most favored countries of Europe: Denmark, even under occupation, managed to maintain roughly its prewar standard of 3000 calories daily; Britain's caloric average before the war (just under 3000) dropped only slightly during the war, although the British distribution pattern under rationing changed notably and provided a distinctly larger and better balanced diet for the lower income groups.

Inevitably the Resistance left a legacy of hatred, all too intelligible, but which produced such post-Liberation excesses as those disfiguring the trial of Laval. But the Resistance also left a legacy—alas, only too ephemeral—of patriotism: common memories of self-sacrifice, of acts of daring clothed in anonymity, of incredible courage in the face of torture. It is one thing for civilians to exhibit courage in wartime when they are surrounded by men they can trust—the situation in the unoccupied countries; it is quite another to operate at the level of nervous tension involved in underground activity when a single false step means betrayal and torture.

For the spirit and flavor of the Resistance, one must go to the rich and varied contemporary documents of the period: to the sets of instructions for the counterfeiters of innumerable official stamps and papers, so many frustrations for the orderly but not always imaginative German administrator; to the superb literary productions of Vercors and his fellows for the *Éditions de Minuit* (stored and distributed incidentally from no less public a place than the Louvre); to the pungent "Advice to the Occupied" ("If he asks you a direction in French, do not think that you are obliged to go along with him to point out the way. You are not on a walking tour together."); to the innumerable accounts of the German-inspired anti-Semitic campaign, like that of the distinguished Jewish lady in Gertrude Stein's village whom the French judge refused to list because she had brought no proof that she was Jewish; or just to the last thoughts of a lad of seventeen before he faced the firing squad—"All the same, it is hard to die." Wrote Jean-Paul Sartre after Liberation:

> To those who were engaged in underground activities, the conditions of their struggle afforded a new kind of experience. They did not fight openly like soldiers. In all circumstances they were alone. They were hunted down in solitude, arrested in solitude. It was completely forlorn and unbefriended that they held out against torture, alone and naked in the presence of torturers, clean-shaven, well-fed, and well-clothed, who laughed at their cringing flesh, and to whom an untroubled conscience and a boundless sense of social strength gave every appearance of being in the right. Alone. Without a friendly hand or a word of encouragement. Yet, in the depth of their solitude, it was the others that they were protecting, all the others, all their comrades in the Resistance. Total responsibility in total solitude—is this not the very definition of our liberty? This being stripped of all, this solitude, this tremendous danger, were the same for all. For the leaders and for their men, for those who conveyed messages without knowing what their content was, as for those who directed the entire Resistance, the punishment was the same—imprisonment, deportation, death. There is no army in the world where there is such equality of risk for the private and for the commander-in-chief. And this is why the Resistance was a true democracy: for the soldier as for the commander, the same danger, the same forsakenness, the same total responsibility, the same absolute liberty within discipline. Thus, in darkness and in blood, a Republic was established, the strongest of Republics . . . [the] Republic of Silence and of Night.*

* *The Republic of Silence* (New York, 1947), pp. 499–500.

5. THE UNITED STATES AND DE GAULLE

This is not the place in which to discuss in detail the course of American policy toward de Gaulle in the months following the invasion of North Africa. We shall need to know far more, especially of the evolution of the Gaullist movement in North Africa and of its Resistance support in France, before we can write anything approaching "definitive" diplomatic history of this period. As of this moment, the principal elements in the situation seem to have been the following:

De Gaulle in the early months of 1943 had far more support in France than the United States was aware of, or at any rate ready to recognize. De Gaulle was himself well informed of the extent of this support. The British were presumably better informed of the nature of his strength than were we.

In the ensuing months de Gaulle exploited this strength, often by methods which annoyed or outraged the allies of France, to win for himself the dominant position in the Algiers government, the Committee of National Liberation. Thereafter, he fortified his position, and finally the Liberation revealed the overwhelming support which he enjoyed within France itself.

The British were consistently eager to give de Gaulle increasingly wider recognition, whereas the United States just as consistently held back. In the end we acted grudgingly and late, and the British naturally gained credit for foresight and generosity. Mr. Hull's persistent and almost sole argument was that we could not take any steps which would compromise "in any way the right of the French people to choose the ultimate form and personnel of the Government which they might wish to establish. That had to be left to the free and untrammeled choice of the French people." *

Unfortunately this statement, unexceptionable in itself, confused the issue. The French people could express its "free and

* *The Memoirs of Cordell Hull* (New York, 1948), II, 1429.

untrammeled choice" only by the election of a constituent assembly and subsequently by the choice of representatives under a constitution drawn by such an assembly. This would obviously be a matter of many months—actually it took more than two years. Clearly the United States could not hope to "supervise" such elections and in any case was not going to wait for this long and cumbersome process before it extended some form of recognition; and it did in fact recognize de Gaulle's as the Provisional Government of France in October 1944.

The immediate problem prior to, and immediately following, D-Day was, not what the final form of the new French constitution should be, but who should govern France *provisionally* during this interim period. Prior to D-Day, the British Cabinet was ready for outright recognition of de Gaulle. The President and Secretary Hull were unalterably opposed. General Eisenhower, commanding both British and American armies, was seriously embarrassed by this conflict and the resulting lack of policy. Mr. Stimson, who fully understood the justifiable annoyance of the President and Mr. Hull with de Gaulle, consistently pressed for a more realistic acceptance of unpleasant truths in the larger interest of preventing a wider breach with the British, of providing for more effective use of Resistance forces, and of organizing a new administration in those areas through which the armies would pass. But even after the invasion, President Roosevelt continued, most unrealistically and contrary to the accumulating intelligence, to expect the appearance of effective French opponents for de Gaulle.*

The art of diplomacy presumably consists in influencing those events which one can alter and in accommodating oneself to those situations which one is unable to change. For reasons which they believed valid—and we have no intention of defending in detail either de Gaulle's wartime policy or

* Henry L. Stimson and McGeorge Bundy, *On Active Service in Peace and War* (New York, 1947), pp. 545 ff.

de Gaulle as a temperament—American policy makers did all they could to discourage the Gaullist movement and to produce rivals for it. It is simply our contention that when it became obvious that this policy was no longer productive—as it did to many close and informed observers in Washington even in the winter of 1943–44—we should have turned to the more profitable task of reaping what advantages we could from a policy which events presently forced us to adopt anyway.

In June 1943, the Committee of National Liberation came into existence in Algiers, with de Gaulle and Giraud as co-presidents. This was an unworkable and inevitably ephemeral arrangement, representing once again the determination of American policy to keep exclusive control of the Algiers government out of de Gaulle's hands. Unfortunately de Gaulle had now rallied most of France overseas to the Fighting French, he had the support of representative political figures, and he was the recognized symbol and leader of the French Resistance. In contrast, Giraud represented nothing in particular, and was politically inept and intellectually hardly a match for de Gaulle.

In the following months de Gaulle eliminated Giraud and his followers, introduced representatives of the Resistance and the major parties into the government, and formed "a reasonably rounded governmental instrument, gradually developing the kind of organization and competence that modern governments require." * This was the one of the two political structures that was to operate the transition to a new regime after Liberation; the other was the Resistance hierarchy in France.

De Gaulle also completed a reorganization and reëquipment of the French Army, with American materiel, and prepared

* On the whole question of the way in which de Gaulle prepared for and assumed power in France, see John E. Sawyer: "The Reëstablishment of the Republic in France: the De Gaulle Era, 1944–45," *Political Science Quarterly*, September 1947.

it for an effective role in the campaigns in both Italy and France. In fact the central concern of the General was to make France militarily strong once again, so that she might resume her place among the great powers; the war he insisted on viewing, unrealistically, as a parenthesis in French history, somewhat in the tradition of 1870. At the same time, he took only a peripheral interest in the great problems of economic recovery, so essential to any program of revived military strength, and he returned to France with no economic plan and then simply let the monetary problem slide.

Following Liberation, the potentially difficult transition to a new government proved remarkably and unexpectedly smooth. The presence of a basically conservative Gaullist government in Algiers and a leftist inspired Resistance mechanism might well have precipitated a bitter struggle for power. Instead, events failed to follow the classic pattern in which political control tends to pass to more extreme and disciplined minorities. The presence of Anglo-American armies in vast strength and the unwillingness of the Soviets and the French Communist Party to breach the war alliance at that time were inhibiting factors of first importance. But Mr. Sawyer has pointed out that there were also significant "internal" factors making for a harmonious transition: The Resistance was a minority in France; its political activists, who wanted to remake France, were a still smaller minority; and the movement was deeply divided. There was no effective alternative organization prepared to overthrow de Gaulle's regime. The overwhelming majority of Frenchmen were opposed to a simple resurrection of the Third Republic, although, as we shall see, they were later to do pretty substantially just that. And de Gaulle himself was a source of confusion—and unity—in that, for the moment at least, he commanded the support of both Right and Left.

Meanwhile the Allied armies had swept eastward over France. Paris was liberated and gave de Gaulle a delirious ovation on August 25. And then, as the delirium subsided and the autumn chill settled over the fuel-hungry capital, precursor of one of the coldest winters on record, the new Provisional Government—now at length enjoying the prestige of official recognition by Britain and the United States—set about the painful and complicated tasks of rebuilding France.

7. Economic Problems

France has rich and varied agricultural resources, including a favorable climate. She is less happy in the industrial field, where she has vast supplies of iron ore but inadequate coal and almost no domestic oil. At the same time she has access to foreign markets capable of supplying her deficiencies, and is in a position to develop a well-balanced economy.

And yet France, in comparison with her leading European competitors, has been laggard in her economic development. This is the invariable verdict of detached observers from abroad. It is the bitter verdict of some of the French themselves in this hour of inventory of their national weaknesses. Traditionalism, caution, individualism, lack of resources, lack of manpower, archaic methods, political instability—these and other factors have prevented the French from making full use of the gifts of nature.

1. AGRICULTURE

The statistics tell us that the number of workers engaged in agriculture—almost seven million—is as large as that engaged in all industrial pursuits combined. They also state that nearly half of all Frenchmen (47.6 per cent in 1936) live in rural communities, meaning those "communes" where the principal "town" is smaller than 2000. But this again is greatly to understate the number of Frenchmen who live under essentially rural conditions.

French literature is filled with pictures of this countryside in all its variety, its regional cachet indelibly stamped in house forms and the architecture of the local church. It is not difficult to understand—emotionally at least—why André Siegfried and so many others have sought to preserve this Attic island against the ugly encroachments of an industrializing Europe. Says Ernst Curtius, the German critic, who has written with such balance and understanding about the French—and he is writing in the early thirties:

> There is a solitude in the French countryside which can scarcely be found any longer in Germany with its dense population. If we desire to get away from the noise and bustle of life, and to break down the bridges which connect us with the rush of the present day, then we must go to France . . . There are regions in which life has gone backwards, regions over which there broods a stillness of death . . . It seems as though time had been drawn back and reshaped into the past. France then appears as the primitive, ancient, mature, mysterious land which it is; the land which has taken on its present form as the result of destinies and forces operating for thousands of years . . .*

Soil, climate, and tradition have favored a wide diversity of crops, ranging from those almost semitropical products of the Mediterranean shore to those which can stand the severe winters of the highlands of Alsace. And these crops run the gamut from conventional wheat, which occupies about a sixth of all the cultivable area, to the rare vintages of Burgundy, Bordeaux, and Champagne. This diversity of agricultural products unites with exceptional transport facilities to provide unique opportunities for that greatest of all French artisans, the chef.

The French countryside is a kind of vast palimpsest on which have been stamped the living evidences of successive stages in its history. Here in the deep soil area between Orléans and Flanders are the larger farms which have felt the impress of mechanization and of more modern agricultural methods. But elsewhere techniques representing every stage of develop-

* *The Civilization of France* (New York, 1932), p. 65.

ment since the Middle Ages can be found, and the characteristic farm is one of 10 to 15 acres broken up into a dozen or more separate—and sometimes distant—parcels of land, all very much a remnant of the medieval manorial tradition. And often the modern and the antique are found in picturesque proximity with only a road separating a field being worked with a modern tractor from a field being tilled by an ancient plow.

But that unending source of delight for the tourist—the archaism of the countryside—is at the same time a deep source of weakness to the nation's economy. Small farms atomized in scattered holdings, addiction to routine, undermechanization, low yields, high costs—these are characteristics of an agriculture which has for decades been progressing so slowly in comparison with its neighbors and especially in comparison with the "young countries" that one leading French writer insists that agriculture has long been in a state of "regression."

The small holding is in many places appropriate to the terrain, and many French farms cannot be profitably mechanized. But there are great stretches of level, deep soil country which are still beribboned by the tiny strips which have no sanction save that of history. Indeed the French agricultural landscape presents a complete contrast with ours, or at least with that part of ours which we incline to view as typically American—the large, mechanized, single-crop farms of the Middle and Far West. France is characteristically a land of small holdings. Almost three-quarters of all French farms include less than 25 acres each. Farms less than 125 acres form 97 per cent of the total number. There is, however, a paradox: the 3 per cent of the holdings larger than 125 acres includes nearly one-third of the total farm area.*

The typical French farm is peasant-owned: three-quarters of all holdings are the property of those who work them. Another 20 per cent is leased to tenant farmers: these tend to be larger properties and more extensively mechanized. Five per

* These figures are for 1929.

cent is farmed by share croppers, generally in the poorer regions.

Small parcels of land inhibit the use of machinery; and one of the prime problems facing current French economic reform lies in the consolidation of small plots to create larger farms.* The individual peasant has lacked the funds to equip himself with expensive machinery. He has been reluctant to submit to the discipline of coöperative organization, although the latter has accomplished a good deal to make effective the pooling of peasant resources. As a result, French agriculture is very much undermechanized: France had, for instance, only one tractor to every 2500 acres of arable land in 1929, as compared with one for every 425 acres in Britain. Again, France and her colonies are very large producers of fertilizers—phosphates, potash, basic slag—so essential to a soil wasted by the use of centuries. Yet French consumption of commercial fertilizer was only 21 pounds per acre of crop and pasture in 1936 as compared with 67 pounds for Germany and 80 for Belgium.

The hand of tradition lies heavily on the French peasant. He is frequently isolated—both geographically and culturally—from the currents of new ideas and techniques. Too often his ideas are those of an age when he still produced for himself and not for the market. For centuries there has been almost no virgin land awaiting his expansion, and he has been completely lacking in the spirit of the Australian pioneer. Agricultural stations have been woefully inadequate, and defective education has reinforced his conservatism. He assimilates scientific ideas slowly, and is inclined to react to innovation in a "spirit of mockery." The peasant, sadly remarks one leading French agronomist, seems convinced that farming is a function of the strong arm, not the head, that its tasks should be accomplished "by fatigue and not by reflection."

French agriculture, then, relies in a far greater degree on

* It was officially estimated, on the basis of an agricultural investigation in 1929, that more than a quarter of all the cultivated land in France was too subdivided to be economically farmed.

manpower than that of Britain, for instance. And it is precisely here that the French have been hardest hit. The difficulties began with the declining rate of population growth combined with the peasant trek to the cities to fill the growing factories. The War of 1914 devastated the peasant class, with 674,000 killed and another half million incapacitated for farm labor. During the war French authorities persistently "combed out" skilled factory workers and left regiments largely filled with peasants. My colleague, Professor André Morize, notes that the war memorial in his town of Lefleix in the Dordogne lists the names of 192 dead in a farming community with a total population of only 1200.

And yet, despite the excessive use of manpower and the emphasis on *intensive* agriculture, yields in France are low: in the case of wheat, the comparative figures are 16 for France, 23 for Britain, and 27 for Belgium; potatoes—110 for France, compared with an average of 191 for Denmark, Holland, and Belgium (figures average for 1932–1936).

The paternalistic policy of the government has contributed a further element to the inefficiency of French agriculture. In the waning decades of the last century, the formidable competition of the grain of the "new countries"—Canada, the United States, Argentina—threatened French prices, and the government sheltered the peasant behind a high tariff wall. The industrial proletariat and urban dwellers generally had to foot the bill for prices kept abnormally above the world figure—and at a time when France needed to lower industrial prices so that she might compete more successfully in the world market. And the vaunted self-sufficiency for wartime, which France had in fact substantially attained by 1914, rapidly disappeared with the mobilization of the peasant: by 1917 France was producing substantially less than half her "normal" yield of wheat.

These are the problems of an agriculture now unhappily devastated by a second war: the French have undertaken to solve them in the ambitious program generally known as the Monnet Plan. Substantially the question is how to render agriculture more efficient so that food prices will decline (thus reducing industrial costs) and so that larger numbers of peasants can be made available to man the factories of a growing industry, in turn essential to the immediate mastery of the dollar shortage and of the export problem in general.

2. INDUSTRY

It is useful to recall again that, prior to the advent of the Industrial Revolution, France led the world in economic power. This is simply to say that in the early eighteenth century she possessed the resources appropriate to economic strength in the context of the then existing state of technology, and that her highly developed "civilization" enabled her to exploit these resources effectively.

Even after the impressive onsweep of Britain during the century after 1750, the industry of France still led the Continent. In the succeeding decades her industry grew steadily and sometimes rapidly. But her industrial strength, *relative* to that of leading competitors, declined, and in overall production she was eclipsed by Germany, the United States, and eventually Russia. We can see that decline graphically in the figures for the total production of energy—coal, petroleum, water power—stated in millions of tons of equivalent weights of coal (1928): United States, 764; England, 242; Germany, 194; France, 60.

The twentieth century has been a period of spasmodic progress for French industry, interrupted by the profound dislocations of war and depression. On balance, it has fallen far behind in the world picture, has been completely outstripped by the new industrial giants, and has raised questions even in the minds of French observers as to whether France can again produce efficiently enough to remain in the race at all. The useful book of Charles Bettelheim * speaks flatly of decline—of *regression*—in industry and the economy generally during the twentieth century. The gross value of French production in 1913 stood at

* *Bilan de l'économie française 1919–1946* (Paris, 1947).

$4.1 billion, but in 1937, even with the incorporation of Alsace-Lorraine, it had reached only $4.2 billion. In 1913 France contributed 14.7 per cent of all European industrial production, in 1937 only 9.3 per cent. The productivity of the industrial world increased 170 per cent between 1910 and 1928, that of France only 30 per cent.

There is of course no simple answer as to why French industry should stagnate in a world of robust industrial expansion. We can only indicate facets of a problem which is in critical need of wider study.

France has bountiful resources in sectors like iron ore and bauxite, but, as we have seen, she has serious shortages in textile raw materials, coal, petroleum, and most of the non-ferrous metals (in 1937 she mined 600 tons of copper and imported 123,000). Such shortages do not condemn French industry to vegetate, but they do mean that she must have an active foreign trade.

A flourishing foreign trade means production of items for export at prices which can successfully compete in the world market. Unfortunately French industrial prices have been generally high, and for a variety of interconnected reasons, to one of which—high agricultural costs—we have already alluded.

The French businessman has in general been much more concerned with an assured profit of modest size than with the more adventurous expansion of some of his foreign counterparts. He has normally turned to monopolistic control of production and price and only too often has encouraged and protected the marginal producer. He has viewed this practice as "socially" desirable—it keeps the small producer in business—and it has enabled the big producer to profit from the higher price required by the least efficient.

Protective tariffs have favored this process. Tariffs tend to promote monopolistic tendencies and to center interest on the domestic market—which is small but which can be more readily and more safely manipulated. This is clearly a situation which tends to produce satisfaction with the status quo and which does not provide the competitive domestic conditions which lead to more efficient production and to prices appropriate to competition in the international field.

The psychology of the French businessman is central to this whole problem. His outlook comes as something of a shock to the more naïve American tourist who seems ready to believe that *homo sapiens,* whether he is encountered in Toulouse or in Nanking, will always react to the same set of economic motives as he would in Minneapolis.

In the first place, the French firm is normally a family business. The various relatives will often be found placing their savings at interest with the family firm, just as we would deposit money in a bank, and withdrawing such sums as they need even for current expenses. "The business is not an end in itself, nor is its purpose to be found in any such independent ideal as production or service," notes David Landes.* "It exists by and for the family, and the honor, the reputation, the wealth of the one are the honor, wealth and reputation of the other."

The French business is normally small—after the War of 1914 more than 94 per cent of all firms employed no more than 20 persons. Large and impersonal corporations have naturally invaded some parts of the economy, but even in the steel business the largest company of all—Les Petits-Fils de François de Wendel—is still a family business.

Smallness is not difficult to explain. These French entrepreneurs are reluctant to expand because they would then need to seek financial support outside the family, a step which might threaten their independence. The object is to make the highest rate of profit possible—an objective which is fully compatible with what we have said of monopoly and tariff protection—and thus to build up reserves for the financing of expansion. Naturally the latter is often much slower than it would be if recourse were had to outside credit sources. The "compulsive urge toward growth" is inhibited both by these conditions and by the

* "Business and the Businessman in France: a Social and Cultural Analysis of Economic Behavior," *Modern France* (Princeton, 1951).

fact noted previously that the French businessman is likely to be concerned with money in so far as it will provide him with "the good life."

The nature of the domestic market is another factor limiting industrial growth. The salaries and wages of white-collar and industrial workers are small, and the purchasing power of the mass of small farmers is low. Even the well-to-do Frenchman makes things do for an incredible period of time, avoids conspicuous expenditure (dangerous in a country where taxation is calculated in terms of "outward signs of wealth"), and is opposed to installment buying. Finally the organization of retail trade has cast a blight on the price structure. There are at present in Greater Paris alone nearly 40,000 retailers engaged in various phases of what we should call the grocery business. The presence of the independent owner of the small "boutique" is a source of social stability, but this altogether disproportionate number of retailers in a country where manpower is scarce keeps prices high. And then, too, it must be remembered that the Frenchman, with a relatively highly developed taste, looks for the individual, the unique, the custom-built item. He does not lend himself readily to the uniform product, mass-produced, even though it is inexpensive.

It is easy to understand why French business, which is small and dominated by the psychology we have described, is also "undermechanized." Capital is not always available for the innovations which new types of machines represent, and the natural French tendency anyway is to use what you have until it wears out. France in 1928, according to one German study, had machines worth 14 marks per capita as contrasted with more than 31 marks per capita for the industrial countries of Europe as a whole.

Manpower shortage has played its part in slowing French industrial growth. The War of 1914 took a staggering toll of an already stationary population. The inevitable result was a massive postwar immigration, making France the successor of the United States as the country which led the western world in immigration. Large numbers of men came to the cities from the country, somewhere between 100,000 and 150,000 annually in the late thirties. The losses of World War II were again severe, although much less serious than in the previous war. And since the last war, the population has, as we have seen, taken an encouraging upswing. Yet clearly labor shortages will continue to be an important bottleneck in an expanding economy: immigration, more efficient agriculture, and a much more effective use of currently underutilized manpower are all parts of the answer.

The political factor, too, had proved a significant inhibiting influence on industry. We have alluded earlier to the effects of political atomization, to the difficulties of finding party groupings in support of a given government which would make it possible to fashion and carry through an agreed economic policy. Never has this been more true than in recent years when parties favoring both planning and "free enterprise" have found themselves the uneasy bedfellows of successive governmental coalitions. At a time when authority and leadership were essential to the execution of unpopular programs, governments have been enfeebled by division on economic questions.

The War of 1914 had sweeping effects on French industry. The French lost—temporarily at least—important foreign markets. The war obliged them to liquidate extensive foreign holdings, making the problem of imports more serious and emphasizing the weakness of the French raw materials position.

Again, the war devastated large parts of ten of the leading industrial departments; crippled virtually all of the coal and half of the iron mines in that area; destroyed 9300 factories employing ten or more workers; and struck a disproportionately heavy blow at the male population 17 to 50, from which most of industrial labor is drawn. It is perfectly true that even this destruction had its more favorable side in that it led to building new and modern factories and to the sweeping renovation of old plants, especially in such key industries as steel. But this very program of reconstruction elicited huge sums from the French government on the supposition that these would be replaced by German reparations, which inconveniently failed to materialize.

These heavy expenditures for reconstruction, in turn, contributed to an ominously mounting inflation which had its origins in the war itself. The franc, which had enjoyed a century of stability, plunged giddily—and has indeed steadily depreciated since, with the exception of brief intervals of recovery. Successive governments contributed their futile efforts to the control of inflation until Poincaré was summoned in desperation and stabilized the franc by rather orthodox methods and above all by the prestige of his name—but not until it had lost four-fifths of its prewar value and spread desolation among wide groups of the population with relative fixity of income. In any event, the conservative Lorrainer laid the basis for the last healthy business upswing of the interwar period, a sunset scene in the years from 1926 to 1930 before the depression closed in.

The war and its aftermath also brought a vast increase in public ependiture. What with paying for one war and preparing for the next, the national budget of 1936 represented expenditures nearly four times as large—in actual purchasing power—as those of 1911. And these increasing economic burdens appeared in the setting of a stagnant national income. The sources of fresh investment for the expansion of private business were steadily drying up.

The changes effected by the war were in turn superimposed on more basic difficulties which had been developing for decades. Whereas in the nineteenth century western Europe was the world's leading manufacturer and source of capital, she found herself in the twentieth with great industrial competitors and with her trade restricted by the rise of nationalism in Asia and Africa and by other drastic changes in the pattern of world relationships. The countries of western Europe then took refuge "in a state of economic siege"—embargoes, quotas, licenses, excessive tariffs, exchange controls, etc.—whose effect on balance was to intensify the distress. This was the situation in broad terms when World War II added its new complications.

3. WORLD WAR II

The sheer physical destruction of the French economy was immense. In the first war it was concentrated in one area. This time destruction was far more widespread. It struck with crippling effect at key economic installations—especially the ports and the transport system. About 460,000 homes were completely destroyed, one and two-thirds millions damaged—nearly 20 per cent of all French real property. With the diminution of stocks and the prolonged wear and tear on personal belongings, the country was probably much more exhausted in 1945 than at the end of the first war.

The bridges of all northern and northwestern France felt the full might of Allied air power at the time of the invasion of 1944, and the French underground made a notable effort in the field of sabotage. The result was that a railroad map of September 1944 shows only six lines of any length still in operation, and parts of the French network are among the densest in Europe.*

The great ports were the special object of German fury, directed to the effective hampering of Allied supply. In some ports, the Germans destroyed what they could in the midst of a hectic retreat, but in others they remained lodged for months to carry out a work of systematic wreckage—and Allied air power and artillery added their destruction. In the first of all French ports, Marseilles, 200,000 tons of shipping lay on the bottom of the harbor and not a single crane was operating when the Americans arrived. Le Havre, the second French port, was a scene of total destruction, with 300 wrecks

* For details on losses in World Wars I and II, see Appendix I.

in the harbor and one crane operating of a total of 276. Lorient was a mass of rubble in which old residents were unable even to identify some of the streets. Along with her ports, France had lost about two-thirds of her merchant marine of three million tons.

German occupation policy added a tremendous increment to the dislocation of the French economy. It is an ironic fact that the French organized a real "war economy" only after the Armistice of 1940. Henceforth the Germans treated the French economy essentially as an adjunct of their own. They pirated vast amounts of industrial equipment, including such key items as machine tools. On a large scale, they diverted French plants from normal peacetime functions to the needs of the German war economy. They swept France almost completely clean of raw materials, so that she had almost nothing with which to operate after the Allies came. The total German exactions in francs of 1938 purchasing power have been estimated at about 300 billion, nearly the size of the national income in that year. In this general setting of economic decay, the productivity of labor declined 50 per cent (1938 to 1943), and the Pétain regime added doctrinal to economic causes in its emphasis on the "return to the land" and its glorification of the artisan.

The economic devastation of war is reparable in a sense in which the loss of men never can be. French losses in the recent war were much less serious than those in the War of 1914, but they were still much more considerable than is generally recognized by the American public. The 150,000 men lost in combat is a figure which makes a sharper impact if we note that, in proportion to the population, French combat losses alone were one and two-thirds as high as American. The comparison becomes more dramatic if we add that total French losses from *direct* war causes were approximately 600,000.*

Modern wars are the breeding ground of inflation. Acute

* See Appendix I, p. 305.

scarcities, a redundant supply of money, and the general dislocation of the economy—to name only three factors—carried the French retail price index by August 1944 to a point more than two and a half times its July 1939 level. But this was only a beginning. Even in the difficult days of the occupation, savings had accumulated—notably in the hands of the well-to-do peasants—and after Liberation this effective unsated demand emerged in a market denuded of consumer goods. The black market, which had during the occupation served in part the patriotic purpose of diverting goods from German hands, now became an inflationary fixture in the economic scene. The French structure of economic controls was wholly inadequate to its task, and the inflationary spiral swung dizzily upward in the postwar years until retail prices in 1949 reached a point roughly 20 times higher than they had been a decade earlier.

We have said enough to indicate that it was a jaded and battered economy which greeted the invading forces of the Allies. Industrial production had sunk to about one-fifth the volume for 1938 and agricultural production was only about 70 per cent of prewar.

4. POST-LIBERATION PROBLEMS

Any attempt to discuss recent French economic problems by themselves at once reveals the weakness of the method we are using here. For almost every economic problem is shot through with political implications, and in the case of developments like inflation the political element is at dead center. Had the French possessed the degree of political unity which the British have mustered in the face of their postwar difficulties, they could have accelerated their recovery and might well have spared themselves the yawning inequities which inflation has produced.

But it is not the political angle alone which is important. Economic problems by their very nature reach out into every corner of the national life, and, in this period more than in most others, they have meaning only in the larger setting of the international scene. At no one place, save perhaps Western Germany and Italy, has the United States made a more massive and concerted effort to block the forward movement of communism than in the field of the French economy. And Moscow, acting through the medium of the French Communist Party, has made a counterthrust in that same area in an effort to frustrate American efforts. The French economy has been one of the principal theaters of the cold war.

In the disorganized condition of France in 1944, the road to recovery was studded with bottlenecks—transport, power, raw materials, manpower. The French brilliantly solved the first, have made notable progress with the second and third, and are scarcely beyond the threshold with the fourth.

The Allied armies had immediate and direct need of the various parts of the French communications system, and they made an important initial contribution to its restoration. But the French carried on with great energy and focus and by the end of 1946 service was normal on all but about a thousand miles of the entire railway system. While traveling in various parts of the provinces in the summer of 1947, I was impressed with the speed and punctuality of trains. Roadbeds had been reballasted, rolling stock reconditioned, and new stations built in the modern style—more comfortable and attractive than the mournful *gares* of another day. The reconstruction of the railroads was a superb achievement.

The story of coal is no less impressive. When the Germans hastily withdrew, production stood at only about half the 1938 figure. The situation was chaotic. Mine timbers were in short supply, the transport facilities were lacking to bring them from distant forests. The food shortage was critical. Machinery was obsolescent and had been abused under the pressure of war demands. Sabotage and absenteeism had been useful weapons against the enemy, but now managers found it difficult at times to control established habits of indiscipline.

The French solved the problem largely by methods which are no longer popular. The workers were deeply suspicious of a management which had collaborated with the enemy during the war, so the government promptly nationalized the principal (northern) coal mines. Then the Communists, who dominated the coal unions and who were at that time part of the coalition government, kept the men on the job. By 1946, coal production had already almost reached the level for 1938, and in 1949 substantially exceeded it.

At the end of the war the French found themselves competitors for raw materials with the entire industrial world, a large part of which had been seriously dislocated. In large measure with Lend-Lease and Interim and Marshall aid, they have overcome the most serious handicaps, but in early 1950 shortages still persisted in coal, petroleum, certain of the nonferrous metals, and parts of the textile sector.

The industrial production targets which the French have set for themselves are too high to make it likely that they can fill their manpower requirements by increased productivity alone. They must also make some addition to the labor force, and for the next few years the increase can only come from immigration. The French have estimated that they will need 300,000 additional workers for the period 1948–1952. Despite the existence of large numbers of unemployed in Italy, Western Germany, and Greece, the prospects for filling these requirements are not bright. The inevitably inadequate housing facilities in France and the difficulties of obtaining citizenship tend to discourage workers from coming. There has been a substantial "spontaneous" Algerian immigration, but the Islamic customs of this group make its members difficult to assimilate.

On the production side, French recovery has been a notable achievement. They accomplished about as much in four years following Liberation as in six years after the end of the first war, and in the early months of 1950 the industrial production index had returned to a point not much below the level of 1929, the best previous year. This achievement is in ironic contrast to the troubled and at times almost chaotic political situation, which permitted the inflation to get out of hand to such an extent that it threatened to compromise the whole recovery program. One shrewd journalist who visited the two countries in the summer of 1948 returned to report that he had the strong impression that "Britain was decaying in perfect order while France was recovering in chaos." Happily the Queuille government, of which nothing was expected, finally curbed the inflation and gave France something approaching a hard currency during its thirteen months of office (September 1948–October 1949).

There are, however, dark sides to the recovery picture as well, and one of the blackest is the failure of the government housing program. The war left about two million homes damaged or destroyed, and French property losses ranked after those of the Soviet Union, Germany, and Poland.

During the initial period–from Liberation to the end of 1947–the program for permanent housing moved slowly at a time when the government was involved in the preliminary task of clearing mines and debris, in repairing partially damaged buildings, in constructing temporary dwellings for more than a million homeless families, and above all in the top priority problems of restoring the economy in general. In the latter connection, there was during this initial period a serious shortage of building materials.

Moreover, the French faced in the field of housing a special problem: restrictions and rent controls, going back even to the period before 1914, had kept rents fairly stable in terms of the 1914 franc despite the phenomenal series of inflations through which France had passed. This situation offered little stimulus to new building by private individuals or groups or to the renovation of rented property by owners. A series of new laws between 1948 and 1950 sought to remedy this anomalous condition. They allowed rents to increase by as much as five times over a period of five years (with, however, significant state rent allowances to the "economically weak"). They opened the way to the formation of housing associations and coöperatives, with greater financial strength resulting from pooled resources; allowed large tax reductions in connection with new buildings; and provided an elaborate system of state building subsidies and loans.

This legislative effort was impressive on paper. In actual fact, however, France had completed, between Liberation and June 30, 1950, only 138,000 new housing units, although the pace was definitely accelerating, with 129,000 units under construction at the latter date. The government has lacked financial resources for this enterprise, as for so many others. One high authority stated in the summer of 1950 that there were still approximately one million destroyed or seriously damaged houses yet to be replaced and that this shortage affected approximately five million people. The implications of a figure of this magnitude in a total population of 42 million are at once evident. The greatest need, moreover, is concentrated in a relatively few highly industrialized areas where the workers are most exposed to the appeals of communism. Meanwhile the new demands of rearmament constitute a fresh threat to the housing program, whose weakness has long been a source of anxiety to American as well as French officials.

For such superb achievements in postwar recovery as the revival of coal production and the reconstruction of the railroads, primary, secondary, and tertiary credit goes to the French themselves. They are the architects of their own salvation. Once again they have revealed that ability for hard work, which runs so contrary to the caricature of the Frenchman popular in the Anglo-Saxon world. And once again they have exhibited the capacity to coöperate in time of crisis, and nowhere more notably than in the planning of the national recovery effort in the Monnet program.

But no country could repair the devastation which France had suffered and at the same time rescue its economy and its political institutions from the shattering effects of war without an infusion of strength from parts of the world which had been relatively untouched by the conflict. When Mr. Roosevelt spoke of the individual's responsibility to lend his garden hose for his neighbor's fire, he was thinking of a wartime situation, but the smoldering fire which threatened postwar Europe rendered the President's metaphor equally valid for that situation. And the country which had the most hose to lend was the United States.

In the United States, the effects of the war had been precisely opposite to those produced in Europe. Where the European economy had been shattered by the war, the industrial production of the United States grew about 50 per cent in volume. And, despite significant shortages in resources and other weaknesses, the American economy has revealed an exceptional stability in the postwar years. On the demographic side, battle losses were relatively small, and, under the stimulus of war conditions, the rate of population growth increased strikingly. In overall military power, the United States emerged from the war in a position of unique strength. The war had accelerated a long-term trend whose direction had become increasingly evident since the turn of the century.

The garden hose metaphor is of course too simple for the situation we are describing. If we had more economics at our command, we should probably embark on a discussion of the refinements of the question as to whether a dollar shortage really exists at all. To a layman at least the problem seems very real.

This American aid effort has had three—often interpenetrating—aspects: *relief*—the emergency feeding and housing of people with whom we have deep cultural ties and sympathies and with whom we now share a common destiny; *recovery*—the restoration of productive activity to a point where it can be maintained; *stability*—strengthening the political and social fabric so that it will be resistant to the corrosive effects of communism. Relief was characteristic of the years just after the war. Stability and the Communist factor will be the subject of the following chapter. Here we are concerned with economic recovery.

The Marshall Plan is only the most ambitious of a series of measures which the United States has taken for the relief and recovery of France. Lend-Lease financed important phases of recovery directly serviceable to military objectives and made long-term credits available to France for "civilian" phases of economic development. Loans from the Export-Import Bank in 1945 and 1946 totaled $1.2 billion. Léon Blum, in 1946, negotiated a loan of $720 million,* of which about $400 million went for the refinancing on a more favorable interest basis of "civilian supplies" obtained under the Lend-Lease arrangement of February 1945. At the same time we wiped clean the "military" aspects of the Lend-Lease slate: there were to be no "war debts" this time. We eliminated a sum of $1900 million, the net French obligation after deduction of $870 million in reverse Lend-Lease. It is not always remembered that France made this very large material contribution to the common effort despite the fact that the country was occupied by the enemy during much the greater part of the war.

Nor is the extent of the American effort in these early postwar years always clearly recognized. We shipped coal to Europe in unprecedented quantities—more than two million tons a month during the latter part of 1946. In early 1946 we cut the flow of wheat to our flour mills and exported it to the physical limits of available shipping. France imported 1,700,000 tons of wheat in the first eleven months of 1946, and 58 per cent of this came from the United States. "Since the end of the war we have been transporting a much greater volume by sea than at any time during the war," was the dramatic report of Assistant Secretary of State Willard Thorp in December 1946.

By the early months of 1947, however, it was becoming increasingly evident that the problem of European aid would

* The second Export-Import loan was also part of the Blum accords.

need much broader and more imaginative treatment than these somewhat tentative, unplanned, and piecemeal efforts suggested. It was at this point that Secretary Marshall appointed as chief of a new Planning Staff in the Department of State, George F. Kennan, a leading specialist on Soviet Russia, a man of deep understanding of the European scene and possessed above all of great breadth and imaginative flair. From the new Planning Staff emerged the concept of the Marshall Plan, developed in a preliminary speech in May in Mississippi by Dean Acheson and officially unveiled in Secretary Marshall's speech at Harvard in June.

In France the situation in the summer of 1947 was disintegrating so rapidly that it was soon evident that the Marshall speech was already several months too late and that interim measures would be necessary to shore up the crumbling fabric of the French economy. With an excessively severe winter and a persistent drought in the summer, the country was about to reap the worst harvest in decades. The Communists, eliminated from the government in May, embarked on a prolonged campaign of strikes for the purpose of forcing their way back into the government. In May, too, General de Gaulle had in effect reëntered the political arena by announcing the formation of the allegedly nonpolitical Rally of the French People (RPF). This step was shortly to add a disturbing new element to the already atomistic situation in the country. By early autumn, the French government was rapidly reaching the bottom of the barrel so far as its dollar credits were concerned, and the country faced an acute situation in the field of foreign trade, despite the fact that it was continuing to make very creditable progress in industrial production.

The foreign trade aspect of French recovery is so central that it deserves substantial elaboration. Planned French recovery will only be complete with the achievement of substantial equilibrium in the balance of payments. "Equilibrium in the balance of payments" is the jargon of the economists for balancing one's budget with the outside world; it means in essence that the goods and services which a country "exports" are equal in value to those it "imports." For this purpose tourist expenditures in France are in effect services "exported," although, just to make the problem a bit more confusing, they are generally referred to as "invisible imports." This equilibrium will involve substantial changes in the foreign trade picture—a large export increase, some diminution in imports, the establishment of a favorable balance of trade with overseas France—as well as a decline in shipping expenditures and a higher income from tourists.

With the generally acute economic and political situation which we have described and with foreign exchange assets and available credits exhausted, the French imposed drastic cuts on imports and appealed to the United States. In the absence of Marshall aid, which became available only in April 1948, the Congress passed the Interim Aid Act and thus made available some $300 million in emergency aid to France.

Aid under the European Recovery Program (Marshall Plan) comes to France in two forms. "Direct aid" covers France's estimated deficit to the dollar area. "Indirect aid" provides France with drawing rights, in their currencies, against non-dollar countries with which she has trade deficits, notably Belgium, the Sterling Area, Western Germany, and Italy. In 1948–49 direct aid to France totaled $980 million, indirect aid $325 million. For 1949–50 these figures dropped to about $675 and $220 million, respectively.

It would be impossible to measure the precise contribution of American aid to French recovery. If, however, we look back at the critical condition in the fall of 1947, it is difficult to believe that a drastic economic situation would not have developed, had American aid come to an abrupt end.* The Communists would have been prompt to exploit these diffi-

* The United States supplied about 40 per cent of the total supplies of wheat and flour, on the basis of which the French Food Administration provided the meager bread ration of 250 grams daily during the winter of 1947–48.

culties under conditions where the American ally could have been pictured as deserting France in her hour of need (this is the other side of the propaganda coin from that of "American imperialism" in Europe which is the one which the Communists currently show). France would have been faced with the possibility of Communist domination, with the probability of paralyzing internal strife, verging on civil war. And the strategic situation of the United States and her democratic allies would probably have been compromised once and for all. No American statesman in a position of authority could have accepted responsibility for such an outcome. Paul Hoffman calls the results of Marshall aid "the greatest bargain the American people ever got for their money."

Even after the experience of Lend-Lease, the whole conception of the Marshall Plan was sufficiently novel so that it was inevitable that it would take time for it to be understood in Europe. Nonetheless by the fall of 1948, and after the European Recovery Program had been in effect only a few months, the extended poll of the Common Council for American Unity * revealed that most Frenchmen believed that it was "A plan to aid Europe by promoting European economic recovery" and that it was "Likely to succeed in aiding European economic recovery." Only "some" Frenchmen said they believed it was "A scheme to promote American domination of European industry," "A plan to promote reactionary policies in Europe," or "Solely a political weapon against Russia." Similarly only "some" believed it was "Just another loan which must be repaid," and a somewhat larger, but still restricted group, declared American foreign policy was "imperialistic."

The upswing of French trade is one of the best indices of the salutary effect of Marshall aid. There was a notable rise in 1948, and 1949 saw a remarkable increase, the latter reflecting also the arresting of inflation and stabilization of the currency by the Queuille government.

* *European Beliefs Regarding the United States* (New York, 1949).

Prior to the Korean crisis and the initiation of rearmament programs in the West, the recurrent question was: How fully will the Marshall Plan have succeeded by the time of its termination in July 1952? What are the chances that the French will achieve equilibrium in their balance of payments by that time?

Authorities differed, of course, but one careful student of this problem * concluded that

> On balance, it appears that the restoration of equilibrium in France's payments position with all non-dollar areas by 1952 at a high level of international trade is well within the realm of possibility, provided that European currencies can be cleared on a multilateral basis . . .
>
> The elimination of the dollar gap is, of course, a more difficult problem concerning which there is less ground for optimism . . . Even under optimistic assumptions with regard to French exports to the dollar area and tourist receipts, some deficit on current account (including amortization of foreign loans) with the United States at the end of the ERP period appears to be probable . . . the deficit might be in the neighborhood of $100–$150 million, although no figure can have precise meaning at this stage. This is an impressive reduction below the immediate postwar level of over $1 billion.

The rearmament program has of course completely altered the question. We are now concerned, not with the question as to whether France can bring her balance of payments into equilibrium but with the problem of the extent to which rearmament may threaten achievements to date in the economic field. In short, how can we effectively reconcile economic and military aid? We shall examine this problem in a postscript to the final chapter.

The French have attacked the problem of recovery in no hit-or-miss fashion. Quite the contrary, in the best French tradition, they have developed a logical plan for the reconstruction and modernization of their economy. This is the so-

* Warren Baum: "The Marshall Plan and French Foreign Trade," *Modern France* (Princeton, 1951).

called Long Term Program, successor to the earlier "Monnet Plan," on which it is based. The Long Term Program originally aimed to achieve an equilibrium in the French balance of payments by the budgetary year 1952–53, and at the same time to bring about "a modest and rising standard of living." To attain this double objective, it scheduled a large increase in agricultural and industrial production.

The original Monnet Plan (*Plan de Modernisation et d'Equipement*) was no scheme dreamt up by a group of economists closeted in the national capital. On the contrary, it emerged from the coöperative efforts of more than a thousand individuals drawn from industry, consumers, trade unions, government, and other groups, and representing political points of view ranging from extreme conservatism to communism. In early July 1947, hence before the breach between East and West over Marshall aid, Benoît Frachon, one of the top Communists, spoke to me with genuine enthusiasm about his part in the formulation of the Monnet Plan.

The Plan emerged from some eighteen different "Committees of Modernization," each entrusted with a particular phase of the economy and each composed of men of high *expertise* or special interest in that area. The result of the Plan's broad base and the general atmosphere in which it was formulated was the creation of widespread public support. In its early history, at least, the Plan was a significant pole of national unity at a time of rapidly growing social and political tensions.

The dynamo of the whole scheme is a small inner group, the so-called General Commissariat of the Plan, whose function is to provide general administration, ideas, and leadership. Presiding over it is one of the best brains in France–short, peppery, dynamic Jean Monnet. From long sojourns in Britain and the United States, he speaks almost flawless English, and his office in the Rue de Martignac is a scene of bustle and efficiency which reminds one more of a wartime agency in Washington than of the more leisurely routines of many French *bureaux* even today. Monnet is a man of "passionate concentration" and great self-confidence. To a pragmatic respect for facts—deriving perhaps from his British and American experience—he brings the Gallic "imaginative ability to see facts that do not exist but might exist under changed conditions," suggests Harold Callender in a recent portrait. Monnet respects and uses technicians, but is convinced that policy must be made by those who are courageous enough to reach decisions well before the technicians have satisfied themselves by buttoning up the very last fact. The plan for integration of French and German steel and coal is also Monnet's. Its daring—both in conception and in its bombshell presentation—is characteristic of the man.

Surrounding this whole effort is an atmosphere of great urgency. The almost poetic introduction to the original report on the Monnet Plan baldly presents the dilemma of France—"Modernization or Decadence." The French economy, states the introduction, was paralyzed during the very years when a revolution was being effected in the productivity of the American worker, who now produces about three times as much as his French counterpart. It is imperative that France increase the productivity of her workers. To do so, she must modernize not only her factory equipment but her industrial methods. If she fails to modernize, she will find herself competing in a world of more efficient rivals, will be able to export less and less, hence produce less and in turn import still less—in short, she will be launched in a vicious circle leading to a progressive asphyxia of her economy.

For all its ambitious nature, the Plan is in no sense grandiose. Said Robert Marjolin, originally Monnet's able aide and more recently the Secretary-General of the Organization for European Economic Coöperation:

> What must France do in reality at the present time, not to achieve the first place among the individual states of the world, nor even the second or the third—that is not the question—but to achieve a production level making it possible to give each Frenchman all the comfort, health and security which are compatible with the devel-

opment of modern technology? For that is the objective we must assign to the French economy. There is no question of making of France either a giant industrial state or a great military power . . .

The agricultural phase of the Program is ambitious and aims to create a fundamental change in the pattern of the French economy. In normal years in the past, French agriculture came within striking distance of national self-sufficiency. The present target is to make France the largest exporter of basic foodstuffs in western Europe.* French planners foresee the difficulty of finding adequate markets for industrial products in a world in which a whole group of competing countries must find new markets if they are to achieve equilibrium in their balance of payments. Hence the French hope to place a larger part of the export burden on food shipments, especially to the United Kingdom and Western Germany.

The general 1952–53 production target is 125 per cent of prewar. Dairy products are to reach 120 per cent, sugar, 151. There is relatively little that can be brought under cultivation in the way of new land. We have seen that the hopes for substantial immigration are not likely to be satisfied. All this means that the program must rely heavily on increased yield per man. That involves in turn a radical increase in the use of machinery and fertilizers, improvement in seed and important changes in other farming methods. And here France lacks an adequate agricultural training and information program.

For much, but by no means all, of the French countryside, greater productivity means increased mechanization. And in most cases mechanization must wait on the consolidation of pulverized farming lands into larger units (with the peasants the French authorities use the tactful word *rémembrement*). The wastage of the system of small and scattered strips—often a serious obstacle to the progress of irrigation, drainage, and mechanization—is indicated by the comparative cost of a bushel

* This is an element of the Long Term Program which differs fundamentally from the agricultural target of the original Monnet Plan which sought merely to achieve overall self-sufficiency for France.

of wheat, which jumps nearly a third if the area of the field drops from two and a half acres to three-quarters of an acre.

The consolidation program is currently a sensitive subject among interested groups in France. Everyone knows that the French peasant is congenitally suspicious and that in this instance he is deeply fearful lest he be the loser in an elaborate series of land trades of the kind here involved. The authorities of the Long Term Program report that requests for consolidation are so numerous that they cannot be satisfied in the face of a shortage of surveyors. Other sources report that the peasants are dragging their feet and that the program is moving very slowly indeed.

As for the agricultural program as a whole, the best informed view seems to be that it is distinctly overambitious and that it is very unlikely that the targets for 1952–53 will be attained. If this view is correct, a more modest agricultural achievement will mean a heavier burden for industrial exports or continued American aid or some decline in the French standard of living. At present writing, and in terms particularly of current international developments, it would seem likely that the solution would include ingredients of all three.

Industrial production targets are also high, but they are much more susceptible of achievement than those for agriculture. The general target for 1952–53 is 143 per cent of 1938 or 110 per cent of 1929. Since production has already passed the 1929 level, it is well on the way to the achievement of the general target.

The central problem is an increase of no less than *one-third* in worker productivity over the 1948 level (there had been a very sharp decline, of some 17 per cent, in productivity during the war decade 1938–48). The French must also reduce real costs per unit of industrial output in order to improve their competitive price position in foreign markets.

It is the opinion of competent observers that French industry can make important strides in worker productivity without excessive cost and in some cases by means of nothing more spectacular than rather inexpensive changes in plant arrangement. Plants are often crowded and badly laid out. Improper work flow and lack of mass production methods are widespread. The French have done relatively little with time and motion analysis, which has become routine in some industrial countries. Faulty assembly organization and assembly techniques are general, and where "modern methods" such as conveyor belts are in evidence, they are frequently misunderstood and misused.

French plants have a strong tendency to fabricate *all* elements of a given product—shoes, for instance—and do not adequately use the subsidiary supplier industries that are common in certain competitive countries. There is lack of national standardization for such elementary parts as bolts and nuts. Cost accounting procedures are lacking or rudimentary.

Plant machinery is very often obsolescent, and special equipment, such as multi-operation machine tools, is lacking. And French factories lag behind their leading foreign competitors in modern machines generally and notably in such essentials as mechanized materials handling equipment. All this means that the French worker must put forth greater efforts than his American or British counterpart, but it is very much worth noting that, despite this fact and the complication of extensive Communist influence with its recent emphasis on "political" agitation, worker morale and effort are high, according to the reports of objective witnesses.

As a contribution to increased productivity in France, the Economic Coöperation Administration (ECA) has in the past year (1949–50) sponsored a program which sends representative groups from various French industries (managers, engineers, workers) for tours of observation in the United States.

So far as the *structure* of French industry is concerned, the Plan underlines and expands interwar emphasis on capital-goods industries. The 1952–53 schedule for steel production for instance, is 14.3 million tons, compared with 8.8 million in 1938 (the Saar included in both cases). Increased fuel production follows naturally from this general trend. Coal, which stood at 62 million tons in 1938, is to reach 76 million tons (again including the Saar). The production of electricity, 31.2 billion kilowatt hours in 1938, is to attain 52 billion in 1952–53. The refining of petroleum products is scheduled for 18.7 million tons in 1952–53 as compared with seven million in 1938. And an expanding agriculture means a much increased production of agricultural machinery: tractors, for instance, the production of which ran only 1700 in 1938, are to reach a figure of 50,000 in 1952–53.

The basic problem in French industry—an increase in worker productivity—means in turn significant investment to render more efficient certain sectors of the French economy. It has been consistently stated that France is devoting some 20 per cent of her total output to gross investment. Since the United States achieved its highest peacetime level of investment at 17 per cent (1948), this level for France would be extremely high.

> A more critical examination of the French national accounts figures [comments Richard Ruggles], reveals that there are major conceptual differences between what the Commission du Bilan refers to as gross investment and what is generally considered to be gross investment in an economic sense. In the first place, the French include current repair and upkeep in their figures of gross investment. Secondly, they include the government's expenditures on armament and all public works such as roads and public buildings. If the French data are adjusted to be comparable to the gross investment concept as used in this country by the Department of Commerce, the investment level in 1949 comes out to be approximately 12 or 13 per cent of total output, instead of 20 per cent.*

In short, France appears to be making a smaller effort in the investment field than is commonly attributed to her and one "which remains low in comparison with most other Eu-

* "The French Investment Program and Its Relation to Resource Allocation," *Modern France* (Princeton, 1951).

ropean countries." The basic question emerges: is this investment program sufficiently ambitious?

In terms of the possible inflationary effects of the program, the answer may well be "yes," although this question is closely related to that of the adequacy of current governmental methods for the control of inflation as well as to a wide range of political imponderables which will come under discussion in the succeeding chapter. In terms of the achievement of the Long Term Program's objectives, the answer is pretty emphatically "no." The level of investment in agriculture and in certain sectors of industry is too low to permit achievement of the assigned targets. Specifically, it seemed very unlikely that the current rate of investment could justify any notable rise in living standards during the next few years even before the complications of the late 1950 rearmament program appeared. French industry to date has achieved an admirable postwar production record, but it was able to exploit extensive unutilized capacity, rendered idle by the acute industrial slump of the occupation period. With the progressive disappearance of these post-Liberation advantages, industry must now set out on the rockier road where production increases depend largely on improved worker productivity. For the period May 1949 to September 1950, French production as a whole had reached a "plateau," above which it could not seem to rise. Unfortunately neither business leadership (the *patronat*) nor labor is disposed to make the effort requisite to increased productivity. The *patronat* generally prefers the ways of the past to the risks and disturbance of new methods. Labor is suspicious that, if it works harder and increases productivity, the additional profit will go in large measure to the employer, and, worse still, that unemployment, the worker's perennial nightmare in France, will follow.

During the long vigil of the occupation, the French Resistance painfully—and perilously—reviewed its country's past: the causes of the collapse of 1940, the weaknesses of the "Old Regime." They concluded that postwar France must find new strength in rather sweeping structural reforms of a generally "socialist" character. In March 1944 the Charter of the Resistance emerged with the broad support of such diverse groups as the Communists, the Socialists, and the Social Catholics, who were soon to found the significant postwar Catholic party (*Mouvement Républicain Populaire*—MRP). The Charter had to be somewhat general—to satisfy its varied supporters—but it did provide specifically for "the return to the nation of the principal industries, of monopolies which are the fruits of common labor, of the sources of energy and wealth, of the insurance companies and big banks . . ." This provision could become the basis of a sweeping policy of nationalization.

The Germans have a useful proverb, that "the soup is never eaten as hot as it is cooked." In post-Liberation France the early drive for nationalization of private business has long since come to an end, and the predominantly "socialist" atmosphere of the early months has yielded to increasing support for a return toward the "free enterprise" situation of prewar experience.

The weakening of the move for structural reform is another reflection of the political disunity of France. The divisions among men and parties tended to be lost in the great compulsive crisis of the Resistance, but these conflicts rapidly emerged as the cohesive force of the German danger moved into the background of less abnormal times. Gradually the support for the reform program declined under political conditions to which we shall come in the following chapter.

Central to the whole reform program were the plans for nationalization, a word which tends to generate more heat than light in this country. In France, at the end of the war at least, nationalization appeared both as an integral and essential part of reconstruction and as a logical development of historical precedents.

On the reconstruction side, the dominant parties were convinced that private capital lacked the will, resourcefulness, and means to undertake the tremendous task of rebuilding and modernizing France's heavily damaged and obsolete economy. The efficient operation of key industries demanded the full co-operation of the workers, and the latter lacked confidence in a management too often discredited under Vichy by industrial failure and collaboration with the enemy.

But it should also be remembered that the nationalization program was not something which the French Resistance had fabricated out of the blue: France had long traditions of state control over important parts of the economy. Some government monopolies went back more than a century and a half. The state had owned the telephone and telegraph system for more than fifty years and at least part of the railroad system since the 1870's. But it was the Socialist Party which generalized the concept of nationalization of the economy for social ends, and the national trade union organization (CGT) which first produced a concrete program in 1920. The short-lived Popular Front government of 1936 took some further steps in this direction at a time when the financial and industrial oligarchy was being attacked for arrogating to itself a position as virtual competitor of the state.

In the months following Liberation, General de Gaulle showed something less than enthusiasm for the implementation of the somewhat vague nationalization provisions of the Resistance Charter. Such an arbitrary transfer of property, he said, should be left to an elected legislature. The General seemed concerned lest reform measures interfere with recovery, and of course his left-wing political opponents stated flatly that all this simply reflected his conservative convictions. The de Gaulle regime did in fact carry through four nationalizations, but none reflected any broad policy of socialization and all were in response to situations which permitted of no temporizing, such as the formation of the *National Coal Mines of the North*, aimed, as we have seen, to stimulate vitally needed production in the principal French coal field.

It was only after the election of the Constituent Assembly

in October 1945 and especially after the retirement of de Gaulle that a broad attack was made on the nationalization problem. First, the Bank of France, which had acquired such wide unpopularity, and the four principal deposit banks were nationalized by an overwhelming vote of the Assembly. In turn the gas and electrical industries, 34 leading insurance companies (representing three-quarters of the nation's insurance business), and finally the remaining coal mines were nationalized in the winter and spring of 1946. Unlike the earlier steps of de Gaulle, these were permanent "structural reforms" which were to create a large sector of public ownership in the national economy and thus in theory to provide the government with "levers of command" for the direction of the whole economy in the public interest.

These major nationalizations reflect a definite pattern. They transferred the property of the companies to the state in its entirety. The banks and insurance companies retain their identity and continue to compete with private concerns, whereas the coal mines and the gas and electrical industries were organized as nation-wide corporations. It is important to note that none of these organizations is staffed by a government bureaucracy or operated directly by the government. Each is in law a financially independent and autonomous enterprise, and is held responsible for the success of its own operations.

Nationalization stopped well short of the initial plans, and steel and other key elements in the economy escaped entirely. The nationalized sectors have been the subject of a systematic campaign of bitter attack in France, but no major party has seriously considered a policy of "denationalization." Production, financial mismanagement, and administrative weaknesses have been the prime targets of attack. A recent and objective American study concludes that the picture must be painted in grays, and not in black or white.*

* David H. Pinkney, "Nationalization on Trial: France," *The Yale Review*, September 1950.

Coal and electricity have impressive production records, and nationalization has stimulated labor to new efforts and greater productivity and has facilitated investment. Although it is virtually impossible to determine the precise financial situation of the national companies, the condition is clearly less alarming than the sensational public exposés would suggest. All of the national companies have achieved, or will shortly achieve, financial equilibrium. The exception is *Gaz de France*, and the latter's deficit reflects a government decision that the national budget should bear a portion of the cost of gas.

On the administrative side, the nationalized companies have a much weaker case. The government's application of the nationalization laws has been extremely dilatory. A law of April 1946, for example, prescribed regional subsidiary companies in the fields of gas and electricity, but in the summer of 1949 the affairs of these two national enterprises continued to be handled by unwieldy national administrations in Paris. Political parties and labor unions have exerted excessive influence in the direction of the nationalized companies, seriously undermining the managerial and financial autonomy which the original legislation sought to achieve. And the companies have been very slow to deliver indemnification bonds to owners of properties expropriated.

The original laws provided indemnification based on the market quotations of the companies' stocks in specified periods during 1944 and 1945 or on evaluations arrived at by special commissions, based on the market value of company assets. The indemnification takes the form of government securities or bonds of the public corporations created by the new laws. These provisions were originally the subject of lively recrimination in 1945–46, and more recent delays in final settlement have stirred these reactions again. The complexity of the task of determining the size of these indemnities explains much of the delay, but the latter has increased private investors' suspicions of both the efficiency and the good faith of the national companies, and the difficulty in obtaining loans on the open market has been increased.

5. ORGANIZED LABOR

In the light of the activities in recent years of the largest national trade union movement (the CGT–*Confédération Générale du Travail*), many readers will no doubt feel that a statement on the French labor movement belongs in the chapter on "Political Problems." It is true that the Communists have sought to subvert the CGT to Moscow's larger political ends, but in longer perspective French labor, like American, has developed a nonpolitical outlook and has addressed itself to the economic problems of the worker. On the other hand, France has never had a strong and stable labor movement which could give continuing and effective support to the needs of the working class.

The movement took form much later in France than in Britain or Germany, reflecting among other things a less highly developed industrial society. Doctrinaire views and factional struggles have plagued it from the beginning. The individualism of the worker and his resistance to the payment of dues have been important factors in the extreme fluctuations in size and the lack of consistently developed, long-term programs. The worker has been highly suspicious of the *patronat*, and yet in spite of his suspicions–which have, alas, been only too fully justified in many cases–the worker has never managed to develop anything like an adequate defense, an effective system of collective bargaining. Both labor and management still have a very long way to go in developing a psychology and in devising the institutional framework which are associated with the smoother functioning of the labor relations process in various other industrial countries. Meanwhile there are very real dangers in a situation in which tensions accumulate with no effective outlet.

The early history of the organized labor movement suggests the doctrinaire and unreal world in which it lived. Shortly after the formation of the CGT, the so-called Charter of Amiens (1906) stated the twin bases to which the organization gave at least lip service down to the Resistance period of the recent war: (1) it was to be nonpartisan; (2) it was to support the principle of the class struggle.

In the spirit of Proudhon, the movement was to seek its ends by economic means and to eschew the political weapon. There was to be no Labor Party, as in Britain. The CGT persistently refused political office, notably when Léon Blum offered it in 1936, at the time of the creation of the Popular Front government. But the organization did not renounce lobbying and other political methods, particularly in the period of its great weakness in the twenties; and the bitter experience of the Resistance finally convinced the CGT leadership of the desirability of accepting political office. By the post-Liberation period the CGT had come full circle since the days of the Charter of Amiens.

The Charter's plank on the class struggle, the CGT proposed to implement in the "general strike." In the years prior to World War I its leadership had constructed a vision of the "grand soir" when the workers with one gesture would lay down their tools and capitalist society would collapse. But the leadership was well in advance of the rank and file (the reverse of the situation in 1936 when spontaneous strikes forced the hand of the Popular Front government), and when war came the CGT took the patriotic line in support of the government of "sacred union."

At the end of the war economic dislocation and the Russian Revolution misled the CGT leadership into believing once again that a moribund and tottering capitalist system invited only a final blow. Strikes and labor disputes became general. Presently the more radical majority broke away from the CGT to form the CGTU (*Confédération Générale du Travail Unifié*), Communist-dominated and emphasizing the class struggle. Both organizations lost strength in the succeeding years—

the CGT because it collaborated with the state and to a considerable degree shed its character as representative of the proletariat, the CGTU because it wantonly used the strike as a political weapon to further Communist aims.

The great depression and the threat of fascism drew the two groups together, and they were formally reunited on the eve of the Popular Front experiment. Membership shot up astronomically for a brief period, as the CGT stressed co-operation and supported the Blum government, and then it dropped off no less strikingly with the deflation of Popular Front hopes and the revival of the strength of conservative forces in France prior to the outbreak of war.

Quite understandably the Vichy government suppressed the CGT, but the organization promptly revived underground and became the center for the remarkable cohesion the labor movement achieved prior to the Liberation. The upper reaches of the clandestine CGT maintained close contact with, and even exercised effective direction over, the legal "above ground" local unions.

In 1943 the CGT took the fateful, and probably inevitable, step of admitting the Communists to its leadership once more, on a minority basis. Since Hitler's invasion of Russia, the Communists had taken a high line of national patriotism, and eventually, as we have seen, played a role of great risk and distinction in the Resistance.

The tragedy of the postwar labor movement lay in the fact that it possessed tremendous power and prestige which it did not know how to use. This "lost revolution" reflected the inferiority complex of the Socialists in the face of the Communists, weaknesses in leadership and vision in the non-Communist parts of the movement, and the reappearance of prewar political divisions. This last named factor was itself sufficient to deprive the labor movement of its earlier promise of effectiveness.

The honeymoon of the French workers was a natural, if unreal, part of the general spirit of national unity characteristic of the months following Liberation. This was a time when the Communists were in the government and when they kept the workers on the job in the interests of national recovery (working days lost in 1946 were only 0.4 of a million man days as compared with 22.7 million in 1947, the era of Communist-promoted strikes). But at the same time they rapidly penetrated the CGT apparatus and by early 1947 were in control of the organization. Hence, when the Communists were forced out of the government in May 1947, they possessed a powerful instrument in the impending struggle between the Soviets and the West. During the succeeding months, hence in the period of France's greatest postwar difficulties, the CGT fomented or exploited strikes on a broad front, until it became increasingly evident to Frenchmen generally and to parts at least of non-Communist labor, that the Communist Party was using the labor movement for political purposes quite foreign to the interests of the worker. The immediate objective was to sabotage the French economy before the hated Marshall Plan could make itself felt.

It was under these conditions that a minority element broke away from the CGT in December 1947 to form the so-called *Force Ouvrière*, whose political connections are with the Socialist Party. This element embraced primarily workers with the more traditional prewar outlook—concern with the immediate economic welfare of the worker. The new organization, it was hoped, would become the magnetic core of a dynamic non-Communist labor wing, essential to the construction in France of Arthur Schlesinger, Jr.'s "Vital Center."

The *Force Ouvrière* has grievously disappointed its supporters. It has fluctuated in strength between perhaps 500,000 and 1,000,000, although French labor union figures are often undependable. As of September 1950, the figure was probably nearer the lower margin. Its leadership is anything but dynamic, and the patriarch of the movement, Léon Jouhaux, is now old and his mind is distracted by a primary interest in international labor developments. When the split took place, the CGT retained the organization's buildings and even equipment down to typewriters and filing cases. FO has lacked funds to replace these and to train cadres and create newspapers, areas where the Communists have abundant funds. In the light of the really dynamic task facing French labor, this is not a reassuring outlook, although some of the ablest American observers are convinced that non-Communist labor contains scattered elements of real strength, whose effective utilization requires only a more imaginative approach.

Not all aspects of the picture are as dark as we have drawn those above. The strength of the Communist CGT has declined from perhaps three million to something between one and a half and two million. It is the universal opinion of non-Communist observers that the CGT, after two unsuccessful attempts, is no longer in a position to produce a general strike, and this despite the fact that it is still the dominant labor group in every basic industry—railways, coal mining, basic steel and metal-working industries, building trades, chemicals, textiles, food processing, maritime and waterside employment. Its capacity, however, to produce strikes of allegedly legitimate purpose and in general to hamper the functioning of the economy is still very considerable. And the fact that the CGT has been able to emerge, shaken but intact, from the loss of two great strikes is itself a feat without precedent in French labor history.

The Catholic trade unions, organized nationally as the CFTC (*Confédération Française des Travailleurs Chrétiens*), are a positive element of strength. The national organization has numbered about a half million members in recent years, but may have had as many as a million members as of September 1950. The political connections of CFTC are with the social Catholic MRP. Like FO, it has a disproportionate number of white-collar workers, but in some parts of France it has important representation in shipbuilding, railroading, the building trades, among industrial workers, and especially in the metal trades, where it has made significant progress in the post-Liberation years. The movement has able and vital leadership, drawn particularly from part of the Catholic youth movement (JOC–*Jeunesse Ouvrière Catholique*). During the Resistance period, the CFTC had worked with the CGT, but fear of losing its identity in a Communist-dominated organization induced its leaders to refuse a post-Liberation invitation for amalgamation.

In the difficult and at times almost chaotic economic situation prevailing after Liberation, the government retained control of wages. As the postwar inflation swept on, the government granted a whole series of wage increases, but how adequate these were remains a subject of warm dispute. The real weekly wages, plus family allowances, of the head of a family with two children employed in industry or commerce in October 1949, may have exceeded slightly his real wages in 1938, and here it is to be noted that hours had generally increased from 40 to 45. But the real weekly wages of a single worker had declined by perhaps as much as a fifth. In the case of the most poorly paid group among the latter, this fall in real wages was drastic in its effect.

In February 1950 Parliament restored collective bargaining, but in the succeeding months both government and the *patronat* vacillated, the latter insisting that credit for any wage concessions given to the workers would promptly be claimed by the Communists. Finally the new Pleven government took the bull by the horns and carried through the necessary first step by putting the essential platform under the new wage structure in the form of a minimum wage. The latter varies from region to region, but in Paris the single worker now receives a minimum wage plus transportation allowance of roughly $47 per month. Those who know current Paris prices, even though they are not those of the workers' quarters, will be able to judge the difficulties faced by the many thousands who have no more than this minimum. A worker must pay for instance more than four dollars a pair for shoes, nearly a tenth of his monthly wage.

The acrid discussion of the minimum wage etched out once again the importance of preserving the wage position of the least favored workers during the new and necessary drive for rearmament. The fresh sacrifices demanded represent simply one more in a series of disappointments for the worker. He expected Liberation to solve the problems of the occupation. When that failed, he looked to V–E Day to bring the return of more normal conditions. When these in turn did not materialize, he put his faith increasingly in the Marshall Plan, but that, too, despite its success in the general field of production and despite the fact that it has rescued the worker from a much worse fate, has nonetheless not solved the problem of more equitable distribution of the national income.

It is against this backdrop of inadequate real wages and disappointed hopes that we shall need to see the current political and international problems of the French, which are the subjects of later chapters.

8. Political Problems

The post-Liberation scene is not unfamiliar terrain to those who knew France before and after World War I. But it does present some strikingly new elements, notably in the strength and character of the extremes—the Communists and the Gaullists.

From the elections of 1945 until the exclusion of the Communists from the Cabinet in May 1947, the governmental majority regularly embraced the Communists, the Socialists, and the Catholic MRP. Although these three parties included roughly three-quarters of the Constituent Assembly (and later the National Assembly), this was in temperament and outlook a left-wing coalition in the tradition of the *Bloc des Gauches*, again a familiar landmark in the French political scene before and after the War of 1914.

Governments since May 1947 have had the support of the Socialists, MRP, and Radical Socialists, plus a varying number of small elements from the Right. This centrist coalition, drawing elements from the right wing of the Left and the left wing of the Right, was a much more characteristic feature of the political life of the Third Republic than was the *Bloc des Gauches*. Rarely was either Right or Left able to poll a majority in an election and form a government supported by parties exclusively of its own persuasion. Much more frequent was the centrist coalition, grouping elements of both. Such a coalition required compromise, often of sharply differing views, and to that extent was representative of the characteristically middle of the road position of the mass of Frenchmen. The center of gravity would shift now one way, now the other—and tended largely to the Right during the interwar years.

In the nature of things, center coalitions found their enemies on the extreme Left and Right—among the "revolutionaries" and the "reactionaries." But pre-1939 coalitions faced enemies whose extremist language few men took seriously or whose power was not great enough to make them a menace to the Republic. That situation has now fundamentally altered. The present center coalition finds on one flank the Communists, possessed of nearly 30 per cent of the deputies in the Assembly, avowed enemies of the existing regime, and acting as an arm of the first military power in Europe; on the other are the Gaullists, with scant power in the Assembly but with extensive, although unmeasured, support in the country and with a program seeking wide but alarmingly vague changes in the existing order. The two enemies to Right and Left account for the term "Third Force" applied to this loose centrist coalition and defining a point of view, a climate of opinion, rather than a political organization. Peace, social justice, liberty are its tenets—hence opposition to dictatorship above all. With some decline in the strength of its opponents and with a new focus of attention on dangers abroad, the term itself has fallen somewhat into disuse.

But the reality is still there. These men of the Third Force are defenders of the Republic in the tradition of Waldeck-Rousseau who fashioned just such a coalition to defend the Republic and its philosophy during the crisis of the Dreyfus Affair. Notes one authority: "The Republic which had divided Frenchmen least in 1873 had become by 1893 the factor which unified them most." * And this was never more true than at the present moment. Unfortunately there is too little else that unites this disparate coalition. The Socialists on the Left support a planned economy and nationalization. The

* On the historic roots of the Third Force, see Edward W. Fox, "The Third Force, 1897–1939," *Modern France* (Princeton, 1951).

Radical Socialists on the Right talk the language of free enterprise and individual initiative. Between them is a divided MRP which speaks in either tongue and for good measure periodically raises the question of state support for Catholic schools, to the great annoyance of both its collaborators. A Third Force premier faces the task of eliciting coöperation from men more different in their outlook than Senator Taft and Philip Murray, and since he is dealing with *various* parties and not the diverse elements within *one* (the American situation), he lacks even such elementary means of inducing compliance as the patronage.

With this initial fragility, Third Force governments have been regularly and viciously attacked by the Communists and Gaullists. At the same time they have faced the complex and frustrating problems of inflation and reconstruction, of Communist sabotage, and more recently of grave international tension and rearmament. The Third Force has often functioned with the slenderest of majorities, and every premier has been obliged to walk the tightrope of compromise. It is slight wonder that the coalition has been reluctant to embark on such courageous courses as tax reform. Nor have these parties, unlike the Communists, had available to them enthusiastic mass support. In a setting of widespread political apathy, Frenchmen vote Socialist or MRP or Radical Socialist largely from habit or *faute de mieux.*

An analysis of the Third Force parties—and then of the extremes—will enable us to understand better the chances of survival of this democratic centrist coalition. First the Radical Socialists.

1. THE THIRD FORCE

The collapse of France and the events preceding it dealt a heavy blow to the prestige of the Radical Socialists. They were in power during the years when France failed to prepare for the great test of 1940. Daladier and Bonnet were architects of appeasement. A large proportion of Radical Socialist Senators and Deputies voted the wrong way in 1940. The Radical Socialist Resistance record was not comparable with that of the Communists or Socialists. At the end of the war they purged only a few of those who had given comfort to Vichy, and there was a widespread feeling that the Radical Socialists were "through."

And yet the Radical Socialists have revived to play a large and even crucial role in French political life. Herriot, grand old man of the Party, returned from a German prison camp to refurbish his prestige and win election as President of the National Assembly. The Party increased the number of its deputies from 28 in the First Constituent Assembly to 43 in the National Assembly of 1946. And, more important, it has furnished two premiers (Marie and Queuille) and a series of ministers in crucial posts during the past three years and has steadily increased its influence in the political arena.

This striking Radical Socialist recovery reflects the fact that it is an old party with long experience and subtle political leadership. It has known how to exploit the numerous opportunities offered by a somewhat chaotic and rapidly changing postwar political scene. Even more important perhaps is the fact that the essentially conservative economic ideas of the party have appealed to an increasing number of Frenchmen at a time when the latter have been inclined to blame postwar hardships on the mismanagement of Communists and Socialists.

In its very conservatism, the Radical Socialist "has been perhaps the most typically French of all parties." From its beginning, it has stood for the "little man"—the peasant, the shopkeeper, the artisan, the white-collar worker—the man of the countryside and of the little town. The Radical Socialists' main idea, said André Siegfried as far back as 1913, "is to defend as if by instinct, everything small against everything big." The peasant and the small businessman have sought protection against the bigness of big business and monopoly.

And latterly they have felt the squeeze from the increasingly well organized Left—the labor unions and the Communist Party. At the time of the Popular Front regime in the thirties, small business was vocal in its complaints concerning the hardships of the 40-hour week and other reforms which big business was in a much better position to sustain.

The result of this bipolar threat—from Right and Left—has been a Janus-like policy on the part of the Radical Socialists. They have faced now one direction, now the other, and these shifts, sometimes sudden in character, have exercised a most unsteadying effect on French politics.

If the Radical Socialist is conservative on economic questions, he is a true son of the French Revolution in his political views. Or more specifically he is a believer in the Revolution of 1789 against the more violent phase of 1793. He is an individualist, first and last, and a profound believer in the dignity of man. He is a Jacobin, a friend of the "little man," but his Jacobinism is by now rather dilute. His enthusiasm for revolution, as such, is expressed on national holidays and has about the same warmth as that of members of our D.A.R. From both the anti-Catholic bias of his forebears in the Great Revolution and from his own strong belief in the efficacy of "science" in the solution of social problems, he is deeply anticlerical, determined to exclude the Catholic Church from the arena of politics and education.

The Radical Socialist Party, like a number of others, took form just at the turn of the century, although it was the heir of the Radical Party, founded some two decades earlier. Its purpose was to defend the Republican victory in the Dreyfus Affair, their friends said—to exploit it, said their enemies. The Dreyfus Case had begun as a melodrama at the expense of an able Jewish army captain. It had presently become the battleground for forces seeking to undermine or destroy the Republic and those determined to affirm it.

From the rarefied atmosphere of the larger stages of the "Affair," the French descended into the fetid air of the post-

Dreyfus liquidation. In the years following, the Radical Socialists played a leading role in the suppression of the Catholic orders and in the separation of Church and State. But with these achievements complete, the Party's battle cry had lost most of its meaning, and anticlericalism became pretty much a thing of the past. Meanwhile, to the social question, which was lifting its head with increasing urgency, the Radical Socialists paid scant attention. Despite its title, the Party was never "Socialist" and only "Radical" in its earlier years and in a comparative sense. Unfortunately this lack of concern with problems affecting the proletariat was only too appropriate to a party with a broad peasant base, functioning in a country in which industrial development was relatively slow.

The interwar years brought the Radical Socialists new prominence and fresh frustrations. Anticlericalism as a flag had lost its appeal. The Party was unequipped in ideology or constituency to move forward to the solution of crying social problems, and, for much the same reasons, it could not grapple with the crucial monetary question in the conservative terms which Poincaré brought so successfully to its solution. The domestic fascist leagues of the thirties drove the reluctant Radical Socialists into the embrace of Socialists and Communists in the Popular Front, but even the mild reforms of Blum impelled them once more toward the Right to complete the unsteadying pendulum swing so characteristic of the Party. With a background of international coöperation, weak and opportunistic leadership, and association with a Right which had largely gone over to appeasement, the Radical Socialists were shortly ready to lead France to the humiliation of Munich.

The rising importance of the Radical Socialists in the post-Liberation period is related to the progressive decline of left-wing support of postwar governments. Ramadier ousted the Communists from his government in May 1947. For reasons that we shall see, the Socialists have wavered in their support of various governments, and actually refused to enter the Bidault cabinet (October 1949–June 1950). In this setting, not only has the traditional conservatism of the Radical Socialists appealed to a wider spectrum of Frenchmen, but the Party itself has become more sympathetic to big business and more conservative in its general outlook on economic problems.

This statement does need qualification, however. Postwar Radical Socialist deputies are a most diverse group, some leaning toward, or even coöperating with, right-wing Gaullists; a few like Mendès-France favorable to planning and having affinities with the Socialists. Moreover, it must be remembered that the Party as a whole is still deeply attached to the French Revolutionary tradition of freedom, and it is this that links it most compellingly to the Socialists and the left wing of the Catholic MRP and makes it hesitant to involve itself too deeply with Rightists whose economic views it shares but who are in many cases hostile to the Republic.

It should also be noted that the Radical Socialists found allies in a small party which has exercised an influence much larger than its size in the Assembly would seem to justify. The UDSR (*Union Démocratique et Socialiste de la Résistance*) was one of the two specifically Resistance groups to emerge and take political form in the post-Liberation period. Representing the non-Communist left wing of the Resistance, the UDSR would logically have coöperated with Socialists. Instead, its members took the bolder course of seeking to make themselves the effective nucleus of what they hoped might be a large political bloc between the two parliamentary extremes. This they did not accomplish, but at the time of the elections to the Second Constituent Assembly of 1946, they did join the Radical Socialists to form the mouth-filling *Rassemblement des Gauches Républicaines* which still exists.

When de Gaulle reëntered politics in 1947, the UDSR furnished a large share of the leadership of the new Gaullist party (RPF). Despite that fact the UDSR has continued to have an independent existence and to play a role of substantial importance: from it for instance came the premier of the recent French government, René Pleven.

Further to the Right a number of small parties have figured in various recent governments. Of special importance have been the Independent Republicans, who elected 28 deputies to the present National Assembly. Larger but less influential has been the Republican Liberty Party (PRL), with 35 deputies. It chose as a symbolic head the son of Georges Clemenceau, has supported economic liberalism, defended big business, and offered a haven to wartime collaborators. It has quite naturally failed to develop any extensive appeal in postwar France.

One of the most interesting facets of the Resistance movement was the emergence of a group of Social Catholics who took an active part in blueprinting the New France which so many left-wing Resistants hoped and believed they could create after the military victory. This group, largely composed of younger men and women, sought to make the Church at home in the modern industrial world, to commit it to the ideals of broad social reform in the spirit of Social Catholicism during the century past. They wanted to render specific the vaguer aspirations of such official Catholic pronouncements as those expressed in the encyclical *Rerum novarum.* At the same time, as true Catholics, they were believers in social peace and hoped to form a bridge between the old possessing classes and the newly self-conscious masses: theirs was to be a "middle way" between capitalism and socialism. The result was the formation of the *Mouvement Républicain Populaire*, which has consistently occupied the "center" in recent "Third Force" coalitions.

The MRP is one of the two parties to which we have applied the term "disintegrating." It was indeed the victim of the rather fluid and altogether exceptional political situation of the months following Liberation in France. For, in addition to the vital core of young Social Catholics, there were also present at

Liberation a large number of conservative Catholics who were clearly unenthusiastic about the social ideals of the core group in MRP but who for understandable reasons did not wish at that time to associate themselves with an outright party of reaction such as the *Parti Républicain de la Liberté*. As a result, large numbers of conservative Catholics gravitated to the MRP, whose leadership was amazed to discover it the second largest—and for a moment the largest—party in France, and no less embarrassed to find among its supporters even a group of collaborationists and Pétainists who had until a few months previously been its mortal enemies. The new Party found itself not only Catholic in its support but catholic in its social and political orientation—a microcosm of the larger France, with representation of both of Goguel's two fundamental political divisions: the Party of Movement and the Party of Established Order.

The fragility of this extraordinary coalition did not at once appear, since the two wings were united in support of de Gaulle, and the MRP became for the moment the "Party of Fidelity." The left wing supported the General as the "First Resistant," their leader during the already legendary days of the occupation. The right wing went along because de Gaulle, a military figure, stood for social "order" and because it became increasingly evident that his views on various issues of social reform were safely conservative.

It was de Gaulle's dramatic resignation as President-Premier, and above all his reappearance as leader of the new national Rally of the French People, the "First Resistant against Communism," that revealed the inherent weakness of the MRP coalition. De Gaulle's action polarized the Party: the leadership and the left-wing "core" group moved away from de Gaulle, particularly during the final struggle over the new Constitution. Presently large segments of the right wing turned to his support as the breach between East and West sharpened domestic Communist activity. Evidence of the magnitude of this desertion is unsatisfactory and comes largely from municipal and cantonal elections. Only a national election can measure it with any precision, but estimates of total MRP losses have run from two-fifths to three-fifths of the 1946 Party strength, although not all of this has gone to de Gaulle.

Again, how much strength MRP might lose in a national election will depend on the voting system employed. The Party greatly benefited from the proportional system used in previous national elections, but the Pleven government is pledged to bring in a new electoral law prior to the next elections. Any substantial move back toward the old single-member constituency (*scrutin d'arrondissement*), with a majority required for election on the first ballot but only a plurality on the second, would weaken the MRP. As a new party, it lacks an effective grass roots organization and local political celebrities such as the Socialists, and especially the Radical Socialists, can produce.

Despite its youth as a party, the MRP stems from an old tradition. Its more remote ancestors were the great figures of the Social Catholic movement during the second quarter of the nineteenth century–Lamennais, Lacordaire, and Ozanam. These men were deeply moved by the social devastation of the spreading industrial revolution and were determined to bring to the social problem a Christian, and not merely a "Socialist," solution.

The more immediate forerunners of the MRP were the Popular Democratic Party and the League of the Young Republic. The Popular Democratic Party, formed in 1924, drew its Christian Socialist inspiration from the papal encyclicals, *Rerum novarum* of 1891 and particularly *Quadragesimo anno*, 1931. For a solution of the evils of capitalism, it would have truck neither with *laissez-faire* liberalism nor with a state-controlled economy, but would provide for the full development of trade unions and their organization in a national Chamber having responsibility for economic and social legislation. This system, however, they sharply differentiated from fascist corporatism by emphasizing that its prime objective was to be the realization of the individual in a broadly humanist tradition. The Party opposed nationalization of any parts of the economy, was anti-Socialist and anti-Communist in its orientation, and tended as a result to work with the very elements favoring a liberal economy which on principle it attacked. Despite its small prewar representation in the Chamber, the Party gained prestige by taking a persistent stand against appeasement of the fascist powers.

The League of the Young Republic was founded in 1912 by Mare Sangnier, better known for the Social Catholic doctrine which he elaborated in connection with the *Sillon* movement, specifically condemned by an encyclical of Pope Pius X. Like the Popular Democratic Party, the Young Republic denounced both economic liberalism and Marxism and sought a humanistic solution of the social problem in Christian corporatism.

Social Catholicism moved forward on other fronts as well during the interwar years. This was notably true in the case of the Christian trade union movement (CFTC) and the various Catholic youth organizations. And these developments took place in a general setting of a reviving Catholicism. The separation of Church and State in 1905 removed the prime stimulus to anticlericalism and gave the clergy a new "spiritual independence." The record of the clergy in World War I was impressive. A large number, regular and secular, served as chaplains, and some 4700 lost their lives. Many other seminarians, not yet ordained, were called and served in the ranks. During the war, and in the spirit of the "sacred union" of all Frenchmen, the government suspended the exile of members of the religious orders. Large numbers of Jesuits, Dominicans, Benedictines, and others returned to open establishments devoted to social work, teaching, and preaching–and they remained after the war.

Aristide Briand, peacemaker with the Church in 1905, resumed formal relations with the Vatican in 1921, and three years later Pope Pius XI agreed to a compromise by which the Church regained legal status, which it had lost by reason of its unwillingness to accept the provisions of the legislation of 1905. Catholicism offered a new haven for many men during these interwar years of intellectual and moral disorientation.

The prime strength of the MRP has come from the important Resistance record of the young left-wing group of Catholics and from the strong strain of social idealism which they had inherited and developed. Before the end of the occupation they had significant roles in numerous phases of Resistance activity, and Georges Bidault had become president of the National Council of the Resistance.

The rapid postwar development of a Catholic party can also be explained in part by the fact that the Catholic Church in general, and not merely the Social Catholic wing, had grown in strength during the occupation period. Many of the lower clergy, as we have seen, actively supported the Resistance. The hierarchy, although supporters of Vichy in the confused initial months, became increasingly critical of Pétain, and bitterly attacked deportation of workers and anti-Semitic measures. With rare exceptions, members of the hierarchy were never pro-German. Rich Catholic laymen collaborated as businessmen and not as Catholics. And prominent individual Catholics—de Gaulle, Bidault, Maritain, Pleven, and others—were active on the Free French side from the beginning.

In any event, the left-wing Resistance group of Social Catholics have discovered a way to separate themselves from the stigma of counterrevolution and to make themselves an effective part of the democratic France in which they believe. This represents a new Catholic revival of significance, and to its vitality the Catholic trade union and youth movements have notably contributed. Thus the MRP offers the Catholic of "socialist" orientation a road which is neither clerical nor reactionary. In support of its views and its candidates, the Party has developed a strong national organization, which has been particularly useful on the propaganda side. It has had the advantage of attracting "new" men, untainted by past political connections.

Alongside these factors of strength, however, are notable elements of weakness. First are the fundamental divisions within the party, which a new national election would only serve to make more dramatically evident. A public opinion poll prior to February 1949 revealed that of a hundred persons who had voted for the MRP in November 1946, only 32 remained faithful; whereas the comparable figure for the Communist Party was 95.

The Party has also suffered because it represents a "tendency" rather than a specific program. It talks in generous terms of a "Humanist Socialism," but its diverse support has made it hesitant to spell this out in really meaningful detail. Moreover, on certain issues, such as a second chamber in the new Constitution, the nationalization of parts of the economy, and state support of church schools, its increasingly conservative attitude has been a source of anxiety and annoyance to its friends further to the Left.

The MRP grew too fast right after the Liberation, and the numbers of its militant supporters did not grow fast enough. It is a big and amorphous party which lacks the tightness of organization and the emotional appeal of the Communists. Its leaders include a few figures of real stature, like Georges Bidault and Robert Schuman, but they are mostly young men, often able but inexperienced. On the other hand, as one leading critic points out, there has been a consistent tendency to exaggerate the significance of the MRP in recent years; it will not do now to make the opposite mistake and minimize its importance.

"Socialism" is easily one of the least understood and one of the most emotionally charged words in the English language. The American public insists on confusing it with communism, and they are abetted by people as well informed as Harold Stassen. Communism, in the usual usage, refers to the body of doctrine elaborated by Marx, Engels, and their followers which predicts, on the basis of an economic interpretation of history, a final violent revolution leading to a classless society. The Kremlin still pays at least lip service to this doctrine. The term "Socialist" has long been used to distinguish those parties which at one time subscribed to this doctrine but which have since taken the "reformist" path: they believe that they can bring about peacefully, over a period of time, and by legal and parliamentary means, fundamental changes of the same general character that the Communists have in mind. At present the emphasis of the great mass of Socialists is on reform and not on revolution, peaceful or otherwise. A great many of them are hardly more than middle-road New Dealers. There is still a small minority that takes its Marxism seriously and some—the Nenni group in Italy is an example—who coöperate closely with the Communists.

The central fact here is that the Socialists form a dominant or a significant element in most of the governments of western Europe. As parties, they are virtually all intent on preserving the free institutions for which we stand. They are on the whole vigorously and even violently anti-Communist. Without their coöperation we could not possibly hope to accomplish our objectives in western Europe. To attempt to turn our backs on the Socialists would alienate a large part of the workers of western Europe, crucial to the present defense effort, and convince them that Communist propaganda concerning the "reactionary" nature of American policy is true.

Like the Radical Socialist Party, the present French Socialist Party grew out of the struggles connected with the Dreyfus Affair, and its evolution has not been very different from that of various other Socialist Parties on the Continent. In the individualistic tradition of the French, the pre-1848 Socialists followed the various "Utopian" schools, with a proliferation of sects. The arrival of Marxism in the seventies was greeted with skepticism and had to meet the resistance of individualist, anarchist, and coöperative strains to mention only three. The first orthodox Marxist party (led by Jules Guesde) was formed in 1879, but already by 1882 it had been weakened by division and the formation of an important offshoot, the so-called "Possibilists," who, as their name suggests, were interested in exploiting immediate opportunities for reform and not in waiting for the "grand soir" of their orthodox cousins. By 1890 there were no fewer than five principal Socialist Parties, three of which were already strongly reformist.

The nineties saw the two left-wing parties—the Guesdists and the Blanquists—turn steadily away from their orthodox persuasion in favor of political action as a means of accomplishing gradualist changes in society. After various vicissitudes, the Dreyfus Affair was the catalyst precipitating the union of the five groups in the face of an attack on free society which, if successful, they believed would have left no place for socialism. The famous Millerand case of 1899 again divided the Socialists on the question of whether a party member might serve in a "bourgeois" cabinet, but the scission was only temporary. In 1905 the final union produced the *Section Française de l'Internationale Ouvrière* (SFIO), which is the party that still exists today. Once again the program of the new party was orthodox Marxist, but the activities of the component elements before 1905 and of the SFIO after 1905 left no doubt that the Party was reformist, and when the great test came in 1914 representatives of the Party entered the Government of "sacred union."

As the conflict wore on, the Party divided, the "Majority" continuing to support the government in its conduct of the war, the "Minority" urging peace without victory. The Bolshevik coup of November 1917 greatly strengthened the latter, which rapidly rose in numbers and actually gained control of the Party in July 1918. Before the end of the war a third, extreme pacifist element appeared.

The formation under Lenin's aegis of the Third International in 1919 precipitated an acrid struggle over support of this new organization. By now successes in Russia and postwar repression in France had greatly increased the power of the extreme Left, and finally at the Congress of Tours in December 1920, the latter found itself with a majority and formed the Communist Party which exists today. The minority withdrew to rebuild its organization, carrying with it most of the leaders and a majority of the deputies into the Socialist Party.

The Socialist Party continued in the succeeding years to carry the banner of reformism and peaceful change. It restated its faith in an elaborate program aiming once again to achieve the "revolution" through peaceful means, and seeking to accomplish along the way a series of reforms valuable to the working class. The Party repeatedly gave evidence of its moderation and of its political and doctrinal flexibility. On more than one occasion it supported left-wing governments against the "reaction." And when in 1936 the Socialists elected the largest number of deputies of any party and Blum became premier, he announced, "We are going to act within the framework of the present regime, whose very vices we have denounced."

And yet despite Blum's moderation, a wave of hysterical denunciation from the Right greeted the reforms of the Popular Front and especially the presence of the Communists in the coalition supporting the government. Blum's brief regime left the prestige of the Socialist Party severely shaken, and internal struggles over the problem of appeasement of the dictators were an added source of weakness as the war drew nearer.

In the confusion of the debacle of 1940, it can be said of the Socialists at least that their record was better than that of the other parties: they cast 45 per cent of the negative votes when Laval asked for full powers for the new Pétain regime. Even so this meant that only 37 Socialists voted "no" of a potential total of 175 Deputies and Senators.

In the Resistance the role of the Socialists as organizers and journalists was significant, but the Party as such "remained inconspicuous, uncertain as to which forms of organization would be best fitted to meet the exigencies of a regained legality."* Nonetheless the Socialists emerged from the Resistance with certain very definite assets.

Léon Blum, the dominant intellectual force and the acknowledged leader of the Party, returned to France from a German prison camp with the great prestige won by his courageous attack on the Pétain regime at the Riom trials. His great distinction, his patriotism, his moderation, set him apart among France's elder statesmen, and he was praised even by many who had bitterly denounced him in the days of the Popular Front. Blum returned with a belief in the possibility of close collaboration between the Party and the trade unions and in the building of a labor party along British lines, a program which ran quite counter to both Socialist and trade union traditions in France. During the occupation he had written and reflected deeply on the humanist sources of Marxism and had now a more fully articulated—and rather highly optimistic—view of the possibilities of the emancipation of the workers in a peaceful setting.

The Party could also point with pride to the Resistance record of its members, and directly after Liberation it set about the overhauling of the party structure, particularly in the interest of carrying its message more effectively to the masses. When the Socialists elected 143 deputies to the First Constituent Assembly in the fall of 1945, giving them roughly a quarter of the total and leaving them only nine votes behind the leading Communists,† it looked superficially as though the virtues and efforts of the Socialists had been rewarded.

These early appearances were very misleading. The disintegration of the Socialist Party has been the most tragic fact in the political development of postwar France. As a result of the next two national elections, held within a year, the number of Socialist deputies had dropped to 105. Even the official Socialist figures showed that dues-paying membership declined

* Henry W. Ehrmann: "The Decline of the Socialist Party," *Modern France* (Princeton, 1951).

† The Catholic MRP was second with 150.

from 370,000 to 140,000 in the three-year period beginning in late 1945. Long before the attack on the Communist trade unions by the Socialist strong man, Jules Moch, the Party "had lost what little working class following it had mustered after the Liberation." Today the Socialist factory cells, never very significant, are all but nonexistent. Once so strong in great *Normaliens* like Jaurès and Blum, the postwar Party has failed to attract intellectuals, a serious commentary on the weakness of its message. Its strong lower middle class support has been hard hit by inflation, has seen itself threatened with depression into the proletariat, and has tended increasingly to identify itself with the proponents of *laissez-faire* and to be highly critical of Socialist "planning." Indeed the Socialists have had to bear widespread and strident criticism of *dirigisme*, and the Party has been made the principal culprit of economic chaos. In actual fact the Socialists have regularly enjoyed the façade rather than the reality of power. They have only once briefly held the crucial Ministry of Finance, and on the contrary have repeatedly administered the vulnerable Ministries of National Economy and Industrial Production.

The Socialists have indeed ceased to be a working-class party. It is true that they are identified with one wing of the labor movement, but it is the Communists, as we have seen, who penetrated, then dominated, the big national trade union organization (CGT). The Communists had money, an effective organization, excellent leadership, and superb prestige from the Resistance period. They rapidly outdistanced their Socialist rivals, and before long had won over the mass of industrial and affiliated labor. The French worker was readily persuaded that Communist efficiency could produce positive results for him, on principle he believed that he would make no mistake in voting as far Left as possible, and in the early years there was little reason to suspect the patriotism of the Communists, who were loyally coöperating with the government.

When the Communists wooed working-class support from

the Socialists, they left the latter with an inheritance from the Radical Socialists—civil servants, some school teachers, white-collar workers in general. More and more the Socialists have become the party of the middle class, especially the lower middle class. This is a serious situation. It means that in the past few French governments there have been no real representatives of the working class at a time when the willing and understanding coöperation of the workers is so essential to the present purposes of democratic forces in France. Not only has the working class been absent from the government, but the majority of the workers have been subject to the control, or to the strong influence, of a party directed from beyond the borders of France and determined to cause the miscarriage of essential foreign and domestic policies.

Once the Communists had embarked on their policy of persistent opposition to the Third Force, the Socialists became victims of an almost intolerable political situation. They were torn between a desire to support the Third Force in the necessary defense against the Communist threat at home and abroad, and the recognition that this coöperation involved sacrifices of the interests of the workers and hence their progressive alienation. This dilemma has become more acute as national elections draw nearer, and the Socialists must presently appeal again for the suffrages of the workers.

Faced by these trying alternatives, the Socialists have supported successive Third Force governments as long as they felt it was politically feasible, have repeatedly overturned these cabinets when they threatened deflationary measures (especially wage freezes), and then ironically have been faced on almost every occasion with a new government more conservative than the last. The governmental instability of these years has stemmed in large measure from the fact that the competition of the Communists has obliged the Socialists to ask concessions from their more conservative colleagues which the latter were unable or unwilling to grant.

The Socialists have been widely criticized for these tactics.

On the other hand, one of their admirers has suggested that the more charitable view would be that they have sacrificed themselves as an institution for the defense of French liberties, that if they had not collaborated with successive governments, de Gaulle or the Communists would have taken over. In any event, municipal and cantonal elections have indicated a striking decline in the Party's strength, and the best view is that a national election would yield a sharp reduction in the number of its deputies in the National Assembly.

Divisions within the Party have contributed to these fluctuations in policy. The big divisions have been two—the Right, with men like Léon Blum, placing the defense of French liberties in the foreground; the Left, with men like Pierre Commin and until recently Guy Mollet, emphasizing the immediate interests of the worker and tending at least for this reason to look toward the Communists. Further to the left the RDR (*Rassemblement Démocratique Révolutionnaire*) is an attempt to create a dynamic non-Communist workers' movement based on Marxist principles and often highly critical of the West. Its principal asset is a newspaper, the *Franc-Tireur*, which has a large circulation and still reaches some Communist readers, a curious debris left by former Communist editors when they jumped ship. It seems very unlikely that the RDR will become the vital non-Communist Left which some of its enthusiastic leaders like to imply. The Party also has a small Trotskyist (Pivertist) group on the extreme Left, who have sometimes been called the only true Marxists in France.

2. THE EXTREMES

From the parties of the Third Force, which for all their diversity represent a middle of the road, democratic, and parliamentary solution of the French political problem, we turn to the extremes. These are currently the parties in opposition, and if one reads uncritically the diatribes of Gaullist and Communist, one carries away the impression that these two parties are in reality poles apart, as indeed they are represented to be by the old political clichés of "Right" and "Left." De Gaulle exalts himself and his followers as French patriots before all else, and the Communists have appeared increasingly as an instrument of Moscow's purposes. And yet the Communists and de Gaulle's Rally of the French People (RPF) have certain affinities which come out more meaningfully if we examine them in terms of DeWitt Poole's ingenious formula, suggesting that we should conceive of Right and Left in terms of a circle, not a line, with the extremes meeting at the bottom. In its simplest terms, this conception gives us liberalism and conservatism at opposite sides of the top of the circle, supporting liberty as a principle and gradualism as a method, and communism and fascism at the bottom of the circle, adhering to authority as a principle and violence as a method.

Political extremism springs from the soil of men's desperation in the face of problems which seem almost insoluble. It is above all the product of the dislocations of war. World War I created the French Communist Party; World War II gave it impetus and opportunity. World War II created the original Gaullist movement and left the postwar disorganization in which the RPF could thrive. Both these movements appeal to the dissatisfied, the disgruntled, the insecure, and both have responded to the rhythm of internal economic and political change: hard times give an impetus to communism, political disorder increases the appeal of de Gaulle. These movements react to each other as well: a sharp rise in Communist strength and activity is an alarm signal for the more pusillanimous members of the Center who rush—momentarily at least—into the arms of de Gaulle.

Both groups are strong believers in the principle of authority, and how far de Gaulle would carry that principle in practice is a question which divides both observers and supporters of his cause. For both parties, the emotional appeal of a "mystique" is central, and in both cases its nature and influence is related to the experience in the last war. Finally, political tactics regularly unite the two: both aim to destroy the Third Force coalition, have attacked it relentlessly and violently, and have voted together against its measures repeatedly.

The questions currently asked about de Gaulle are: What is his future? What kind of regime would he give France if he came to power? The fluidity of the political situation in France makes prediction desirable; the complexity of the forces at work make it hazardous. We shall be able to answer these questions more adequately if we look first at the topography of de Gaulle's ideas.

Perhaps the most striking element is a strong predilection for authority. This we can trace back to the writings of the prewar period. What he wrote before the war antedates his political ambitions and has, therefore, a certain disinterested candor. In his *Philosophy of Command*, for instance, we find praise for the "leader," the man of character, the man to whom others turn in the hour of crisis. Here, too, there is a certain contempt for the politician. This is the authentic accent of the soldier, and de Gaulle is a soldier before he is anything else.

Authority is essential to the realization of national power, and the greatness of France has been the consistent and primary concern of the General. Like Winston Churchill, he is deeply read in the history of his country, and the grandeur of the French past shines through his pages. He will tolerate no parochial or selfish interest tending to diminish national power. He denounces the excesses of the trusts, on one hand, and of the labor unions, on the other: in the past three years he has talked in vague terms of corporatism, a word strongly redolent of fascism.

During the war de Gaulle's penchant for authority appeared in diverse forms. The Consultative Assembly was a parliamentary façade, behind which de Gaulle exercised the substance of power. Diplomacy and military affairs, inevitably involving the most important wartime decisions, he reserved for his own action. His negotiations with other powers, notably with Britain and the United States, bore only too often the stamp of querulous authority. He insulated his power by surrounding himself with "yes men"—stalwarts "of the first hour." His supporters of course could claim that all this was a reflection of the exigencies of war and of the relative insecurity of the political structure de Gaulle had so daringly contrived. There is a strong element of truth in this point of view, but one cannot overlook the fact that the General's outlook and methods during the war were not different from what had preceded or from what followed.

The months following Liberation furnished numerous examples of de Gaulle's deep concern for "order" and authority, but his final struggle for a strong executive was the crucial instance. With the submission for the first time, on January 1, 1946, of his resignation as President-Premier, he hurled a bristling challenge: "Do we want a Government which governs or do we want an omnipotent Assembly selecting a Government to accomplish its will?" De Gaulle was stating the case for a "strong government" not merely from preference for authority but because he sought to arm France politically to play a great role in the world and because the memories of her weakness in 1940 were vivid in his mind.* But de Gaulle's plea for a strong executive, followed soon afterwards by his abrupt final resignation, caused widespread misgivings concerning his usefulness as the head of a democratic and parliamentary regime. These doubts have scarcely been quieted by his subsequent elaboration of the nature of the regime he would establish.

De Gaulle's new constitutional structure would aim above all to assure effective power to the executive. It provides a strict separation of powers, a second chamber virtually coequal with the first, and a president subject to indirect election—perhaps an intentional departure from the direct method used by Louis Napoleon who has in recent years been all too frequently compared with de Gaulle. The president would be arbiter among the three powers, but would also occupy a position above any of them. His supervision would be felt particularly in areas

* John E. Sawyer, *Political Science Quarterly*, September 1947.

"connected with his role as guardian of the integrity of the national territory and of respect for treaties: foreign policy, national defense, the French union . . ." He would choose the premier, and the latter would in turn be responsible to the chamber. But when a ministry was overturned by the chamber, the president would have the option of naming a new premier or dissolving the chamber and calling new elections. This power to maintain a chamber which was friendly or to destroy one which was not, would place enormous powers in the hands of the president. But this is not all. The president would also have a plebiscitary power, the right to call for a national referendum in cases of grave conflict between himself and the parliament. This is the description of a regime whose misuse could rapidly lead to dictatorship.*

That brings us to the inevitable question: Is de Gaulle a fascist? The concept itself has proved highly adaptable to the particular national soil in which it has grown. For the present the General rejects the more sinister elements in the fascist regimes of Hitler and Mussolini—racism, predatory war, mass brutality, rigorous police supervision of private life. Yet we find disjointed but disquieting elements in a variety of Gaullist pronouncements that could be elements in a fascist philosophy: respect for the "leader"; concern for national power; balancing and integration of pressure groups by a strong executive; a single party; concern for "order" in society; shock troops; "emotionally charged" public meetings; a pervading mysticism; and a perhaps calculated vagueness of doctrine—André Malraux, himself significantly an ex-Communist and one of de Gaulle's principal left-wing advisers, states the case: "We have no faith in programs, but only in objectives." These are only timbers; nowhere has the General tried to build them into a coherent structure. Very probably his mind does not work on the theoretical level which would make this tempting, even if he considered it politically wise.

* H. Stuart Hughes, "Gaullism: Retrospect and Prospect," *Modern France* (Princeton, 1951).

Those who defend the General as one deeply attached to free institutions invariably point to the fact that he made "no effort" to create a dictatorial regime following Liberation when his enormous prestige, they claim, would have made such a step possible. There are two answers to this view.

During the heroic period of the Resistance de Gaulle had seen Frenchmen of almost every political stripe coöperating in the larger national interest. He appears to have felt that a large measure of this unity would carry over beyond the war and would support a program of national regeneration—which meant in effect *the program* which he represented. As soon as the Constituent Assembly met and it became evident that a majority would oppose his plea for a strong executive, he resigned. In short, de Gaulle *did* try to create a strong government, one in which he would obviously occupy the position of power and one which his enemies and critics feared might just conceivably become a dictatorship. However, he did not succeed.

Did de Gaulle really have at any time the choice of which his admirers loosely speak? Could he have succeeded in the establishment of a dictatorship during the delirium of unity which immediately followed the Liberation? The answer seems to be clearly no. So radical and unexpected a step would have alienated and disillusioned the Resistance and the great mass of Frenchmen who fully anticipated the reëstablishment of democratic institutions. It would have flouted the Communists, when they were under Moscow's orders to be highly coöperative and when de Gaulle was actively seeking an alliance with the Russians. It would probably have precipitated civil disturbances at a time when the Resistance was still armed, and would have called down upon the General's head the wrath of the Allies who were still deeply engaged in fighting the war with the Germans. De Gaulle did not seek to achieve a regime of authority following Liberation because it was not politically feasible and because he believed Frenchmen would remain united in his support when the time came to propose the new institutional arrangements which would give France a "strong government."

Following his resignation as President-Premier in January 1946, de Gaulle remained in retirement for more than a year, emerging only to blast the two successive constitutional drafts of 1946. In the spring of 1947 he reëntered the political arena and presented his countrymen with the Rally of the French People (RPF) which he carefully described as not a political party but as an opportunity for collaboration of all non-Communist Frenchmen who espoused the high purposes for which he stood. The movement grew rapidly and the internal situation degenerated at a corresponding tempo, so that by autumn de Gaulle was ready to have the RPF frankly enter the electoral lists in the municipal balloting. The result was a great triumph, and Gaullists claimed as high as 40 per cent of the vote. It would, however, be very difficult to translate the results of the municipal elections into any meaningful terms applicable to a national election of deputies, since the electoral system used for the latter would be different and because various local influences are at work in municipal elections. Moreover in the municipal elections of 1947 most of the Radicals ran on RPF lists.

Since the Gaullist "high" of the municipal elections, the strength of the movement has fluctuated—with a decline under the sound and firm Schuman administration in the early part of 1948; a revival during the August-September crisis of that year; an all-time low at the time of the cantonal elections of March 1949; a gain in strength again with the 1949 drought, the rise in prices and the fall of Queuille (October); and a decline again in 1950, especially since the rearmament program has enabled Pleven to steal the General's nationalist fire.

These fluctuations suggest clearly enough that we cannot write off the Gaullist movement. Domestic economic or political difficulties, a fresh threat to French security abroad—these are the stimuli to Gaullist revival. The mass of non-Communist Frenchmen recognize the great service of de Gaulle to France in the hour of her direst peril, but they will support him now only as a *pis aller*, only if the crisis becomes threatening enough to become intolerable, menacing enough to make them willing to risk free institutions for the security which a regime of authority might bring. Meanwhile, the "normal" support of the RPF comes from Catholics of conservative and traditionalist outlook, some remaining monarchists, Vichyites, some outright fascists, parts of the business world. The General has a much more limited following from perfectly republican Radicals, from authentic members of the Resistance, and from a wide range of people who are attracted by his great prestige and his earlier services to France. But the mass of his current following is essentially conservative, even reactionary. He has, for instance, made little progress on the labor front.

French national elections will come at the latest in October 1951. The size of the Gaullist vote will depend in some measure on the nature of the electoral system adopted and above all on the domestic and international situation of France at that time. If the Gaullists should receive only 25 per cent of the vote and the Communists should drop to 20 per cent (which is by no means inconceivable), a coalition government of the type we have had since 1947 might continue to exist, although its majority would be fragile. If the Gaullists were included in a government with de Gaulle at its head but with at least half of its support from other center parties, it might still be possible for the MRP and the Radical Socialists to exercise a moderating influence on de Gaulle and especially on his entourage, various ones of whom have always been the subject of bitter and probing criticism. If, however, the elections returned the Gaullists with anything approaching a majority and a "pure" Gaullist government followed, the results for the United States and the West generally could be serious.

With a penchant for authority, and with men in his entourage who believe in it even more, de Gaulle might be tempted —or driven—to assert his power. Moscow might well decide to present us with a fascist or pre-fascist France by precipitating serious Communist disorders and a consequent abridgment of civil liberties, alienating French Socialists and supporters of the parliamentary regime generally. A fascist France would be a source of acute embarrassment, to say the least, to the United States as leader of the cause of democracy in the West, and the impact on Italy and Germany could be most serious. And in all this de Gaulle could perfectly well persuade himself that he was acting as a French patriot, and from the highest motives.

It is often loosely assumed that de Gaulle would be able to restore "order" to France because he would be willing to use "strong" methods. Of some 400,000 coal miners, 250,000 are Communists or Communist sympathizers. Large numbers of these even spent four years under the German yoke learning the arts of sabotage. How readily de Gaulle could compel compliance from such a group is a nice question. And coal is at the center of the functioning of any industrial society.

De Gaulle is far from being a man ideally suited to cope with the complex economic, political, and international problems which France now faces. He had an opportunity to deal with the economic legacy of the war, and the record was unimpressive. He is said to have relatively little direct interest in economic questions. Remarked one shrewd observer: "He knows economics on the same level as a woman knows a carburetor."

On the political side, one candid but friendly observer notes that, although de Gaulle has exceptional qualities—lucid intelligence, broad and profound views, courage, integrity, disinterestedness—he lacks precisely those ordinary qualities so much needed by the politician. He lacks the expansiveness of a Jaurès, the capacity to win men and to tap their resources in the easy give and take of familiar political intercourse. In the months after Liberation he centered his attention on the things which commanded his primary interest—military problems and diplomacy—and in the case of economic and political questions was too often content to be counseled by his "experts." When he discovered the depth of national disunity, he retired in disillusionment. If he returns to power, asks our critic, will he have learned to deal with parties or will he have been disgusted with democracy and turn to authority of a type not resting on the consent of the majority?

In the international field, American officials in the last war learned how difficult it was to get on with de Gaulle. He has been persistently dissatisfied with the role assigned to France in western defense arrangements. And at present the problem of rapidly forging a defense instrument among the Atlantic Pact powers is already growing so complex that few on either side would wish to complicate it further by adding the ingredients of de Gaulle's temperamental nationalism and hypersensitivity.

This probing and highly critical discussion of de Gaulle must not blind us to the fact that the French parliamentary system has profound weaknesses, that de Gaulle's program aims definitely to remedy certain of these, that Frenchmen as a whole have long been deeply discouraged with the inefficiency of their political arrangements, and that the Third Force has proved to be anything but stable or consistently resolute. It is perfectly possible that conditions may arise which will make de Gaulle seem desirable—even to the present writer!

It is almost inappropriate to deal with the Communists in a chapter on French political parties. Without yielding in the least to the influence of current hysteria concerning the Communists, we can say quite flatly that their organization in France is something of a quite different order from that of other political parties.

A party in a democratic community is a group of men freely associated, having a set of political tenets (sometimes vague and even conflicting), and aiming to achieve political control through the machinery of free elections. Let us admit at once that there is inevitably an inner group which controls party finances and exercises an altogether disproportionate influence on such crucial questions as the selection of candidates. But in a free society there are always present the strong correctives of a free press and the possibility of successful "revolt" within or without the party. Above all, the party has objectives that fall within a "national" framework: no matter how narrow the class or group interest, it is not one which consciously seeks the good of another state in preference to that of its own.

The organization of the French Communists has various outward trappings which strongly suggest a party—national congresses, election of deputies, and so on. But the differentia are sharp and significant. Hierarchy, control, discipline, are the order of the day. We have to do here essentially with an army. Decisions proceed from the French Politburo down through the levels of the hierarchy and usually permit of no discussion, except perhaps with reference to implementation of policies. The press carefully follows the party line. The deputies are sent to "school" after election and before they take their seats, and then regularly are briefed on the appropriate attitude toward each measure so that they invariably present a solid front.

Control within France is, however, only the beginning of the story. It is the Kremlin that makes the big decisions, and these are dutifully carried out by the French Communist Party. De Gaulle denounces them as "séparatistes," men who love Russia more than France. Moreover, the Kremlin makes decisions for the French Communists which respond to the global Soviet policy in the cold war and which often run quite counter to French national interests. We are faced here with an internal peacetime fifth column which is in fact an arm of the Kremlin, prepared to carry out the latter's will on the political or military level.

The documentation of these statements does not come from anything as clear-cut as intercepted messages between the Kremlin and French Communist leaders. It doesn't seem to happen that way in any case. But French leaders do occasionally go to Moscow, they meet Russian representatives at Cominform conferences, and there is always the Soviet Embassy in Paris. Again, there is plenty of indirect but very relevant evidence on this relationship. A careful correlation of the propaganda line in Soviet *Pravda* and *L'Humanité*, the official organ of the French Party, for the years 1936–1939 shows the characteristically persistent parallelism. When Thorez denounced the projected Marshall Plan at the Communist Strasbourg Congress of July 1947, just at the moment when Molotoff was arriving in Paris to negotiate for the possible coöperation of the Soviets in the Plan, he was obliged to make an all too obvious retraction on the following day, stating lamely that he had been misquoted in the press (including *L'Humanité*). On February 24, 1949, Thorez made a statement that ran so counter to French patriotic sentiments that it deeply offended many Communist sympathizers, namely, that in a war with Russia in which Soviet armies were obliged to pursue "aggressors" on to French soil, the French workers (and people) could only welcome the Soviet army in the tradition of the satellite states.

The other side of the coin shows only a small defection to Titoism. The so-called "National Communist Movement," whose members do not refer to themselves as Titoists, had about 4000 members in September 1950. It published *La Lutte* and various other papers. Some 1500 to 2000 students and workers went to Belgrade during the summer of 1950 to work on the new *Cité Universitaire* and to see selected "sights" in Yugoslavia. The Communist Party takes consistent and anxious notice of this group—in *Humanité*, for instance—but there is nothing yet to indicate that it will grow to significant size.

Close observers declare that the Communist Party has been losing ground since the middle of 1947. And they cite such evidence as that of elections, loss of circulation of Communist newspapers, and alienation of their following occasioned by the politically motivated coal strike in the fall of 1948, which was followed by the dropping away of a certain number of peasants and members of Communist "front organizations." Here again the weakness in our analysis is that we apply to the Communists the criteria normal in our judgment of political parties, and are influenced by such barometers as the fluctuation in party membership. If instead we focus our attention on the Communists as an instrument of the Kremlin's objectives, then a decline in membership may simply signify a hardening of purpose through the elimination of waverers (and in fact recent party policy seems to have been directed at producing just this result). Our questions should be: how effective is the Communist Party as an instrument of peacetime sabotage (and here we must think not merely of loss of production but especially of the more subtle problem of the sapping of morale), and, on a more sinister plane, how effective will it be as a wartime instrument of clandestine military aid for an attempted Soviet invasion? It has been claimed that the large-scale strike failures of the Communists demonstrate that a successful general strike is beyond their powers. This may be so. Their recent quiescence might also mean that the Soviets are awaiting a more useful peacetime opportunity or that the "hard core" is being carefully conserved for "D Day." Meanwhile the French Communists have again revealed their versatility by transferring the Korean instrument of "war by proxy" to the domestic front. In the Stockholm peace campaign, they may have enrolled five to six million "peace partisans," most of them non-Communists of course, but these are well meaning citizens who do the Communists' work for them by contributing to the spirit of neutralism and apathy already so widespread. The Communists have organized large numbers of these peace partisans in communal and factory committees.

The organization of the French Party is a tight and cohesive hierarchy. At the top is a Politburo in the Kremlin tradition, but receiving its directives from Moscow. The directives of the Politburo in turn guide a Central Committee, which is said to have varied in size from 13 to 80 members; and the latter exercises vertical control through regional committees, *rayons* (usually five to a region), *sub-rayons*, and cells. The last named are the smallest units and are formed in factories, villages, specified streets of urban centers, and in the armed forces. On a horizontal plane, the Central Committee includes sections on agitation and propaganda, colonial work, foreign laborers in France, agrarian problems, and "self defense" and paramilitary organizations.

The Communists also have a hierarchy of support. The leadership is Moscow-trained or oriented, able, unscrupulous, and deeply compromised with its Kremlin masters—not a single Communist leader of importance has deserted the Party in the last fifteen years. Supporting the leadership is a hard core of Communist Party members, men and women who have a fanatical belief in the fair land of the future and often a deep hatred for the selfishness and Philistinism of the capitalist world as it is painted in their press. The strength of the Communist Party discipline is suggested by the support of prominent intellectuals—Joliot-Curie is only one—nourished in a tradition of notorious independence. These are people ready in mind and training for great risks.

It would be idle to state a figure for this group (after all, the gradations are subtle), but since the total number of party cards is estimated at about 600,000, they might include 200,000. Of the remainder of those with Communist cards, many surely would actively aid their brethren if war came, but others would be lost as the anti-French character of Soviet purposes became clearer.

Beyond party members, the Communists regularly received some four and a half million votes in the post-Liberation elections. These came largely from urban workers, but there was also substantial support from agricultural workers and even from the peasantry. If war came with a patently democratic government still at the helm in France, overt Communist coöperation with the enemy would certainly alienate large elements of this non-Communist support, particularly that of the peasants. On the other hand, if it were preceded by an authoritarian government which took strong measures against the Communists and in so doing abridged civil liberties generally, then working class support might be widened by the addition of many left-wing Socialists.

The Party's concern with the French peasant warrants at least a word. On principle, the peasant is a fundamental Communist interest. In the case of France, the peasantry's "ferocious individualism and its petty bourgeois outlook" posed a formidable barrier from the beginning. But the Communists also had advantages: the Jacobin tradition induced many peasants regularly to vote for the extreme Left; a rural proletariat and semi-proletariat was present, and a large number of very small owners who were resentful of growing capitalist concentration in agriculture.

The Party painfully laid the foundation of its peasant campaign in the decades after 1921, but the great successes came only after Liberation. The Party line set collectivization as a long-term goal, but it wisely emphasized hereditary land rights for all working peasants and practical reforms along the way, responding to the profit motive. The Nazi-Soviet Pact of 1939 destroyed the Party's position in the countryside, but the Communists recovered much of their influence during the Resistance period and emerged from the war with about 2500 Committees of Peasant Defense and Action in 33 Departments in the Center and the South (old areas of Communist penetration).

Since Liberation, the Communists have boasted unashamedly that they have helped to raise agricultural prices—at a time when urban workers, their principal supporters, were being caught in the squeeze of unequal price and wage inflation. They have also paradoxically supported lower taxes for the peasants, and at the same time higher public investment for the modernization and mechanization of farms.

A confidential Party publication of 1947 showed 12,060 rural cells, and *Humanité* claimed as early as April 1945 that the number of Party members in agricultural regions had increased by 253 per cent since 1937. In the three national elections following Liberation, the Communists gained little over prewar in the Paris region, but their share of the vote doubled or tripled in almost every rural district. In the post-Liberation elections the Communists polled less than 10 per cent in only two Departments, and no area now lacks a network of village cells.

Since these elections, bitter Communist hostility to the Marshall Plan and reports of purges and collectivization in the satellite states have produced a diminution of their rural strength. The total decline in the Communist vote since 1945, as measured by the partial cantonal elections of March 1949, may have been as much as 20 per cent. And yet one close observer declares that if the condition of the peasant should worsen again—and various farm prices did slump in 1949 for the first time since prewar years—the "Communists alone are fully prepared to take advantage of rising discontent." *

The Party possesses numerous advantages for the accomplishment of its purposes both in factory and field. First of all, financial power: the Socialists and opposition labor groups bitterly complain that the Communists have money for every necessary purpose, from propaganda (invariably more lavish than that of their opponents) to the training of specialists for each one of their many purposes. The sources of their financial strength are numerous. During the chaos of Liberation they seized convoys of gold belonging to the Bank of France. They were in a position to sell protection to "mild collaborators" after Liberation. In the initial years, they made a profit on certain of their large circulation newspapers, although deficits followed later. The Communist treasury takes part of the salary of deputies and of various other officials. And the Party does get some help from Moscow for purposes which the Kremlin is convinced are useful, although it is said that the latter is strongly economy-minded in matters of aid to "foreign" Communist Parties.

* See the article by Gordon Wright, "Communists and Peasantry in France," *Modern France* (Princeton, 1951).

At a time when the press of other parties had been hard hit by the war, Communist newspapers appeared on every side. *L'Humanité* came above ground again and attained a top circulation of around 530,000 between November 1944 and June 1945, but, with an increase in price, had dropped 100,000 in the next six months. Second to *Humanité* was *Ce Soir*, with a comparable evening circulation in Paris. In addition, the Communists were operating in December 1946 ten newspapers with circulations of 8000 to 115,000 in principal provincial cities. The influential agrarian weekly, *La Terre*, attained a circulation of nearly 300,000 in 1946,* and scattered throughout the countryside were innumerable local weeklies speaking to the parochial interests of each given region.

Schools for Communist indoctrination included, in March 1947, 17 *Écoles Centrales*, 14 of them designed to produce "militant Communist specialists," particularly in the propaganda field; 234 "Federal" or "Interfederal Schools" with 4453 students; and a whole series of *Écoles de base* offering courses in preparation for electoral campaigns (in which Party leaders participated in Paris) and courses in "Marxist-Leninist formation." There were also offered an interesting "course of study for the Communist deputies to the first Constituent Assembly and a course of study for Communist representatives in Parliament in January 1947" which an official handbook described as "veritable Party schools which were attended with assiduity and profit by every one of our elected representatives."

The detailed history of the Party need not detain us. We have seen how it came into existence in 1920. It grew unevenly until the Depression and then reached its interwar high point at the time of the Popular Front election of 1936, following the 1935 Comintern decision that Communist Parties everywhere might coöperate with left-wing "bourgeois" parties to oppose the rising tide of fascism. The Party weakened with the failures of the Popular Front and was suppressed and

* All these figures are from the Party and prepared for internal consumption.

driven underground with the announcement of the Nazi-Soviet Pact and the beginning of the war. It first attempted to sabotage the war effort and then collaborated with the occupying Germans.

With the Nazi invasion of Russia in 1941, the Party executed an about-face and rapidly developed its underground organization to combat the German occupation and aid in the eventual defeat of the Nazis. It is widely admitted that the "Parti des Fusillés" made the largest single contribution to the Resistance, and it emerged from the war with a superb record, although one that was exaggerated both by Communists and by the emotional reactions of its non-Communist admirers, many of them people of very conservative outlook.

The Communists exploited to the full the honeymoon following Liberation, when the world was gripped by a widespread conviction that the Soviets and the West could coöperate to achieve a peaceful world. Party members were persistently in the government until May 1947. The Party coöperated effectively in the early phases of recovery, and notably in such outstanding achievements as the reconstruction of the coal industry. Meanwhile, following a vigorous and ingenious propaganda campaign, the Party emerged as the largest in France, and during the same period the Communists made themselves masters of the dominant national trade union movement, the CGT.

The breach between the Soviets and the West was already widening when the Communists were ousted from the government, nominally because they were attempting to support one view in the cabinet and another in the Assembly. When the Soviets refused to participate in the Marshall Plan on the terms which the American government had offered, the French Party at once swung into line with a propaganda campaign against "American imperialism," and it has repeatedly sought to cause the miscarriage of the European Recovery Program, notably by attempts to produce general strikes in the autumn of 1947 and again a year later. On the latter occasion the spearhead of the strike was in the northern coal fields where the Communists took a most drastic step in calling out the workers who manned the pumps and the security equipment. The obvious political motivation of the strike alienated some non-Communist labor support and caused a further decline in the numbers holding Party cards, although not necessarily, as we have noted above, of Party "strength." Since the coal strike the Party has been further purged of "unreliable" members. As we noted earlier, the fall strikes in 1947 resulted in a scission in the Communist-dominated CGT and left only some two and a half to three million workers under Communist control of a total which had once been above five million.

Despite certain evidences of "decline," the Communist Party remains a primary threat to French security. It can still cause persistent losses to the French economy through long-range sabotage. It could probably cause widespread economic dislocation, if the Soviets should elect to call for an all-out effort. And its threat as a wartime fifth column has caused French authorities to take drastic security measures at a time when it is believed that the illegal apparatus is becoming more significant than the "above ground" Party organization. In this difficult task, France faces the paradoxical situation that, whereas the Kremlin is using the movement for its own purposes, large numbers of its adherents have a fanatic attachment to the Party, among other reasons, because in a period of profound moral confusion communism appears to offer men a firm belief to cling to. France and the West need to find a new objective for the aspirations of mankind compatible with the humanistic traditions of western civilization but offering the security and satisfactions which many men find in this competing belief. "The question," suggests Vera Dean, "no longer is whether France or other Marshall Plan beneficiaries will have enough to live on by the end of ERP, but whether they will have something to live for."

9. France Overseas

Continental France is a land of modest proportions. But overseas she controls an area which would make 22 of France and one and a half of our country. The French Empire is second only to Britain's in size, and, although the greater part of it is concentrated relatively near to France and in the northwestern third of Africa, it does extend at intervals in a broad belt encircling the earth. Airfields permitting, a plane with a good deal less radius than the B–29 could circumnavigate the globe touching nothing but territories under the French flag.

In size, the French Empire resembles the British; otherwise, it contrasts sharply with it. Almost all the French possessions –North Africa is the important exception–lie in the tropics, and their products are largely complementary to those of her metropolitan economy. On the other hand, the most highly developed of the British Dominions lie in the temperate zones, and their products have in recent decades come into sharp competition with those of Britain, contributing to the loosening of the ties of empire. The British Dominions, at least, are self-governing; all parts of the French Empire stood in varying stages of colonial subordination prior to 1939.

The French Empire was the product of no outpouring of national energy, of no universal desire of Frenchmen to see the globe splotched with the national colors. On the contrary, almost all of this vast area was acquired in a period of national weakness, following the defeat by Germany in 1870, and was the work primarily of a small, active, able, and enthusiastic nucleus of "colonialists"–diplomats, explorers, generals, missionaries, propagandists. These men, moreover, accomplished their impressive task in a setting of national apathy, and in the face of acrid criticism by a minority. And yet in these years since Liberation, the majority of Frenchmen, who had shown little interest in the acquisition of the colonies, have been concerned that France should not relax her grip on them—to lose this symbol of power would be one more evidence of weakness in a world where the international position of France has already been diminished.

Parts of the empire lie at great distances from the Metropole (Continental France)—difficult to defend, embedded in areas dominated by other powers. Since the war, France has lost its possessions in the Levant and has been struggling desperately to maintain a foothold in Indochina. Years ago the great naval theoretician, Admiral Castex, argued that France was greatly overextended, that much of her expansion had taken place in the wrong parts of the world, and that she would do well to consolidate her position by trading territories in the Levant, the Far East, the Pacific, and the Caribbean for defensible lands which would round out her African possessions.

1. WHAT OVERSEAS FRANCE INCLUDES

Of the seventeen big and little French possessions in Africa, it is the three in the northwestern corner of the continent which command our attention—Morocco, Algeria, and Tunisia. These three are economically more valuable to France than all the rest of the Empire together (see map, page 220). To the south lie the inhospitable reaches of the Sahara, organized on military lines and attached to the office of the Governor General of Algeria. Adjacent on the south and west is the huge expanse of French West Africa, well over half the size of the United States, the producer of a significant crop of tropical products for the Metropole. Still farther south and extending over the Equator is nearly a million square miles of French Equatorial Africa, much of it jungle. These, then, are the vast and contiguous colonial territories of France in the northwest third of Africa. The fact that they are continuous has limited significance, however, since nature has interposed tremendous obstacles to movement, and the transport system is rudimentary. The only other very significant African possession of the French is Madagascar, an island about the size of California lying off the southeastern coast.*

Whatever may be said for or against colonialism as such, the strategic value of her African possessions to France is unquestioned. The control of the North African shore has given her command of the western Mediterranean, and access to the Continent through Sicily and Italy. The campaigns of 1942 and 1943 etched out again the strategic relations of this area to Europe. West Africa's Dakar is a window on the narrows of the Atlantic, and was a source of serious anxiety to the Allied command so long as it was controlled by men who were collaborators of Hitler. French Equatorial Africa served as a vital link in the trans-African air ferry route over which men, planes, and Lend-Lease supplies reached Cairo during the critical period of the defense of Egypt.

In the Levant, after the first war, France received mandates over Syria and the Lebanon, where she had had interests, particularly of a religious and cultural nature, for more than a thousand years. Rising nationalism, Franco-British wartime promises of independence to the two countries, the obvious reluctance of the French to implement these promises, and finally the blundering reinforcement of the French garrison in May 1945 at a critical point in the negotiations ended in intervention by the British, ostensibly to protect communications routes to the still flaming war in the Far East. Amid feelings of great resentment, the French were presently forced out of the area entirely.

* * *

* For the economic importance of the overseas French possessions, see Appendix I, p. 294.

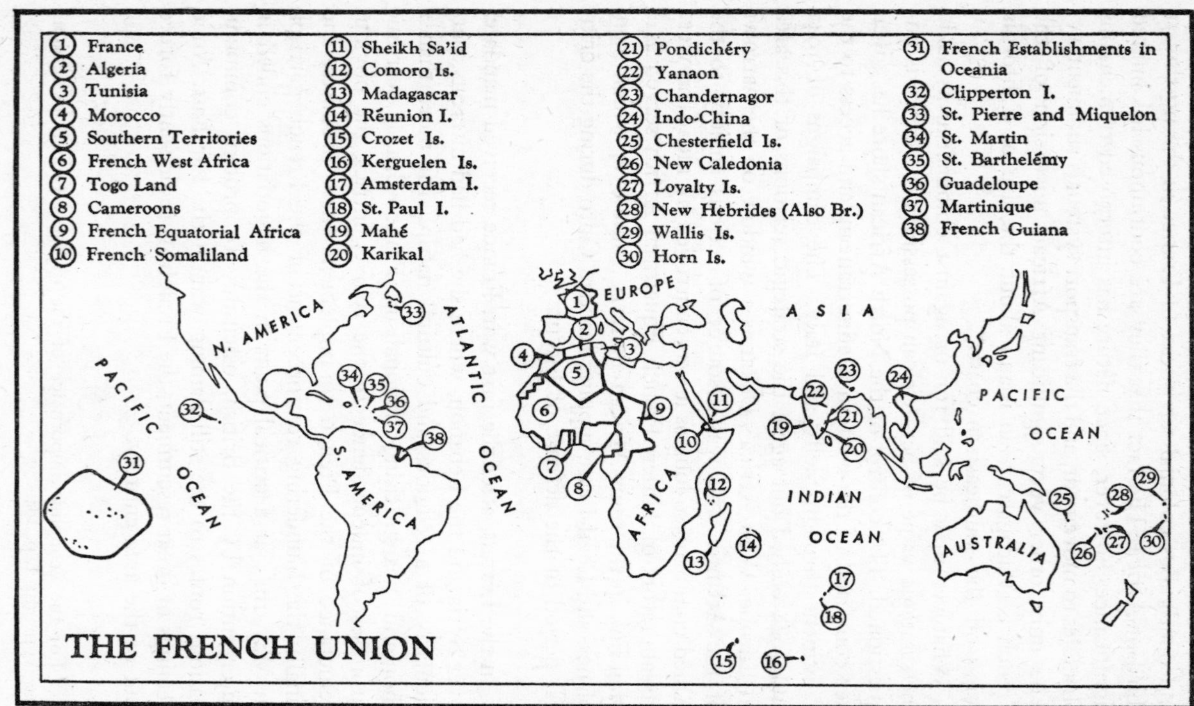

THE FRENCH UNION

From the great days of their eighteenth-century Indian Empire, the French now retain only five commercial ports in that subcontinent. These have considerable economic—and sentimental—importance, but no independent strategic significance, embedded as they are in India.

The pearl of the French possessions in the Far East is of course Indochina, which we shall discuss presently at some length. The New Hebrides Islands, which the French hold jointly with the British, and New Caledonia lie at a considerable distance off the northeastern coast of Australia. It was in New Caledonia, which had promptly joined the Free French, that the Guadalcanal offensive against the Japanese was mounted. The latter island also abounds in various metals, like chromium, essential to modern industrial processes.

French Oceania includes hundreds of islands strung across the central Pacific below the Equator, with tiny Clipperton farther north and only 900 miles from the coast of Mexico. However rapturously Pierre Loti and others may have described Tahiti and her sisters, the brutal fact is that during the later decades of the nineteenth century the islands were sinking into a state of economic somnolence, and where the French hoped that the Panama Canal might revitalize Oceania, the result, alas, was rather to open the area further to American commerce and Protestant missionaries. The islands have strategic importance only in the setting of the naval coöperation of France, the United States, and Britain.

In the Western Hemisphere, French possessions are mere remnants of the empire of the eighteenth century. The Islands of St. Pierre and Miquelon, off the southeastern shore of Newfoundland, are the center of the French codfishing industry, supplied by the annual catch of Breton fishermen off the Grand Banks. The Islands enjoyed a brief notoriety during the days of Prohibition when they warehoused large stocks of liquor for destinations in the United States. In the West Indies the French have Martinique and Guadeloupe, famous as sugar islands before the competition of the beet. Strategically, they are now important only in the context of the American wartime bases leased from Great Britain.

France also possesses a colony in Guiana, on the northern shores of South America. The latter includes a large penal colony and substantial gold mining; but its economic possibilities are almost completely undeveloped.

2. FRENCH COLONIAL POLICY

When the French faced the problems of a new empire overseas in the late nineteenth century, they did so with a ready-made policy, legacy from the mid-eighteenth century when French territory lay in a great arc from Louisiana to India. It was natural to the age of the enlightenment to believe that French civilization, which had been so hospitably received in the more sophisticated societies of Europe, should be equally welcome to the backward areas which had fallen under their imperial control. These new territories were to constitute in reality a "France d'outremer," a New France beyond the seas endowed with the institutions and ideas of the Metropole. The colonies were simply parts of France separated from the mother country by the accidents of geography.

In the application of this policy of "assimilation" in the late nineteenth century, we meet a paradox. The French, with characteristic logic, had founded this new version of an eighteenth-century policy on the principles of 1789. But, whereas these principles imply the right of free men to choose their own institutions, the French now fixed the institutions of metropolitan France on the colonial peoples under their control, and where this process created tension and conflict with native cultures, the latter had to yield.

Still another paradox. In fact, as opposed to theory, the French were less concerned with the export of their own institutions than they were with the subordination of the colonies to French interests. In this context, racialism and other attitudes foreign to the French in France—where it must be admitted, however, that the French do not face these problems in any very acute form—developed in a way quite irreconcilable with the generous principles of the Great Revolution.

Nowhere did French interests appear more starkly than in the economic field. French policy has consistently sought to build a protective wall around the colonies so that they should constitute free trade preserves for France. But the crowning inconsistency in this regime lay in the requirements that colonial products pay duty on entering France, on the theory that the colony ought financially to support the colonial administration, for which, moreover, it had never asked. A colonial merchant could very properly complain that he was French when he bought but only half French when he sold.

The whole theory of assimilation in its more extreme form was clearly destined to break down in the face of native resistance and domestic criticism. Timid harbingers of a new decentralizing policy appeared in the early years of the present century—a separate budget for Algeria in 1900, widening powers for the colonial Governors General in the succeeding decade. The pacification policy of Galliéni and Lyautey was another straw in the wind. The growing humanitarian movement played its part. But the new policy of "association" did not fully emerge until after the first war.

The policy of "association" declared in effect that, if the larger interests of France were to be served, the colonies must be viewed not merely as markets but as societies. And this does not mean to imply that many Frenchmen in positions of colonial responsibility had not previously taken a broad humanitarian view of the native problem. In any event, it was now clear that all natives could not be made Frenchmen even though a small but significant minority had in fact become so. The pursuit of such a policy could only produce tensions of a potentially dangerous type. It was both safer and wiser to permit the development of these individual native societies along lines appropriate to each but still in the general framework of French leadership and control. The natives would share to a larger degree in political life, especially on the local level. But at the same time there was no thought that these colonies were being prepared for anything so radical as eventual independence.

A new economic policy was the clearest indication that the colonies were to continue in subordination to the interests of the Metropole. Following the first war, Albert Sarraut, who had enjoyed a broad colonial experience, enunciated a policy which envisaged the colonies no longer as economic preserves of French industrialists but as interdependent parts of a great organic system of which France was to be the center. Tariff policies were to favor the economic development of the colonies on a mutually interdependent basis and in such a way as to bring maximum benefit to the whole. France could only prosper if the colonies prospered. But in whatever language this economic aspect of the policy of "association" was dressed, the fact remained that the Metropole continued to occupy the central and dominant position and that the colonies were still viewed as primarily intended to serve the interests of France. And it should be emphasized that, even with the change in outlook implied in the policy of "association," the concept of "assimilation" continued–and still continues–to be a very significant force in French colonial administration.

To those sensitive to the great qualities of the French as a people, analysis of their colonial policy is an ungrateful task. In meeting the challenges of dynamic change in this field, they have, it is true, repeatedly altered their policy, but, like the Poles in another day, they have almost invariably been ready for concessions "one river too late."

During the interwar years French colonial policy was eroded by the forces of nationalism and incipient communism. Behind the tariff walls of the Sarraut economic system, the colonial share in French imports doubled in a decade, but critics in the colonies loudly protested that they paid too high a price for a system which advantaged primarily the French Metropole. The emphasis on agriculture complementary to that of France, it was declared, sacrificed self-sufficiency and forced the colonies to turn to outside markets for foodstuffs. The tariff regime diverted trade from natural channels offered by neighboring countries. The discouragement of colonial industry prevented the development of a better balanced economy. In the absence of a corps of indigenous engineers, young men found few opportunities in this important profession,* and at the same time their opportunities in the civil administration and in economic activity generally were severely limited. With the lack of industrialization and the ruin of handicraft industry by the competition of factory products from France, a jobless proletariat appeared and turned to anti-French and anti-capitalist agitation.

In short, the French hold on the colonies was loosening at the very time, during the thirties, when her domestic difficulties were at their height. Then came the war, which profoundly stimulated nationalist movements in the empire.

The defeat of 1940 dealt a heavy blow to French prestige, essential element in the rule of native peoples. German and Italian propaganda in North Africa fanned the fires of nationalist discontent. And the Allied invasion of 1942, following the ringing phrases of the Atlantic Charter, opened the floodgates to native agitation, which in the case of the "Manifesto of the Algerian People" (February 1943) went so far as to demand self-determination, equality of all groups within the population, and the confiscation of the estates of the French *colons*.

The French were in a difficult position. They were militarily weak. The Gaullist French Committee of National Liberation was deeply in the debt of those colonies, such as West

* Exceptions are to be noted in such cases as that of the *Société Indochinoise d'Électricité* which employed engineers of Viet Nam origin as plant heads with excellent results so far as their loyalty to the French at the time of the Japanese "invasion" of Indochina was concerned.

Africa, Equatorial Africa, and New Caledonia, which had given the Free French loyal support at an early date. At the same time de Gaulle, intent on the restoration of French power and prestige, wanted effective and well-controlled support from the empire.

The eventual result was a compromise which came to be known as the "French Union." The nature of the struggle to determine the form of this new French Union indicates above all the wide divergencies of view in France as to how this thorny problem should be solved. A very able group of liberal colonial specialists, men who had devoted their lives to the disinterested solution of these problems, wanted to give to this new "French Community," as it was known originally at its inception at the Brazzaville meeting of 1943, the form of essential equality among autonomous governments, coördinated by a "supra-national" element. This would have represented a vast step forward and the creation of a structure not fundamentally different in spirit from the British Commonwealth of Nations. One of the leading spirits in this movement was Paul Mus, presently to become the distinguished director of the *École de la France d'Outremer* and who actually suggested the name, *Union Française*, late in the summer of 1944.

This liberal group did in fact get its ideas expressed in the preamble to the Constitution of 1946. Unfortunately the *articles* of the Constitution, adopted one by one, took away what the preamble had granted and restated an outworn conception of the French colonial system. This victory for the forces of the past was due in considerable measure to the activities of Alexandre Varenne, a deputy and former governor general of Indochina. Varenne was supported by French "colonials," who returned immediately after the war in great numbers to Paris, which they had not been able to visit for years, with ideas which were often suitable enough to the prewar period but which were no longer applicable to the post-1945 developments.

The result in any event was that France, in yielding to the

forces of the past, lost a great opportunity for moral and political leadership in this field. During the early stages of public discussion of the Union, one heard enthusiastic praise of the possibilities of this new solution. But these opinions contrast all too sharply with the terms in which the Constitution finally resolved the problem.

The President of the Union is the President of the Republic. He presides over a High Council which includes a delegation from metropolitan France and representatives from the Associated States (Morocco, Tunisia, the Indochinese Federation), and has the vague function of assisting the French Government "in the general conduct of the affairs of the Union."

It is significant that the Assembly of the Union has half its members representing metropolitan France and half drawn from all the overseas components, and that its functions are to give advice on matters submitted to it by the French Government, the National Assembly, or the Governments of the Associated States. It may also submit spontaneous opinions on matters within its competence to the National Assembly, the French Government, or the High Council of the Union. But the Assembly has no independent legislative power of its own. These somewhat shadowy institutions actually began to function during 1949, but it remains for the future to show whether they are to develop any real substance and significance.

The Constitution also provides for an elective Assembly in each of the overseas territories, but again the composition and powers are to be determined by a law of the French Parliament. The Constitution likewise declares that the nationals of these territories "shall have the status of citizens, in the same capacity as French nationals of Metropolitan France or the Overseas Territories," but it carefully hedges again by noting that "Special laws (of the French Parliament) shall determine the conditions under which they may exercise their rights as citizens."

In the creation of the French Union real power remains with metropolitan France while the shadows of concession have been given to the overseas elements. Clearly the postwar "colonial atmosphere" in French governing circles has been very different from that prevailing within the Labor Government in England during the period of the revolutionary changes in the Commonwealth. The danger is that in the case of France the brutal march of events will overtake the too deliberate and cautious steps of a policy which failed to embrace the liberal and dynamic possibilities offered by the post-Liberation world.

3. POST-LIBERATION PROBLEMS

The French have faced problems of great difficulty in their overseas possessions since Liberation. Nationalist movements, stimulated by the war, encouraged by French weakness, and supported by the French Communist Party, have sought to achieve independence, or at least autonomy. There have been risings of one kind or another in widely separated parts of the empire, and a serious situation developed in the "strategic front yard" of France—North Africa.

In North Africa the nationalist movement gains strength from the fact that it is religious and, paradoxically, "international." "Islam is everything," says one observer, even though there are important nuances among the nationalist parties. The religious kinship with that band of peoples extending almost continuously from Morocco to Indonesia makes North African Moslems highly sensitive to the nationalist activities of Moslems everywhere. In Algeria, one party (that of Messali Hadj) will accept nothing short of independence, another (that of Ferhat Abbas) will settle for a wide autonomy. Both have been stimulated by the economic dislocations and hard times following the war; both have responded to the tensions and irritations of the Algerian social structure where for generations now the well-to-do French landowners (the *colons*) have exploited and spurned the natives and have developed a psychology quite peculiar to themselves.

In Morocco the nationalist movement (Istiqlal) has grown tremendously since 1942 in response to the feeling that France is in serious difficulties. One close observer suggested to me in 1947 that "the theme of independence in Morocco appears to have reached the proportions of a quasi-national psychopathic obsession." The Sultan has aligned himself with the nationalist youth which dominates the movement and has in fact made his person "the living symbol of the nationalist aspirations of his people." Here we have the curious and arresting phenomenon of a theocracy of the Middle Ages allied with a rabid nationalist youth of the twentieth century.

Communism in the colonies is a problem closely allied with nationalism. In the years just after the war, when the Communists were represented in the government, they sought to strengthen the French state at a time when it was still coöperating with the Soviets. When the breach between East and West came, the Communists in the colonies shifted their ground and attempted to use nationalist movements for their own ends. In Indochina they allied with the nationalists and contrived to play the dominant role. In North Africa, on the other hand, the Moslem nationalists have been highly suspicious of the Communists, and the latter have had to be content for the most part to give their support unrequited but in the hope that independence would free them from French police control or that the chaos of revolutionary conditions would offer them an opportunity to achieve their objectives.

In this connection, many of the French have come to think of Soviet Russia and the United States as the "big bad wolves" in this whole question. The Russians have stimulated colonial nationalism in order to weaken the Metropole and permit the Communists to fish in troubled waters. The Americans have similarly contributed to the growth of anti-colonialism, through the influence of their troops in North Africa, for instance, and above all by their "misguided" policy in the Philippines.

Despite the unpromising picture we have drawn—and Tunisia has its difficulties as well—the atmosphere in North Africa has notably improved in the past three years. But the problems which the French face there are still enormous. The native population, for instance, is increasing at the rate of 100,000 a year and creating new tensions in an economy which is already inadequate, even by very modest standards, to the support of the existing population. The success or failure of French policy elsewhere in the colonies—and especially in Indochina—will inevitably have repercussions of a most significant kind in this key sector of the empire.

In the face of these frustrating difficulties, French policy has been lacking in the flexibility needed to meet a dynamic situation. The French have chosen to fight a rearguard action of concessions. The very fact that other imperial powers have yielded, or have been forced to yield, to nationalist demands for independence—in the Philippines, Indonesia, Burma, India, Pakistan—has given fresh stimulus to nationalist movements within the French Empire and notably in Indochina, which is literally embedded in a sea of rising nationalism. At the same time, the very psychological scars of defeat have made the French reluctant in the present to yield what, as we have seen, they were never eager to acquire in the past. They have—quite understandably—tended to cling to the empire, and they show excessive sensitivity to foreign criticism of their policies.

Finally, there is a fundamental, logical inconsistency in the French colonial position which they have never squarely faced. However great the contributions the French may have made to a given colonial people, this alone is not enough to convince that people that it would not prefer to rule itself—in accordance, indeed, with the high principles of 1789. The French in France—and very comprehensibly—have resisted the imposition *upon themselves* of ideas from the outside, however "preferable" these might demonstrably be. No people welcomes improvement at the hands of another. All these, and other problems, are illustrated in the case of Indochina, where the French have met their most serious challenge in the postwar world.

4. THE FRENCH IN INDOCHINA

French difficulties in Indochina begin with the geographical situation. Indochina is remote from France and reached by sea routes traditionally controlled by the British. In our postwar world it is situated in a power complex dominated by the British and Americans. In short, Indochina is inaccessible to the French, and has been held at the sufferance of other powers.

The area suffers from a further disadvantage. It is adjacent to China. Here the relationship is implicit in the population statistics: Indochina has about 25 million people, China perhaps 400 million. For millennia the Indochinese have felt the vast weight of their neighbor. For centuries—and at two different periods—the Chinese dominated Indochina politically. Annamese culture, the most important in the area, is sodden with Chinese influence. The Chinese have settled in a great diaspora over Southeast Asia: there are some 400,000 of them presently in Indochina. And the recent triumph of Mao and the Chinese Communists poses the problem of Indochinese independence in a new and dramatic form.*

The French brought Indochina under their control during the latter half of the nineteenth century. They found a society characteristic of much of Southeast Asia, where the peasant cultivated the land with a simple technology, depended primarily on one crop, irrigated rice, and possessed a communal organization with "an immediately comprehensible, human and

* The problems of this whole area are considered in detail and in a different focus in other volumes in this series: John K. Fairbank: *The United States and China;* Lauriston Sharp: *The United States and Southeast Asia;* W. Norman Brown: *The United States and India* (the last two to be published shortly).

rewarding series of duties and inter-personal obligations." Set apart from the peasantry but still forming "a deeply integrated and unquestioned cultural entity" with them, were the king and aristocracy living in a magnificent capital city and concerned with hierarchy and power rather than "simple communal democracy."

In an earlier day the European had been greeted as just another type of foreigner by what was an exceptionally tolerant society and one comparing most favorably in this respect with the highly developed and even intolerant ethnocentrism of the West. For three centuries the European in Southeast Asia profited from the tolerance—and cupidity—of the ruling class, but in the end he brought a superior technology and either reduced the princes to pawns or liquidated them.

Meanwhile the European had developed, alongside the essentially subsistence economy of the peasant, a second economy, a plantation system responding to the demands of the West for sugar, coffee, tea, and rubber. With the repercussions of imported labor and of periodic world depressions and falling prices, this system struck a blow at the traditional peasant culture. By the twentieth century the European had grown in numbers, and both he and his exploitation were obvious and resented.

In the meantime European ideas had penetrated the East—political democracy, social humanism, Marxism, and nationalism among others. The ruling class had bifurcated, and alongside the "museum piece" remains of the old aristocracy had grown up a vigorous group of intellectuals, Western-trained and fully capable of using these new ideas as weapons for their own ends. Above all, nationalism, previously unknown in the East, became the dynamic for the extrusion of the colonial powers. The European was convicted of an unanswerable inconsistency: the rights of nationalism which he asserted for himself he denied to the "backward peoples" whom he had conquered. "In the nineteenth century," concludes Cora DuBois, "Europeans devised the white man's burden as a rationalization of the inconsistency between nationalism as a positive virtue and the establishment of colonial empires." *

The term "Indochina" embraces a diverse topography, population, and culture. Substantially larger than metropolitan France, it is a country of extreme contrast, notably between the wild and generally forest-clad mountains and the intensely cultivated lowlands. The principal mountains, the Annamese Cordillera, hug the eastern shore all the way from Tonkin to Cochin China. There is a great delta in Tonkin, another in Cochin China, and the population is crowded largely into these two areas. With a narrow seacoast lowland connecting the two, it is often suggested that the country resembles a bamboo pole with a rice basket at either end.

It is this bamboo pole–rice basket area that is inhabited by the Annamese, nearly three-quarters of the total population. The Annamese are the most vital and dynamic of the Indochinese and have recently been the spearhead of Indochinese nationalism. In the southwest are found the Cambodians, bearers of an ancient Indian culture but characterized by "a fatalistic indolence." In the west are the less developed Laotians, a Thai people like the Siamese, who live in scattered communities and form only a small minority of the total population.

In the midst of this population of some 25 million Asians have lived a mere handful of Frenchmen, about 20,000 before the recent war. Alongside the French are some few thousand *adoptés*, Annamese with French education who have become wholly French in outlook and sympathy. Next are some tens of thousands of *intermédiaires*, men with French education but closely knit into the economic life of the indigenes. The remaining millions of the natives are, as elsewhere in Southeast Asia, peasants.

In this social setting, French rule has faced huge and complex problems—problems which grow in part from the mere

* See Miss DuBois' stimulating *Social Forces in Southeast Asia* (University of Minnesota Press, 1949).

physical difficulties of the situation. With mountainous terrain and lush vegetation, roads are difficult to build and few in number. Movement is further impeded by the southwest monsoon, which blows from about May till October, brings heavy rains, and makes outdoor activity repellent. Then, too, few of the French speak Annamese, a difficult language. For these and other reasons, the French have lacked effective means of reaching the people and of gradually creating for them a newly structured national life. The inaccessibility of the people to the French has of course been an enormous advantage recently to the Annamese nationalists who have possessed precisely the advantages in this regard which the French lack.

As of the turn of the century the French system of control worked reasonably well. It worked because the French had left the Emperor of Annam as the *chef de la vie nationale;* and by a people still deeply influenced by their Confucian inheritance from the Chinese the Emperor was held in tremendous respect. This was in fact a dual system: the Emperor continued to rule through the Mandarins, the French through the *intermédiaires.*

Unfortunately for the position of the French, a revolution in the power structure took place during the decade preceding the recent war. The young Emperor, Bao Dai, had been raised and educated in France, and his Empress had become a Catholic. The latter step offended the Annamese and weakened the position of the Empress, unfortunately just in a period when the stabilizing power of Confucianism was also declining. Simultaneously, the French disrupted the previous equilibrium of the dualist regime by attempting "in the best Cartesian style" to create a military system with the Emperor Bao Dai firmly under their control. Hence the Emperor came to be viewed as a French puppet at the very time when his prestige was declining anyway and when Annamese nationalism was making significant strides. It is this same Bao Dai who was returned to Indochina by the French in 1949 and whose regime in early 1950 was recognized by both the British and the Americans.

Nationalism in Indochina was the product of many forces.

The military success of Japan, an Asiatic power, against Russia in 1905, stirred national sentiments widely in the East. The upsurge of Chinese nationalism had important repercussions in Indochina, and Sun Yat-sen maintained headquarters for a time in that country. The use of Annamese soldiers and workers in Europe during the War of 1914 was a further stimulus.

The presence of the French themselves has of course also been a significant source for the growth of native nationalism. Any objective observer will readily admit that French rule has had its very beneficial sides in Indochina—peace and order, schools and hospitals, control of famine, farm-land reclamation, to name only a few. And for these modern innovations, the Vietnamese peasant was grateful to France, particularly during the period from about 1902 to 1920 when these things were new and were definitely identified with the French. But French rule has also deeply irked the Indochinese through its heavy financial demands on the population, its waste and inefficiency, and its insistence upon economic policies which refused to permit the country to pursue an independent industrial and commercial development but instead held it subservient to the interests of the metropolitan French economy.

This is the background for understanding the psychology of the numerous Annamese students who went to Paris during these years. They were infected with nationalist—and even revolutionary—ideas, as so many students before them had been over a period of more than a century. They returned to Indochina eager to realize for their own countrymen both the national independence and the personal freedoms which they witnessed in France and in which inevitably as visitors they shared. In the schools which the French founded in Indochina, the teacher formed the student on the basis of the ideas of 1789 which, particularly when they are not fully understood or are taken at their face value, can have explosive effects. The French provided the Annamese with the ideas of free men but failed to create the institutions which would give form to these newly awakened aspirations. They gave the Annamese *rights* when the latter asked also for *responsibilities.* When something looking to eventual dominion status was in order, the French maintained the old paternalism, the screen of the *intermédiaires,* which prevented them from making contact with the people and from understanding the full implications of the situation.

The recent war gave a tremendous impetus to nationalism all through Southeast Asia. Whatever his faults, the white man was clearly recognized to have possessed *power* before the war. Now he was suddenly and unceremoniously swept aside by self-assertive yellow neighbors of the Indochinese. Japan, too, had been profoundly stirred by the currents of Western nationalism, but her advantage over China and the countries of Southeast Asia was that she had also been successfully infected by Western technology and so possessed both the will and the power for expansion. Western ideas, borrowed in their pristine vitality, if not always in their original intent, provided the dynamics of nationalist development in the East.

The outbreak of the European war in 1939 alerted the Japanese; the fall of France in 1940 opened the door to a policy of adventure. Indochina was the strategic key to Japanese expansion in Southeast Asia; the Vichy regime offered vigorous verbal opposition but could do little to prevent the progressive military infiltration of the Japanese. By the end of July 1941, Japan occupied the whole of the country and then proceeded rapidly to organize it as a base for the lightning thrusts against Thailand and Malaya which followed Pearl Harbor.

The inevitable weakness of the Vichyite French *Gouvernement Général,* viewed as a puppet auxiliary of the Japanese, did little to maintain the prestige of a militarily depleted nation, although the effects of this weakness were little in evidence in the provinces. Then as the war drew to a close, the Japanese, in a calculated move, swept aside the Vichy regime (March 1945) and granted "independence" to the three states of Indochina. Thus, they left to the French the ungrateful task of reconquering peoples who had already been permitted to assert their political freedom, and, to complicate the problem, they contributed arms to the Annamese nationalists.

Only the unwary or the prejudiced will discuss the postwar Indochinese situation with full confidence in his data, or will reach conclusions of the black and white variety. The following statement includes the main lines as they appear to the writer.

Following the Liberation of France, the greatly altered French international position and the changed situation in Indochina convinced the Provisional Government that concessions—nominal at least—were in order. Accordingly, in March 1945, it announced a plan to give Indochina, organized on a federal basis, an autonomous position in the new French Union. Unfortunately this plan was vague.

During the following months, the French saw their colonial prestige still further weakened when they were obliged to return to Indochina, in the tradition of Louis XVIII, "in the baggage of the Allies." For it was the British and the Chinese who effectively liberated the country and then divided it for occupation, north and south. The British further damaged the eventual position of the French by using the Japanese to maintain order.

The French finally arrived to confront a vigorous and assertive nationalist movement, the most significant element of which, the Viet Minh, had originated in 1939 and grew to power under the wartime protection of the Chinese. The Viet Minh, "League for the Independence of Viet Nam," was led by one of the most elusive figures in the conspiratorial history of our century, Ho Chi-minh, a Moscow-trained Communist. When he came to France for the Fontainebleau meetings in the summer of 1946, Ho was asked whether it was true that he had used at various times twenty different aliases. He replied that he had more than that number currently!

Well before the return of the French to Indochina, Ho had become President of the newly proclaimed Republic of Viet Nam ("Land of the South," traditional name for the Annamese parts of Indochina), the Republic having succeeded to the Empire of Bao Dai, who had abdicated as Japanese support dissolved.

Viet Nam authorities were exercising complete administrative control when the British and Chinese first arrived. There is evidence to indicate a general willingness on the part of the Viet Namese to accept the return of the French so long as the full autonomy of Indochina, on a reliable and specific basis, were guaranteed. This sentiment was undoubtedly related to fears of Chinese power and to the belief that the French would be militarily weak. Unfortunately, the British, supported by the French, ousted Viet Nam officials from Saigon and precipitated bitter guerrilla warfare in the south.

The conflicting objectives of the Viet Namese and the French doubtless made the final conflict more or less inevitable. The Viet Namese were determined to assert for the Annamese parts of Indochina (Tonkin, Annam, and Cochin China) a very large measure of independence and were unwilling to accept a return of the French on anything like the prewar basis. The French were ready to grant on paper rather wide concessions, but their acts suggested that they were unwilling to implement these promises in any thoroughgoing way. Each side was intensely suspicious of the other, and the French were undoubtedly concerned that this movement, led by a Communist, although containing a wide spectrum of nationalists, might one day fall under Moscow's domination.

In March 1946, Ho and the French signed an agreement which recognized the Viet Nam Republic as a "free state" within the Indochinese Federation and enjoying political, economic, and military autonomy. A referendum in Cochin China was to follow to determine whether that province should be included in Viet Nam, along with Tonkin and Annam. The Viet Nam government was to receive the French Army on a friendly basis.

The agreement itself was vague. When the two sides sought to implement it in a series of conferences, the effort miscarried.

Meanwhile, the French had recognized an independent Cochin Chinese Republic (although still promising to hold the referendum with reference to the reunion of the three provinces). This step Viet Nam supporters considered an act of bad faith.

Suspicions now mounted rapidly, and it is known that by fall both sides were preparing for, and expecting, an armed conflict. The war broke out in the north in December 1946. The unfortunate massacre of a large number of the civilian population of Haiphong by the French artillery, and the corresponding Viet Nam attack on Hanoi in an attempt to wipe out the French and mixed populations of that city served to widen the breach between the two contestants.

Ho's weapons have been both political and military. The Viet Minh had earlier framed a sweeping program of social and political reform, but the exigencies of war have substituted the secret police for personal liberties, and reforms have been put on the shelf. An exception is the program to extend literacy, in which Ho has an understandable stake and which is reported to have made notable strides. Ho's military strength is of course related to the topography and dense forest cover of much of the country, greatly favoring guerrilla operations. Until recent months, the Viet Namese have avoided open engagements with the French and have resorted above all to nocturnal sabotage of transport.

The result of the first three years of the war was that the French were able to hold only certain key centers—Saigon, Haiphong, Hanoi, etc.—and even these were almost islands in a sea of fluctuating guerrilla power. During this period American opinion was generally critical or even hostile to the French. The public had little sympathy with the attempt to reëstablish the French colonial system just at the time when the Americans and British were moving out of the Philippines, Burma, and India. On the other hand, the public had little conception of, or interest in, the larger political and strategic implications of a complete victory of Ho and a possibly Communist-dominated Indochina.

The victories of Mao in China dramatically magnified these dangers. As British and American policy makers became increasingly concerned with the whole future of Southeast Asia, the French saw opening before them a last chance to save their almost hopelessly compromised position. In the spring of 1949 they returned to Indochina ex-Emperor Bao Dai who had meanwhile been satisfying his playboy instincts on the Riviera. Bao's mission was to use his prestige as a focal point for the rallying of nationalist support, in theory leaving eventually to Ho only the convinced Communists. The French government promised a wide autonomy to a Viet Nam * headed by Bao, and this promise was implemented by a treaty ratified by Parliament in January 1950. Viet Nam was to enjoy autonomy, but foreign affairs and key elements of defense—here was the nerve center of the agreement—were to remain in French hands. Viet Nam was to have its own army, with full control in peacetime but integration with the French in wartime. The French were to have naval and air bases and such French troops as might be necessary for the protection of the latter.

Even close and sympathetic observers of the Indochinese scene originally viewed the Bao Dai venture as a somewhat desperate final expedient. Only the Right generated any real enthusiasm about it, and the Socialists seem to have gone along in the hope that Bao might be useful as a "mediator" and could become the instrument of saving both "face" and the army for the French. The number of Ho's supporters who have come over to Bao Dai has been disappointingly small. But the shift in the fortunes of Bao is related, not primarily to domestic events, but to the dramatic change in the international situation.

Helpless before the onsweep of Mao's armies in China, American policy makers have been searching for a barrier—or even a secure toe hold—from which they might hope to repel the flow of communism toward Southeast Asia. They believe

* Since then the term Viet Nam has regularly been applied to Bao's followers, Viet Minh to Ho's movement.

that they have found this position in the still dubious military struggle in Indochina—and as of January 1951, it would be sounder to call this a toe hold than a barrier. The new position took concrete form in the recognition of Bao Dai by the United States and Britain, which came just at the time when Communist China and the Soviet recognized Ho. Hence the line of defense against communism in Southeast Asia has been drawn and hardened, and that unfortunate country seems outwardly to have become another Greece.

Indochina, however, is Greece with a difference. In both countries the West has sought to repel the Communist danger, with its far-reaching political and strategic implications. With outside military aid, the Greeks have been able to maintain their independence, making it possible, though by no means inevitable, that they will move on to the creation of a liberal regime. In Indochina the colonial presence of France has confused both the issues of independence and of the achievement of free institutions. Asian opinion has been deeply fearful that the triumph of Bao Dai might lead simply to the reassertion of French colonial power and the consequent miscarriage of hopes both for independence and free institutions for Indochina. And as the supplier of arms and other forms of support to the French and to Bao Dai, the United States has inevitably involved itself in the widespread Asian criticism of French colonialism. If the United States were in the end to be the instrument of the restoration of the French colonial position in Indochina, our prestige and influence in Asia—and that of the West in general—would severely suffer, and our policy would play into the hands of Communist propagandists in Asia and throughout the world.

Happily, these anxieties have been somewhat allayed by the action of the French government and parliament which took steps in November 1950 to guarantee independence (within the French Union) to the three Associated States of Indochina—Viet Nam, Cambodia, and Laos. Jean Letourneau, Minister of

State in charge of the Associated States, announced on November 22 that all internal administrative services had been transferred from France to the Associated States, that financial and economic powers would soon be so transferred, and that the Associated States would send representatives to Washington and London. This is clearly a significant step in the right direction, but the way in which this still somewhat vague promise of independence is implemented will be crucial so far as its effects both in Indochina and in Asia generally are concerned. The problem of who possesses military power is central in this connection, and here again the French are making an important contribution by the rapid training of Viet Namese forces. This later step is part of a larger development in recent months.

It has become increasingly evident to the French that they cannot indefinitely sustain the losses in men and the financial costs entailed in the Indochinese war, especially in the light of the heightened danger in Europe and their rapidly growing commitments there. The cost of the Indochinese military effort is approximately $600 million a year, and this in an area in which the total French investment is about $300 million. Losses in men have also been very heavy: it has been said that the yearly rate of officer casualties had reached a figure comparable to the size of the annual class graduating from Saint-Cyr even before the defeats of the autumn of 1950. The French recognize, too, that if Bao Dai finally wins out, he will inevitably be under great nationalist pressure to push the French out in turn. The French naturally ask themselves why they should make these tremendous sacrifices simply to achieve their own eventual elimination. Why not instead let the Americans bear the cost of repelling communism and let the Annamese do the fighting for their own independence? Hence the trend toward arming and training native troops, which can have useful effects in reassuring the Viet Namese and strengthening the nationalist support of Bao Dai. On the surface the situation is complicated by the fact that Bao Dai's followers constantly talk, for public consumption, of the desirability of eliminating the French at once, whereas of course nothing would be more disastrous for Bao than the immediate departure of French troops and the consequent overrunning of Indochina by the Viet Minh forces.

American arms and supplies on a rather massive scale would be necessary to achieve an effective native armed opposition to Communist forces. But the West has a large stake in preventing the further spread of Communist domination in Southeast Asia, and a military aid program, such as we have already initiated, can be the means of sparing the United States the military losses and the political embarrassment of direct armed intervention. Fortunately the United States has sent to Southeast Asia an important mission to survey the military, economic, and other problems of that area on a broad base. It has a very specific interest in health and agrarian problems in Indochina. This is a significant recognition—important for Asian peoples in general—that the military problem is only the most immediate of those needing solution if we are to win Indochina to our side over the long term. We are inevitably competitors of the Communists at the rice roots.

Meanwhile the Communist-led Viet Minh has won important victories in northern Tonkin and has compromised the position of the French in that whole frontier area. The Communist Chinese have been training Indochinese troops, perhaps on a fairly large scale, and the latter have appeared with equipment and tactics which raise them out of the guerrilla class and render outmoded the French measures of defense. The Chinese have developed both roads and air-drop as means of strengthening supply to the Viet Minh. All this adds up to a picture not unlike that in Korea. Mao can train and equip Viet Minh troops almost endlessly and, if this pressure is not sufficient for victory, he can, if he is willing to take the risks, once again introduce Chinese troops on a large scale.

Meanwhile the still slender military resources of France and the United States are being depleted at a time when they are sorely needed to reinforce the thin lines in Europe.*

Recent American policy in Indochina has given rise to harsh criticism—particularly before Korea took the spotlight. In this connection it is well to remember that the Indochinese problem—like the Korean problem—does not exist in a vacuum, and cannot be solved alone. Like almost all other international problems of importance, it is part of a world context. The public in this country, as in others, tends to focus its attention on one problem at a time and to insist that the solution of that particular problem is the touchstone of the capacity and honesty of public officials. Unfortunately the Secretary of State cannot enjoy the luxury of solving one problem at a time but must keep steadily in view the world as a whole, and must constantly assess the interrelationship of all his problems. It is his function not to produce an ideal solution for problem *X* but to obtain a maximum satisfaction of American interests on a world plane.

* Happily, since the above was written, the French and Viet Nam forces, under the distinguished leadership of General de Lattre de Tassigny, have inflicted a defeat on the Viet Minh forces, created a strong defensive position (perhaps analogous to that of Korea), and have created new prestige and morale.

10. The International Scene: France and the United States

Rapid change in the fortunes of the individual usually means reluctant—and often painful—readjustment. The average man has developed a high degree of adaptation to the station which he occupies in life, and his ambitions usually aim to better, only rarely to make revolutionary changes in, his status. When such a radical change does take place, carrying him either up or down the social ladder, he finds himself constrained by the inertia of the old habit patterns, willing and able only gradually to make his peace with an unfamiliar environment.

So it is with nations. Their position in the international power picture is subject to rude and even revolutionary change. Every nation which has at one time in the past enjoyed a position of unquestioned leadership has later had to relinquish this position. So it will be one day with the United States and Soviet Russia. Our immediate concern is with the past war, which left various countries—Britain, France, Germany, Japan, Italy—with a diminished power status, and elevated others—Russia, the United States, China—to places of new power and responsibility. In the case of France and the United States, these new roles were alien, and in both cases they were resisted.

1. FRANCE IN THE POSTWAR WORLD

The results of World War II then were fundamentally to alter the old situation in which a series of powers of roughly equivalent strength made possible the creation of a balance of power and prevented the domination of Europe by any one of them. In the new Europe Russia emerged with something close to a monopoly of military power in the period following demobilization in the West and clearly possessed of the capacity to sweep over Western Europe at will. Henceforth the concept of balance of power was applicable only on a world scale and, when the breach came between East and West, could be conceived of only as polarized about the United States and Russia.

Meanwhile France has less power absolutely than she had in 1939, and the threat to her security is greater. The Soviets not only possess power on the Continent unique in modern history, but they threaten France internally through the operation of a peacetime fifth column, the Communist Party. The degree of France's "independence" in foreign policy has sharply declined, and the war has left her at times more a victim of international politics than a positive agent in their direction.

The drastic changes in French foreign policy since Liberation are a measure of the extent to which France has adapted herself to this fundamentally new situation in the world. For France, however, as for the other democracies, the character and implications of this new world were accepted grudgingly and only after Soviet Russia had made them manifest by repeated and unmistakably aggressive acts. It is a sad commentary on the slowness with which men learn that only as a result of Russian aggression have the United States and France been willing to accept the new roles forged for them by the events of the past decade.

The German problem is an excellent example of French adjustment. Whatever may be said of the rights and wrongs in the baffling conflict of these two peoples, it is clear that during the past three-quarters of a century a brooding sense of insecurity has oppressed the French in their relations with the Germans. The explanation is simple enough. In economic power and population—twin bases of war potential—Germany rapidly outdistanced France in the later nineteenth century. In three wars fought within the memory of some men still living, the Germans thrice invaded France; twice France went down to defeat in a matter of weeks, and on the third occasion she avoided catastrophe by hardly more than inches.

With the end of the last war, the French attacked the German problem with the mandate of both logic and history. After the lesson of three wars, the Germans must never be permitted to become strong enough to strike again. But this was to cast the problem in terms antedating 1939 and to ignore the potential nature of the Russian threat. It led directly to the Franco-Russian alliance of late 1944. It led also to the French territorial and political program for Germany.

The French territorial program was threefold. It sought to remove the Rhineland, the Ruhr, and the Saar from German control. The objective was primarily security and secondarily economic, and the two were closely interrelated.

To the French the Rhineland was a great strategic springboard which the Germans had repeatedly used to launch an attack on the West. Marshal Foch had described it as "the most formidable military base known to history, both in offensive and defensive." The French wanted to separate this crucial base from Germany, to allow it to manage its own affairs under a regime of autonomy, but to leave it permanently demilitarized and at the same time subject to Allied military control.

The French were even more intent on separation or control of the Ruhr, the heart of the economic and war-making potential of Germany. The Ruhr includes the most important coal field in Europe, and in 1937 produced almost a third of all European steel. On the economic side, the French steel industry has needed a large supply of Ruhr coke and has feared German competition in foreign markets.

The Saar the French have sought from the beginning to detach from Germany primarily because they need its important coal production to supplement their own glaring deficiencies.

Of this drastic and ambitious program, the French have succeeded only with the Saar. The British and Americans consistently opposed the separation of the Rhineland, convinced above all that such a step would serve only to crystallize German irredentist spirit and would present a superb opportunity to Soviet propaganda. Britain and the United States have opposed successive French plans for separation of the Ruhr for these same reasons but above all because of the area's overriding importance for the economic recovery of Western Germany. In the case of the Ruhr, as in that of the Rhineland, the French have been obliged to retire from advanced positions to others more tenable, the most recent represented by the Schuman Plan for a "merging" of the coal and steel of the Ruhr with that of the rest of western Europe.

The Saar is a very different case from the Rhineland and the Ruhr. Here the French have been able cleverly to exploit the deep changes effected by the war and to win the temporary support at least of the Saarlanders, a dramatic reversal of their attitude of the thirties when they voted to rejoin Germany. It is a case well worth studying by those who are overimpressed by the stability of national sentiment.

The Saar is a small territory, parts of which have belonged to France at times in the past. Its production of coal and fertilizers is of prime interest to the French in a period of industrial and agricultural reconstruction.

After the War of 1914 the French wanted to annex the Saar outright. They were forced to content themselves with economic incorporation, ownership of the coal mines, an international regime under the League of Nations, and a plebiscite in 1935. At the end of a vigorous Nazi propaganda campaign, the Saar in 1935 voted 90 per cent to return to Germany.

With the German economy distorted at the end of this war, the French took prompt measures to woo the Saarlanders. They adopted a policy of *economic attachment* of the Saar to

France but of *political autonomy* for the area. They granted the Saarlanders larger rations than were current in other parts of the French zone of occupation. They focused attention on the coal problem and rapidly won the coöperation of the miners. They wisely used German-speaking managers and technicians and rapidly repatriated former Saar miners among the German prisoners of war. They gave the miners housing priorities, increased rations for themselves as well as their families (an important point), canteen "extras," points for consumption goods, rewards for attendance records, and privileges in the matter of scarce goods, such as gasoline and tires for commuters. By the early months of 1948 coal production had attained once again the rate of 1936, and had incidentally moved up much more rapidly than that for the Ruhr and for Britain, the two coal areas of critical importance in western Europe.

The French enjoy only a *de facto* status in the Saar. At the Moscow Conference in the spring of 1947, Britain and the United States agreed to support the French position in the Saar, but the Russians refused, and so no formal international charter has ever been drawn. Such a charter could stabilize the situation by making the French feel more secure in their economic rights and the Saarlanders more adequately protected in their political autonomy.

Meanwhile the Saar has continued to be a source of substantial discord in international politics. The French have sought to fix their economic control more firmly through the negotiation of a fifty-year lease of the coal mines. The Saarlanders have been restive under the political limitations of a regime in which they enjoy very considerable autonomy * but in which the French High Commissioner exercises an absolute veto over all Saar legislation. And the recently created West German government has loudly protested that the Saar is Ger-

* The Saarlanders have been given a constitution with an extensive bill of rights and a single chamber elected on the basis of universal suffrage and having the right to choose the premier.

man and that only a plebiscite can establish justice in the area. Again, the Schuman Plan has placed the Saar issue in a context which may make solutions easier.

On the political reconstruction of Germany, French policy has faced the same type of progressive adjustment as that involved in their program for dismemberment. Once again their objective was the weakening of Germany, and to this end they proposed its political atomization. While the Americans proposed a federal system, the French sought to move considerably farther by enlarging the powers of the separate German states (the *Länder*), in the tradition of the old German conception of a "Confederation." Moreover, the French would accept a central government for Germany only with very limited powers defined in a constitution cautiously prepared and instituted under the aegis of the Allied Control Council.

The resistance of the French to Anglo-American proposals on governmental arrangements for the new Germany, which earlier took the form of repeated vetoes in the Control Council, finally succumbed to the solvent of the cold war. It became increasingly obvious to the quite understandably schizophrenic French that Russia was a greater threat than Germany and that to preserve themselves from the Soviet threat they might soon be obliged to work with the Germans. The logic of events now moved on rapidly to accomplish this end.

The somewhat sensational Schuman Plan is testimony at once to the distance which the French have traveled on the German problem since 1945 and to the seriousness they attributed to the world situation even prior to the Korean crisis. The Plan, dropped like a bombshell into the meeting of the Foreign Ministers in London in May 1950, aims above all to create by *indirection* a wider unity in Europe which the more *direct* attack of the Council of Europe has failed to produce. The means are economic, the pooling of the coal and steel resources of western Europe, but the objective is political. Schuman himself stated flatly that the French were determined to bring about the "unification of Europe and to settle in large part the eternal Franco-German problem." And Jean Monnet, the imaginative formulator of the Plan, said in the beginning: "Don't ask about economic details; this is a political problem."

That the Plan is not primarily economic in inspiration is suggested again by the opposition of the French steel masters, and also by the great vagueness in economic details—perhaps intentional—in which it was originally presented: Kurt Schumacher, the German Socialist leader, although generally favorable to the scheme, acidly stigmatized it as "a frame without a picture." The French insisted that the Plan should first be accepted in principle; since then months of negotiation have followed in an effort to settle the many and complex economic problems.

Above all, the French view the Plan as establishing close links between the two countries under conditions where German war potential would be subject to supra-national control and the danger of war between the two countries largely dissipated. The Plan has also facilitated the development of a new French attitude on the German manufacture of war materials and recently of a more accommodating view on the German contribution of troops to the combined North Atlantic forces.

The Schuman Plan also has important economic implications for France. The French see it as a logical outworking of longstanding policy which during the interwar years sought to move the industrial center of gravity from Germany to France, a policy receiving vigorous governmental support in the form of subsidies, loans, favorable distribution of industrial credit and capital investment, and high tariffs. The present Plan would not make the French steel business more important than the German, since the latter has both larger current capacity and greater natural economic advantage. But the French undoubtedly view it as a means of accomplishing something like the rough equalization of the two industries. To this end the French need larger quantities of Ruhr coal and coke, with an end to the German system of double prices (one for coal consumed in Germany and a second and higher price for that exported), and a wider market for iron ore, of which they possess the largest field in Europe and for which they meet in Germany the sharp competition of higher-grade ores from Sweden. The French government has also spoken of the salutary effect on the French industry of foreign competition in the interest of lowering prices to the consumer, although it is to be noted that much of the French steel business has now reached a rather high level of efficiency, reflecting among other things postwar plant renovation.

The British refused from the outset to accept so "vague" a scheme in principle and hence have taken no direct part in the negotiations. The British position is understandable. Men who are in the process of nationalizing the British steel business are quite naturally concerned about the possible impact of independent decisions by a supra-national authority on questions of wages and prices and the possible repercussions on the whole national economy. On the political side, there is the traditional fear of being too closely linked with the Continent and especially of entrusting British destinies to the decisions of an international authority. Responsible French officials tend to see Britain as still not quite a part of Europe and believe that it is better that they have elected to stay outside the Schuman Plan whose nature would probably otherwise have been diluted at British insistence. The French Socialists are regretful that they did not receive at least some encouragement from British Labor: the idea of European Union has deep roots in Socialist thinking and their support of it is a kind of sublimation for their inability to dominate the French domestic political scene.

Nowhere is French adjustment to the new world situation more evident than in the contrast between the outlook of de Gaulle, in the autumn of 1944, and official French policy in the summer of 1950. It was inevitable that de Gaulle, influenced by temperament, military background, deep patriotism, and above all the humiliations beginning in 1940, should assert French rights in the world in season and out, and should proclaim his determination to restore his country to her position of power and influence: French unity, power, prestige—these are sentiments that run like a red thread through de Gaulle's wartime speeches. Characteristic was the address to members of the French armed forces everywhere on June 22, 1940, following the German armistice, when he proudly declared: "One day, I give you my promise, our forces—a picked French army, a mechanized land, sea and air force—in common action with our allies will restore liberty to the world and greatness to France."

There is no question that, with the Liberation of France, de Gaulle's reiteration of his belief in her "eternal greatness" had important positive effects on the shattered confidence of the French. But in the last analysis he was describing an unreal world, and since that day the French, like the Americans, have had to shed a good many illusions which were created by the war.

When de Gaulle promptly turned to the Soviets for an alliance against the German menace, he was at once making a bid for French independence and taking a step consonant with old and tested French traditions. His enthusiasm for the Russian connection cooled when France was excluded from Yalta at the behest of the Soviets. But in the fall of 1945 he could still assign a large role to France in a world in which the disagreements between East and West were already mounting:

> In the world as it is today, there are two very great powers, and we lie exactly between them—the extremity of Europe toward the West, the bridgehead of Europe with the East! We have only to look at the map to understand that in this situation, our vital interests command us to hold a rigorous balance.
>
> In the measure that it depends on us, therefore, we propose to follow a policy of friendship, to the East and to the West, with our eyes open and our hands free . . . we know that our balance is identified with the balance of peace, and we are fully decided not to

abandon it, certain that after various oscillations, it is our attitude which will finally determine the balance of the needle for the good of all.

De Gaulle was given no opportunity to test the practicability of this appealing but difficult formula, for relations between East and West had already so far disintegrated in the ensuing two months that before he left office in January 1946, he had already decided that France must align herself with the West. Indeed it is hardly too much to say that Soviet intransigence has carved out for France the place she occupies in the world today. Russian policy has been responsible to a large degree for French economic and military dependence on the outside world. In a relatively peaceful world, France could have carried through her economic reconstruction at a slower pace and with less foreign aid. Instead, the internal threat of communism was so insistent that both France and the United States were ready for a massive program of aid to build rapidly a barrier of economic prosperity against the Communist tide. Again, in a more normal world, France could have rearmed slowly and at a speed appropriate to her reviving economic strength. But once more Soviet aggression has greatly accelerated the arming of western Europe which can only be accomplished at this speed with extensive foreign aid.

Frenchmen have not been happy with this posture of affairs for many reasons. The Communists of course have used bitter invectives regarding the "warmongering" of the West, these "lackeys of American imperialism." But the mass of Frenchmen have been deeply disturbed by the increasing danger that Soviet armies would sweep over western Europe before the Atlantic Pact powers are able to build up an adequate defense. Prior to the Korean crisis there was question of the will of the United States to do its part, and criticism of the slowness and the small-scale nature of our military aid effort. These factors, in the deeper setting of French losses in two world wars, induced a widespread sense of popular apathy, or even futility, in the face of mounting peril in the East.

This neurosis took an extreme form in the case of a small but vocal group which urged that in a hypothetical war between the Big Two France remain neutral. In the long history of a country whose destinies have been inextricably associated with those of the rest of Europe, this is a striking innovation. It is unlike American isolationism in the sense that the United States had, in the nineteenth century at least, the justification of physical remoteness in an age of undeveloped transportation. The early phases of the Korean crisis appear to have dealt a blow to these dreams and to have strengthened the conviction that in a general war France can only be saved if the Russians can be excluded by force.

Even in this more restricted setting of partnership, France has a large and important role to play. Physically, France is, as de Gaulle suggested, a beachhead. Hers is the territory over which, in a general war, armies will fight or be supplied. At this writing, France is still a beachhead of weakness, but it is the belief of widely informed civilian and military observers that she is susceptible of becoming a central element in western European strength.

The French economy has strength. We have seen it accomplish an extraordinary work of reconstruction. It can, for instance, contribute notably to the manufacture of military supplies for the West, provided it is given adequate aid and sufficient time to organize.

France has a great military tradition. She has been a leader in the development of the science of war in modern times. Her officer corps is the product of a superb, though in some respects limiting, system of education. Her troops have characteristically fought with *élan,* nowhere more so than in Italy during the last years of the late war. Her *poilu,* oftenest of peasant stock, is a patient, courageous, and resourceful soldier.

The French have been slowly remaking their army since the war. They have emphasized new weapons, mechanization, and the things generally which the high command neglected in the thirties, despite the warnings of de Gaulle, Reynaud, and others. They have deserted the old urban barracks and emphasize troop-training in open country. The high command has persistently purged the army, and especially the officer corps, of Communists. It is enlarging and equipping the army with new weapons as rapidly as resources will permit, but it goes without saying that this effort, like that of the other members of the Atlantic Community, has been far slower to date than the nature of the Soviet danger would justify. And of course a large part of French military strength has been drained off to Indochina.

France has another important source of strength, well-developed diplomatic and administrative "know-how." For centuries she played a large—often the largest—role in international diplomacy. She has a numerous and resourceful corps of experts, educated in the setting of a long national experience. The postwar *École Nationale d'Administration*, which has a monopoly of training men for the foreign service and a variety of administrative posts in the national government, is making a vigorous and imaginative attack on the problem of developing young men for the complicated tasks of this new world. There are still certain areas, however—economics is one—where French *expertise* is notably weak.

The Schuman Plan has again strikingly demonstrated that France can offer ideas and leadership in the international field. For a considerable period following the war, French policies, notably on the German problem, were so much at variance with those of her allies that her efforts were largely lost in friction. Now that events have brought basic Allied policies much more in line, France has been able to assert effective leadership again. Imaginative leadership in the international field may well prove one effective avenue for the recapture of French influence in the world.

If it comes to war, the effectiveness of the West's effort will depend in no small measure on the solidity of the French home front. There is, first, the Communist danger. The French

Communists have unquestionably prepared elaborate plans for a wartime underground. They have probably succeeded in hiding considerable stores of small arms. They will inevitably benefit from the rich experience in the Resistance during the last war. They have apparently strengthened their membership through the recent purges of "waverers" and others. And a large number of non-Communists who vote for Communist candidates at election time may well have been so much influenced by Party propaganda that their attitude toward a war against the Soviets would be unsympathetic—or at least apathetic.

During the past three years the French government has learned a great deal about how to deal with French Communists, particularly in the person of the strong man of the Socialist Party, Jules Moch. The latter has repeatedly held the critical Interior portfolio and has been widely praised for his masterly handling of two large-scale Communist-inspired strikes.

As Defense Minister in the Pleven government, Moch has undertaken in effect to merge the interior police with the army (July 1950) in the interest of creating effective "vertical defense" against fifth column uprisings preparing bridgeheads for air-borne invasion. On the basis of various traditional units of the French "police," Moch is creating real military units and multiplying their strength four or five times. All these units will be heavily and appropriately armed for their special task —with anti-aircraft artillery, antitank guns, and bazookas. They will be highly mobile, but will be recruited from, and normally stationed in, their home areas where they know the local Communist situation and personnel. They are to be drawn from an élite group of men with previous army service.

Naturally the observer can learn very little about the methods and means of governmental penetration of the Communist apparatus. It may be useful to note in passing that the FBI has had considerable success along this line in the United States and that the French have had a far longer experience with subversive organizations. Prompt action in a crisis might immobilize the leadership and cripple the rank and file.

The delicate problem of French morale in a hypothetical war forms part of this chapter's concluding section on the reaction of France to the Korean crisis.

2. THE UNITED STATES IN THE POSTWAR WORLD

American experience in the last war was not entirely different from that of the French. We, too, began with overwhelming defeats, which reflected lack of preparedness, lack of military imagination, and a feeling that we were secure behind our Maginot Line, which in this case was the broad Pacific. Happily our humiliations did not include occupation of our homeland, but that, too, had some connection with geographical accidents.

Precisely because our country had not been occupied, we emerged from the war with a less confused, but still unreal, view of the world. President Roosevelt repeatedly proclaimed the political objectives for which the war was being fought. But the public is inclined to view these questions in simpler terms and to feel that when the fighting ceases, the war has been completely won. This view was undoubtedly strengthened by Mr. Roosevelt's invention of the term "unconditional surrender." The public's outlook of course missed the elementary point that wars are, or should be, fought for political objectives, and that if a war is to be "won," these objectives must be achieved during, and especially after, the fighting.

As a result, the American public greeted the military victory as the end of an experience which had been ugly, painful—or just inconvenient—and asked for nothing so much as to put this unfortunate parenthesis behind them and return to the pleasures of what Warren Harding once termed "normalcy." They wanted our huge armed forces quickly returned and demobilized, civilian controls eliminated, and an unfettered opportunity to enjoy the fruits of a burgeoning economy. Unfortunately the Congress and the administration were in an all too coöperative frame of mind and presently, despite the resistance of the President on food price controls, we had disarmed ourselves in the face of both the enemy abroad and inflation at home.

Hindsight always permits a cheap victory over the past, and it is easy now to see that we dissipated our wartime strength with a negligence that has placed the security of the nation in acute jeopardy. The painful and disillusioning discovery that we could not march hand in hand with the Soviets to create a peaceful world required a profound readjustment in the attitude of the American public. At the same time it was revealed to us that, as the nation with the greatest economic power, the war had left us with the responsibility of leadership in the western world. As a people, we resented both discoveries, but, like the French, we have in the past three years been painfully adapting ourselves to this new role.

This new world is one very different from that we had imagined in 1945. In place of sinking into an undisturbed siesta of prosperity, we found ourselves in the autumn of 1950 engaged in a difficult military action in one part of the world and anxiously on guard against possible outbreaks in other, widely separated, areas. This crisis, coming at the end of nearly five years of progressive revelation of Soviet intransigence, has finally carried conviction to the man on the street of the nature of the Soviet danger. He sees, what had become increasingly evident to close observers, especially since the spring of 1947, that the Kremlin is determined to expand its power, that weakness invites aggression, and that apparently only strength can hope to induce compromise. The short-run, bipolar validity of this thesis has been demonstrated by the Russian retreat in the face of the success of the Berlin air lift and by the aggression of the North Koreans against what the Kremlin had obviously assessed as weakness. The widespread acceptance of this thesis by the West has led to the policy of "containment," the building of strength to oppose aggression and induce eventual compromise.

The policy of "containment" makes sense only on a global scale. The Soviets, with Communist China and the satellites, occupy a vast strategic fortress extending over much the greater part of Eurasia. Their opponents, as we have noted, occupy various parts of the periphery and most of the outlying islands. None of these peripheral (largely peninsular) areas is capable of independent defense and some of them are extremely weak and contain important elements which are apathetic or favorable to the Soviets. Non-Eurasian power is available principally from the United States, but the latter suffers from serious disadvantages: (1) the logistic (supply) problem to any one of these areas is tremendous, and is further complicated by the fact that the United States must use "exterior" lines of communication (as contrasted with the more efficient "interior" lines of the Soviets); (2) the most significant weapon in the American arsenal is the atom bomb, which is generally unsuitable for "peripheral" operations such as that in Korea; (3) the initiative, in the nature of things, lies with the Soviets, who can coördinate their resources and objectives in longer term plans and can strike at the West in places and ways of their own choice. This last factor means that the West is obliged constantly to strain its resources and distort its plans in order to reply effectively to the latest Soviet initiative.

Under these conditions, the position of western Europe has become critical, and the time for united action by the North Atlantic powers is short. For the present, western Europe is just another Allied foothold on the periphery of the Eurasian Continent. It is obviously far more impressive than Korea or Indochina, since it possesses vast economic strength, large potential military power, and a centuries' old tradition of independence. But like Korea, western Europe occupies a peninsula which does not offer very large opportunities to trade space for time. The enemy would benefit from extensive fifth column organization, notably in France, Italy, and western Germany. Soviet military power is available to strike rapidly and, for the present, would presumably meet no force capable of impeding for any length of time its march to the Atlantic. The Russians are even training and equipping what amounts to an army for eastern Germany, which could not now, like the North Koreans, strike an "independent" blow at western Germany without precipitating a general war, but which, given such a war, could play a useful military and political role in the invasion and "unification" of the "new Germany."

The policy of containment is one of *peace*. During the initial period—the years immediately ahead—hopes for peace rest in large measure in the belief that the great disparity in the Soviet and American stockpiles of atomic weapons and the inadequacy of radar defenses of the principal Russian industrial centers are such that the Soviets will seek to avoid a general war. When, however, the Soviets have built up a comparable—though presumably not equal—stockpile of atom bombs, have developed their long-range bomber force, and have perfected their radar screens, they may then feel that the total world situation justifies an attack on western Europe with the massive ground forces which they possess. At that time they could argue that they had full power of atomic retaliation on the United States and that, in the best situation (for them), the mutual threat of the atomic weapon would be so great that it would not be used by either side.

It will probably be precisely at this juncture that the next acute period of danger will arise. At this point the Soviet decision as to whether to strike at western Europe will presumably depend in large measure on their assessment of the power of resistance of Allied ground and tactical air forces. This is the basic argument of the supporters of a rapid defense build-up in western Europe. If these forces can be rendered sufficiently formidable, the Russians, they argue, will be deterred from war and can then be induced to seek in negotiation a *modus vivendi*. If this analysis be adequate, Congressional and other opponents and disciples of half-measures and delay are involving themselves in a very heavy responsibility for the security of the nation. Meanwhile, in the present writer's view, this policy should never preclude or limit our willingness to negotiate: as long as there is, in George Kennan's words, "a one-thousandth chance that a major world conflict can be avoided . . . let it not be said of us that we allowed any hope for the avoidance of war to die, like an unwanted and unappreciated child, by abandonment and neglect." *

The alternative to this difficult role in Europe is to withdraw and attempt to go it alone. The neo-isolationists who propose that we do withdraw to the Western Hemisphere on a defensive basis need to provide convincing answers to certain conclusions (December 1950) of the National Security Council, which has once again reviewed this question with great care: (1) Such a step would "enable the Soviet Union to make a quick conquest of the entire Eurasian land mass." (2) This in turn would give the Russians military resources and economic power "vastly superior to any that would be then available for our home security," as well as a strategic position "which would be catastrophic to the United States." (3) This development would so unbalance the power situation in the world that peaceful negotiations would no longer be possible. (4) We should, therefore, have either to accept imposed terms or fight without allies.

In this western European "foothold," France has a central place. "Containment" involves the substitution of a spearhead of strength for the spearhead of weakness which is now ominously thrust into the flank of Soviet power in central Europe. Economic strength comes first, and no viable Europe is possible without a sound and recovered French economy. That first task is far progressed, but on its foundation must now be built military strength. Here again France, whose military recovery we have described, must inevitably make the most im-

* "Let Peace Not Die of Neglect," *New York Times Magazine*, Sunday, February 25, 1951.

portant European contribution to land forces. But the task of France must in any case be related to that of the other North Atlantic powers.

The Atlantic community realized a new cohesion with the signing, in April 1949, of the North Atlantic Treaty, in which two American and ten European states pledged themselves to consider an attack against any one of them as an attack against all. The North Atlantic Council, central organ provided by the Treaty, has been handicapped by the fact that it has been able to meet only infrequently at the ministerial level. Accordingly, at its London meeting in May 1950, the Council provided for continuous exercise of its functions through the appointment of deputies, one by each government.

To complement the Treaty and provide the sinews of war, the American Congress accepted a military aid proposal not unlike the Marshall Plan in the economic sphere. Under the Mutual Defense Assistance Program, the United States furnishes large dollar grants to the member states * with the understanding that each will respond with self-help and mutual aid to further the objectives of the North Atlantic Treaty. Roughly a billion dollars was allocated in 1949–50 and again for 1950–51 to the Treaty nations, before the crisis of the summer of 1950 precipitated a rapid expansion of this program, with an added appropriation for 1950–51 of four billion dollars. France will in the nature of things receive a large slice of this aid.

As is the case with the Marshall Plan, both the executive and Congress have been much concerned that the defense effort of the European states should be "integrated." In May 1950 the North Atlantic Council urged the different governments to concentrate on "balanced collective forces," each country to supply what is needed to make the accepted general defense program effective, and to eschew the development of arms which prestige, predilection, or narrowly parochial security considerations might dictate. It was emphasized that

* And actually to certain other countries.

integrated defense was essential both to achieve maximum security and to avoid creating impossible burdens for the economies of Europe and the United States.

These burdens are a greater danger to the economies of Europe than to that of the United States. Even with substantial recovery, the former still operate on much smaller margins between bare subsistence and very modest comfort. As late as the May 1950 meeting of the Council the final communiqué could state that

> the combined resources of the members of the North Atlantic Treaty are sufficient, if properly coördinated and applied, to insure the progressive and speedy development of adequate military defense without impairing the social and economic progress of these countries.

These were brave words, but premature. With the vastly enlarged military effort of the succeeding months, it is clear that, even with extensive American aid, the European powers must plan for somewhat less butter so that they may speedily have a larger supply of guns.

Military aid to France—and other countries—takes three forms. Certain essential items of military equipment, the United States supplies directly. We send personnel to Europe and also provide training in this country in connection with the use of recently developed weapons. We undertake to send machinery and materials for the purpose of increasing production of military equipment in France and other pact countries. In return our agreement with France provides for the production and transfer to this country of "raw and semi-processed materials required by the United States as a result of deficiencies or potential deficiencies in its own resources, and which may be available in France or dependent territories under its administration."

The size and distribution of European forces projected by the North Atlantic Council was still in the discussion stage as this chapter was being written. Newspaper reports suggest that the Council is thinking of 55 to 60 allied divisions on the Continent as necessary to the task of holding the enemy in the initial stage of a hypothetical conflict. Winston Churchill on July 27, 1950 roundly declared to the Commons that the "preparations of the Western European Union to defend itself certainly stand on a far lower level than those of the South Koreans," that in contrast to the 80 divisions the Soviets are believed capable of placing in Europe, the states of the Atlantic pact had only 12. The French are now prepared, with appropriate aid, to increase their armed forces in France from five to 20 divisions by the end of 1953.

On the eventual soundness of our military thinking, the layman can make no very useful comment. The success of such a defense as is proposed for western Europe is related to the effectiveness of the new weapons, about which we have heard a certain amount in the press, but from which no doubt only a corner of the curtain has been lifted. It is connected with such problems as the tactical usefulness of the atomic bomb. Naturally we know all too little about Soviet developments in the field of offense, but we should have to face in Western Europe a very resourceful enemy who has been spending an altogether disproportionate part of his national income on the military establishment and one who is psychologically prepared for acts of great daring and the reckless expenditure of men. With the inevitably greater regard for human life, characteristic of the democracies, we face the further handicap of higher financial cost and a longer period of preparation in the interest of reducing casualties. The "cheap" mass armies of the Soviets and the Chinese may themselves constitute a new weapon of great importance.

The United States has vast power in this new world. It has correspondingly great responsibility for the use of that power. This latter concerns not only ourselves but the rest of the world—in peace or in war. The way in which we use this power is of crucial concern to those states, like France, which occupy geographically exposed positions.

The French recognize that in a common enterprise such as the North Atlantic Pact, leadership will gravitate to power and that the United States must necessarily play a role that bears a rough relationship to its strength. The French are very much disturbed, however, lest the United States use its power unwisely, and especially lest its use involve them prematurely in a conflict for which the West is not yet prepared and for which they, the French, would pay the frightful price of Russian occupation—even though the West might eventually "win" the war. The disillusionment of another occupation, Communist indoctrination, and the decapitation of the Western European élite might render impossible the reconstitution of a society with which the United States could again establish a coöperative relationship.

It is extremely difficult to learn to play a new and unaccustomed role. It is especially difficult to do so when the urgency of crisis obliges the learner to practice what he learns before he has mastered it. The tragedy of our situation could prove to be that we have the power for success in this difficult role but that we will bungle it in the end because we lack the higher "know-how."

We lack personnel for this complicated enterprise. The United States has a small but devoted corps of permanent Foreign Service Officers, many of them very able despite the cheap *clichés* that circulate in parts of the press. In recent years we have drawn into the State Department, the Economic Coöperation Administration, and other parts of the government concerned with the foreign scene, some very able top-level officials, but they are new to their jobs, necessarily operate as inspired amateurs for a long initial period, and too often retire before they have reached the upper level of their effectiveness.

We need to go forward rapidly in the development of young men who are specialized in areas such as Russia, China, Southeast Asia, India, the Near East. It is a scandalous fact that, for such a crucial area as Soviet Russia, we had in all the United States in 1945 only a handful of men who could be considered in any real sense "Russian experts." Leading universities accepted this challenge with energy, and postwar "area programs" have made a promising start in these and other fields. It is clear, however, that, if an élite, in numbers adequate to our new responsibilities, is to be developed, Congress must be willing to make—and *maintain*—appropriations at a much higher level. Very able young men will be consistently attracted to this field only if the relevant government agencies offer challenging opportunities under imaginative leadership, and under conditions where the future is not subject to the budgetary whim of Congress.

Beyond personnel lies the larger problem of policy on the world level. In the summer of 1950 the policy of "containment" enjoyed, in name at least, the support of the overwhelming majority of the American people. The 1948 Wallace-ite conception, that this policy is provocative and that one can successfully "negotiate from weakness," had largely disappeared in the solvent of events. On the other wing, however, was growing a third, distinctly minority but potentially dangerous, view—that we should proceed forthwith to preventive war.

The execution of a policy of containment presents very great difficulties. Success will require the greatest diplomatic (and military) skill. We shall need to keep clearly and unwaveringly in mind our long-term objective—to recover strength, block Russian expansion, and oblige the Kremlin in the end to negotiate. This will require infinite patience on the part of both officials and the public, and the capacity to absorb, in the tradition of the new diplomacy, a large volume of abuse and mendacity.

Nor are the *means* for the achievement of our objects well understood. The rapid creation of additional military strength here and in Europe is the most obvious and widely accepted step. But even this policy involves important choices. Between 1946 and 1950 we prepared for an atomic war directly with the Russians. Instead, the Kremlin presented us with a small-scale war in Korea, where the use of the bomb was unsuitable and where our meager ground forces, which had been allowed to dwindle to some eleven divisions, were basic. Quite logically we now propose to build up the latter, but we can be very sure that the resourceful Kremlin will by that time seek out another weak spot in our armor.

The importance of strengthening our economy for the great strains it must bear has been unexpectedly emphasized by the noisy objections to sudden price rises by the consumer himself, impelling a reluctant and election-conscious Congress to grant to a reluctant President broad stand-by control powers. The public apparently has no desire to repeat its inflationary experience either of the early war period or of that following the postwar elimination of price controls.

In the end, however, even sound economy, military strength, and a well-conceived and skillfully executed strategic plan will not be enough. The policy of "containment" is, as the word suggests, a negative conception: this is a holding operation against the Soviets and their allies. But by its very nature a holding operation, in the military use of the term, suggests a regrouping behind the lines, a reorganization for eventual victory. So in this instance, the peoples for whom this policy will offer immediate protection will inevitably expect much more. They need to be assured that we offer them not only a safer but a better world. It is precisely this latter promise which the Soviets are everywhere making—recklessly, insincerely, but often with great effect.

What can the United States offer the rest of the world? Like other peoples, we Americans suffer from the handicap of nationalism, which in our case has a strong overtone of evangelism. Too often we yearn to make other people over in our image, and the fact that in certain respects, notably in technology, we are in the van of modern developments gives this emotional drive rational support. One senses a widespread impression in the United States that we can reasonably expect that over the years the rest of the world—or at least the non-

Soviet world—will come to have a political, economic, and social complexion not unlike that of our country.

One has only to examine attentively the social structure and psychological outlook of one of the peasant economies of the Far East to be convinced that this outlook is unreal. Centuries of poverty and authoritarian rule cannot be transformed overnight by the touch of the democratic wand. To the more sophisticated eye it is clear that the "adaptability" of even a developed industrial society like that of France is severely limited by its own traditions. Our problem is not to rationalize the economy of western Europe so that it can be mistaken for our own, nor yet to transport the New England town meeting to Sumatra. It is something quite different.

We need to win friends abroad, peoples who will have good reason to prefer us to the Soviets. To that end, we should speak to each of these peoples in language which it will understand. Naturally our words must in every case conform to the broad tenets of our democratic belief, but within that hospitable range our message can vary immensely in content.

In the Far East we need to ally ourselves with "nationalism" but above all, in the words of John Fairbank, with its most dynamic component, "reform." We should aim to make real for the peasants the alluring promises of the Soviets. This program would put us on the side of a revolutionary process in Asia and, although there is a chapter in our history called the American Revolution, the word has come to have certain terrors for a people operating a highly successful society whose essence is stability. We find ourselves in the difficult position of a people with a set of ideas quite appropriate to our domestic situation but unsuited for export to "underdeveloped areas." And yet the yawning inequities which agrarian reform seeks to cure fall clearly within the western tradition with its deep concern both for social justice and economic efficiency.

In the case of France, and western Europe generally, the situation is very different. France is a democratic and industrial society, one "comparable" with our own despite the significant differences which we have so frequently emphasized. Our problem here is to contribute to the strengthening of the French social and economic fabric so that the average Frenchman can enjoy a fuller life and so that, in a soil relatively free of major social discontent, democratic institutions can continue to exist and to flourish. We can make important contributions in technology and "know-how." The French need, perhaps above all, an effective modern tax system and a vital non-Communist labor movement. In both instances our experience can be valuable. The French have important strides to make in such fields as industrial rationalization. On the other hand, we must not expect our friends in France to use our technology in just the ways or always just as "efficiently" as we do. There are many reasons—some representing no more than social inertia but some reflecting deeply weighed convictions—why their society will not accept all the implications of our modern industrialism.

There is one area where we shall inevitably have difficulties. If we give vigorous support to agrarian reform in underdeveloped areas, we shall probably accelerate the loosening of the ties between the Metropole and France overseas. A development of this kind has larger strategic implications, for example, in the case of North Africa, and these we need to keep steadily in mind. The French, somewhat like ourselves, face a paradox in dealing with the revolutionary demands of agrarian nationalists: their own system stems from a great revolutionary act in the eighteenth century, and this faith they have carefully instilled in native leaders whose pretensions they now combat.

With reference to our methods, it is clear that we need to make a much more effective explanation of our case to the world as a whole. We appear to be doing an understanding job of telling our story to the French, both on the cultural and informational sides. This is in sharp contrast to the anomalous situation existing in the summer of 1947 when Congress cut appropriations just as the Marshall Plan was being launched and thus sharply curtailed the already well developed informational program in France. The expanded program which is now envisaged faces the very real problem of finding additional personnel who have that rare sensitivity to the French scene which comes only from years of contact. In any event, we are over the hump in explaining the European Recovery Program to the French, but we must now embark on the more difficult task of explaining the American conception of the defense of Europe.

On the cultural side, American professors coming to France are making a useful impression, particularly those teaching in the field of American civilization. The French have now made a place for the teaching of American civilization in the secondary schools, the *lycées*, but the textbooks exhibit various errors and misconceptions and the teachers to date are inadequately trained in the subject. It remains only too true that we Americans, for all the inadequacy of our knowledge, still know and understand Europe far better than Europe knows and understands us. At a time when mutual comprehension and coöperative action are crucial, this can be a dangerous situation. It has been proposed that an institute of American civilization should be created in Paris, staffed by a rotating group of American specialists in different fields, and operated in the tradition of "area studies" in the United States, somewhat along the lines of the Summer Seminar at Salzburg. Available to Europeans generally—students, scholars, public servants, journalists, and others—this could be the means of bringing a new range of understanding of the United States to the French and their European neighbors.

For more than mere information, however, we need to use the propaganda of fact. The Marshall Plan is the outstanding example of the successful use of persuasion by fact. We have indeed succeeded in Europe where we have failed in Asia, and we should emphasize our successes as well as our failures.

But American action abroad, important as it can be, is not the whole story. Our friends and potential friends abroad need also to see America in action for themselves. The ECA has made an important beginning here by sending managers, engineers, and workers in selected industries to visit plants in this country. The managers have apparently been deeply impressed by the productivity of the American worker, the profit possibilities, the relations between capital and labor. The workers have been no less impressed by the massive increase in real wages achieved by American labor since the turn of the century and by the present well-being of the worker as evidenced, for instance, by the widespread ownership of automobiles. It is altogether in keeping with the story of the Soviet official who asked to be taken for a trip through the New York slums only to discover that his guide could find no vacant spot in which to park his car. French students, too, are coming again to the United States and are often pursuing fields different from those frequented before the war—economics, public administration, electronics, engineering, American civilization.

There is a distinctly greater comprehension in France of American progress in the intellectual sphere, perhaps even a recognition that much of this progress has been made possible by the wealth created in the amazing industrial development of the past few decades. And there is, too, a clearer recognition that the current American scene cannot be dismissed in the shabby generalizations about materialism which were so characteristic of certain French travelers here in the twenties; a better understanding that the intelligence, ingenuity, confidence, and resources of this country have contrived a civilization which, for all its serious defects, has done more than almost any other, through lavish production and equitable distribution, to alleviate the hardships of man's existence. For, despite the conservative terms in which we frequently describe our institutions, we have in fact taken some very radical measures along the road to social justice. The income tax, when examined in terms of its full social implications, is only one. The negative reactions of American labor to the blandishments of communism are striking evidence of the success of these measures and of the "American experiment" as a whole.

This book has been deeply concerned to make clear the great contributions of France to the western world, the important role which France still has to play. The United States, too, has a message for the world. It is a message more difficult to convey, because we have emerged so recently into a position of significance and leadership. It is to be hoped that, in our interest and in that of the French and others, we will have the skill, the patience, and the humility, first, to understand that message ourselves, and then to make it understood beyond our borders.

3. POSTSCRIPT, SEPTEMBER 1950

The observations that follow are based on a brief visit to Paris in late August and early September 1950. It will be clear to every reader that they do not apply in every case to early January 1951, when the final touches were being put on this manuscript, and will probably apply even less to the situation existing when this book appears. Both the reverses in Korea and the dramatic resurgence of isolationist sentiment in the United States have had profoundly disquieting effects in French official circles and on the public in France: the French see the international threat gravely magnified just at the moment when there is even some talk of the United States deserting the Atlantic Community. More even than in September 1950, the time element has become of crucial importance. Despite these significant changes in emphasis, we believe that the basic picture remains the same, and we have decided not to bring this section "up to date," as that would have involved using largely published sources of information, much less valuable than those which were available to us in Paris.

1. We shall no doubt evaluate the importance of the Korean crisis with more assurance a decade hence. But it is already clear that it is not just one more in a series of clashes between

East and West. It has induced a qualitative change in the world atmosphere. The more pessimistic suggest that it marks the subtle shift from "postwar" to "prewar" which we had known in the mid-thirties. It has opened a wider vista on the purposes and methods of the Soviets. The crisis has brought a new conviction to millions of Americans that a policy of strength alone can offer any real hope of security. It has at the same time brought to millions of Europeans the conviction—which many of them lacked—that the United States is ready to accept the challenge of armed conflict. And it has added a vast new element of urgency to the policies of the West.

2. These changes were strikingly evident in the France of early September 1950. When the writer had visited Paris in 1949, he had written a piece, "France Turns the Corner," which was almost exclusively concerned with the surmounting of production, and especially monetary, difficulties. Recovery and the related internal defeat of the Communists were problems of such magnitude that they tended to obscure the danger abroad, especially at a time when the Russians had capitulated on the Berlin blockade. In September 1950 every eye was riveted on the urgent problem of military security, although the economic implications of preparedness were at the same time the subject of anxious speculation.

It is unfortunate that this book must be completed in the midst of what the military would call a "fluid situation," which is a euphemism to express the fact that it is sufficiently confused so that intelligence officers really do not know what the score is. The easy—and probably the only honest—thing to do is to take refuge in that ancient academic haven which is a statement of the factors on both sides. First the "positive" factors, those inducing some degree of optimism.

3. The Korean crisis has given the French confidence in the readiness of the United States to take the highest risks and consequently a distinctly enlarged hope that a defense force adequate to stand off the Soviets may now be developed in Western Europe. Prompt American and British decisions to

reinforce their garrisons in Germany have added to this cautious optimism. Meanwhile there has been relatively little criticism of lack of preparedness in the United States, and considerable understanding of our difficulties by a country which knows only too well the hazards of waging war in the Far East.

4. The crisis has induced a distinctly greater sense of unity among Frenchmen of non-Communist persuasion and notably among those diverse elements supporting the present government. This unity is evidenced in the sweeping nature of the initial French preparedness plan, although there is still skepticism in some American circles as to how rapidly and thoroughly the French government will carry out its commitments. It is to be seen in the sharp decline of that curious brand of "neutralism" which professed to believe that France could in some mysterious way remain aloof in a Soviet-American conflict. Newspapers of widely disparate views on other problems now agree that salvation for France can lie only in a united military effort of the Western powers.

5. The prompt and rather far-reaching official French reaction on rearmament is a positive element in the situation. In response to the American request for information on what the various Atlantic Pact powers proposed to do, the Pleven government pledged the creation within three years of fifteen new full-strength divisions (to add to the five now in France and some five in Indochina) and this at a time when their budget is being drained of some $600 million annually by the military effort in Indochina. The French are said to be willing to supply eventually as many as half of the land forces required in Europe, but they insist that in the light of their losses in the past two wars they cannot incur a heavier responsibility in manpower. The French have also made an increase in the conscript term of service from one year to 18 months.

6. The events in Korea have given a new impetus to the really remarkable evolution of French thinking on the German problem. It is a long road indeed from the immediate post-Liberation policy of partitioning Germany and atomizing the

country politically, to the bold partnership of the Schuman Plan and the agreement of the French on a limited form of German rearmament. On the other hand, we need to keep steadily in mind the fact that, although the French understand the inevitability of a German contribution to a rearmed western Europe, the precipitation of our policy of rearming Germany has had a distinctly alarming impact on French public opinion. Numerous French leaders have complained persistently and bitterly over the years of Anglo-American policy toward Germany between 1920 and 1938 and have asserted that World War II could not have taken place if France had been permitted to take the steps that she felt essential to her own security or if Britain and the United States had lived up to what were construed by the French as binding promises given in 1919. Many of these same men now feel that there is every indication that Britain and the United States will follow the same course once again.

French leaders do not see the immediate threat of German rearmament as lying in the danger of an attack on France by an "independent" German army. Rather, they are deeply concerned lest such an army become an offensive instrument for the unification of Germany, thus precipitating a general war, which they seek to avoid, and subsequently recreating the strong Germany they fear. Or, alternatively, they see a German army as a bargaining weapon with the Soviets.

7. The Pleven cabinet itself was an element of strength, even though its capacity to carry out its sweeping program could be tested only in the subsequent reactions of Parliament. It had strong men in key places: Pleven as Premier, Schuman as Foreign Minister, Moch as Minister of Defense, Petsche in the critical Finance Ministry, Queuille at the Interior. Each of these men had reputations for strength and accomplishment, and in varying degrees each enjoyed a large measure of political independence. The present Queuille government has substantially the same personnel.

8. And finally—although this is unconnected with the Ko-

rean crisis—the French had already achieved a fairly sound economic basis for rearmament, despite the weaknesses in the fiscal structure and although observers agreed that it would have been very desirable to give the French economy another two years of development without the compromising burdens of new military outlays.

The "negative" factors in the situation were primarily two: the profound sense of apathy, futility, even resignation on the part of the mass of Frenchmen in the face of what, until the summer of 1950, at least, they were convinced were hopeless odds in favor of the Soviets in any war which might break out in the coming months; and the fear that the rearming of France might compromise her economic recovery or at least depress the real wages of workers at the bottom of the scale, those most exposed to the attractions of communism.

9. The morale problem is a sensitive one. The mass of the French people is profoundly anti-Communist and convinced that a Soviet occupation would be far worse than that which they knew under the Germans. The French have a great military tradition. They fought exceptionally well during the later phases of this last war and they have demonstrated time and again that they are tough and courageous soldiers. But their tremendous losses in two wars and the discouragements and frustrations of the post-Liberation period are no background for bold initiative and risk-taking in the international field. The plain fact is that in the summer of 1950 the French, an essentially skeptical people, saw no hope of restraining a Soviet invasion in the existing military context. Why then should they sacrifice large numbers of men in a hopeless cause? No nation, they argued, can be expected to fight in a hopeless cause. The problem clearly was one of creating such strength in Western Europe that reasonable hope of resisting the Soviets would return and with it the confidence of the French.

10. At the same time the French were deeply anxious lest rearmament be purchased at the price of undermining their very substantial economic recovery, primary bulwark against

the internal threat of communism. It would be idle, they argued, to prepare for the enemy without by opening the gates of the citadel to the enemy within. The crucial problem was the real wages of the lowest paid urban workers. The latter have been caught in the squeeze of postwar inflation, and would suffer again from a fresh inflation induced by diversion of effort to the "nonproductive" armament sector. Unmarried workers at the lower levels exist on a real wage which is derisory by the standard of almost any Western European industrial country.

Inadequately organized, the French worker faces a business community which is, as we have noted, all but universally recognized as being highly arrested in its views on labor and production. The members of this group have made substantial or even very large profits since the war, but have shown an acute unwillingness to share these profits with the workers. Quite aside from the problem of the social justice involved, the *patronat* cannot see the economic value of a contented labor force nor the profit implications of increased purchasing power in the hands of the workers. The ECA French Mission has made useful progress in this direction, through the groups of industrialists, engineers, and workers which it has been sending to this country to inspect American plants. But the fact remains that the French businessman simply has not had over the decades the experience of his opposite numbers in Britain and the United States in dealing with well-organized and responsible labor unions. Here is perhaps one of the biggest and most challenging jobs in adult education in the world today.

The United States is in a position to make a contribution in the case of both of these "negative" factors in the French situation.

11. At the end of August 1950, it seemed clear that no single act would inspire as much confidence in France as the prompt dispatch of additional troops to Germany. Happily President Truman and Prime Minister Attlee followed almost at once with decisions to do just that. The sending of additional Amer-

ican troops to Germany ("Send them by way of France but don't leave them there," suggested one journalist) will demonstrate that the United States is ready to risk men as well as dollars for the defense of Europe. The French are convinced of our capacity to make this contribution since they remember vividly the great preponderance of American troops in the push on Germany in 1945 at a time when we were also making a major effort in the Far East.

12. But sending troops is only part of the picture, and as this is being written the Atlantic Pact powers are planning a unified and balanced force for Western Europe, subject to a single command. The French will give meaningful support only to a scheme which welds the powers effectively into a common enterprise in which the risks are shared and financial burdens are commensurate with economic strength. All the way from planning to the fabrication of weapons, it is of the first importance that the French energies and talents be fully enlisted in this effort, and that the French feel that they are full partners in every sense.

These are among the steps which could, over a period of two or three years, produce an armed force in Western Europe capable of withstanding Soviet power. Such a force, to which France would have made a large contribution, could in turn infuse a new confidence in the French and restore the will to resist by restoring reasonable hope of successful resistance.

13. The present writer is one of those who believe that this plan can succeed provided always that we act with the speed and skill which existing dangers demand. The French are a people of great human resources—of energy, intelligence, courage, ingenuity. If they can draw new confidence from swift and bold action by the West—and here we should recall the dramatic conversion of the Germans of West Berlin from apathy to determined resistance almost overnight by the successful air lift—they will ask only a fresh challenge to be enlisted in great enterprise. The French have the pride of centuries of leadership in Europe. Like the artisan deprived of his

tools, they will, we believe, be eager to return to their creative tasks.

14. The United States is also in a position to help cushion the impact of the rearmament program on the French economy. It is clear that the French must pull in their belts and make sacrifices. Controls will return and there will be some inflation and hardships even under the best conditions—after eighteen months of stabilization, prices began to rise again in August 1950. The problem for the French is to keep these new sacrifices to a minimum, to prevent their affecting those workers who are in the weakest economic position, and to reassure the workers that sacrifices will be evenly distributed, that their share of the national income will not once more decline.

15. The development of a much more effective non-Communist labor movement which could more adequately represent the worker's interest in the face of the *patronat* must be given most active consideration. But it is a problem which lends itself more to the technique of the rifle than the shotgun, hence one requiring time and patience. More immediately promising are plans focusing on the weak spots in the workers' position, such as housing, where, as we have said, France has lagged in a most lamentable fashion. Provision of adequate housing in key industrial areas, or in those where new factories are projected and with rentals which workers can afford, would meet a prime source of worker discontent.

16. In a better ordered world the notoriously defective French tax system could be made to yield a far larger revenue. This problem has been the constant concern in this postwar period of all who are involved in a sound budgetary and monetary position for France. Some progress has been made during the past year by means of tightening up administrative procedures, but this is clearly homeopathy where surgery is needed. The well-known resistance of the patient, however, is such that only the most audacious believe that a really radical solution is possible.

17. Meanwhile the United States has a vested interest in maintaining as nearly as possible the economic gains in Western Europe, for the achievement of which we have spent a good many billions. We shall continue to support economic recovery with substantial appropriations under ERP, although as our own budget skyrockets the natural tendency in Congress will be to cut any appropriation which can be made to seem in any sense "peripheral" to the military effort. The most recent military aid appropriation of four billion dollars happily includes a figure of $475 million which is available for flexible purposes in Western Europe such as the building or activating of armaments plants. This can be the means of lessening the diversion of existing plants from the production of consumer goods and of adding to total worker income. It can be the means also of giving the French a more active share in their own rearmament, an important psychological consideration and a means of obtaining lower production costs than those normal in the United States. Despite all the difficulties involved in this transition, there are those who believe that the rearmament process, given substantial foreign aid, might lead to a snowballing economic expansion (paralleling on a smaller scale what took place in the United States during the last war and providing, in a war boom, a solution for the dollar shortage in Europe and for various problems which are now the source of real anxiety). In this connection it is to be noted that some factors in the recovery program, such as the provision of certain types of steel producing equipment, will only make themselves felt sometime hence.

18. There are two final elements, of much larger than French dimensions, which are of importance. Crisis conditions will precipitate decisions of a far more sweeping character than were possible previously. The French rearmament program and the further rapid evolution of the French attitude toward Germany are only two evidences of the striking changes of these crisis months. The new French government at least is distinctly more disposed than its predecessors to

move rapidly and to avoid the stigma of "dragging its feet" and of relying excessively on foreign aid.

19. In the second place, the crisis is moving on ineluctably "to make Europe" in the expressive phrase so common today. The new Europe will certainly not emerge tomorrow in terms of the blueprint dreams of Council of Europe speakers. But irresistibly events, forged from the perils about us, are moving men to the building of some unifying elements, at least, in a still rambling and amorphous structure.

20. The statesman of six countries are making tremendous efforts to create a new political and economic unity with the Schuman Plan. Despite the enormous difficulties facing them, the North Atlantic Treaty powers are moving forward on a broad front to create a common defense for Europe. The Marshall Plan has already made a superb contribution to the economic recovery of Europe, and the experience of its staff, in Europe and the United States, can be of tremendous value in various other enterprises looking toward unity. Specifically, the Office of the Special Representative, administering Marshall aid for all of Europe, and the Council of Deputies under the North Atlantic Treaty are currently taking steps toward substantial integration at both the top and working levels. The Office of European Economic Coöperation offers another framework for European action, and it should not be forgotten that the Atlantic Treaty powers together wield a tremendous influence in the United Nations.

21. France is then a part of a larger setting. Her policy and efforts must inevitably be related to those of other powers. In a very real sense, a book on *The United States and France* is now an anachronism. On the one hand, the French no longer view themselves as capable of effective action except in this larger context. On the other hand, the very fact that the French are part of a larger unity of rapidly increasing strength is a source of reviving confidence. They see the Schuman concept as essential to their future safety with Germany. Military security is only possible in association with the Atlantic Treaty

powers. Economic stability can likewise only be a product of coöperative action in that same setting. One of the most compelling evidences of a new unity in Europe—and in the West—is the conviction of the French that they can move forward to a safer, and perhaps eventually a more prosperous, world only in close and coöperative association with their neighbors in the Atlantic Community.

Appendix I. Some Vital Facts about France

Compiled by Aaron Noland

POPULATION AND AREA
(1946 Census)

	Area, Sq. Miles	*Population*	*Density of Pop. per Sq. Mile*
France	212,659	40,518,884*	190

In 1946, the urban population was approximately 21,550,000. The rural population was approximately 18,952,000.

Source: France: Institut National de la Statistique et des Études Économiques, *Annuaire statistique*, 1946, p. 18.

FRENCH EMIGRATION

Total number of Frenchmen living outside Metropolitan France			1,740,000
Total number in colonies			1,200,000
Algeria		853,000	
Morocco		156,000	
Tunisia		108,000	
Indochina		30,000	
Total number living abroad without intending to return			540,000
Europe		225,000	
Asia		11,000	
Africa		24,000	
North and South America		275,000	
United States	127,000		
Argentina	80,000		
Canada	25,000		

Source: Estimates by A. Demangeon, *Géographie économique et humaine de la France* (Paris, 1946), I, p. 13.

* Includes 1,670,729 foreigners, but not 312,105 merchant seamen and members of the armed forces who were outside France when the census was taken.

MOVEMENT OF FRENCH POPULATION

Birth Rate		Death Rate	
Year	*No. of live births per 1,000 inhabitants*	*Year*	*No. of deaths per 1,000 inhabitants*
1938	14.9	1938	15.8
1939	14.8	1939	15.5
1940	14.0	1940	19.3
1941	13.4	1941	17.5
1942	14.8	1942	17.1
1943	15.9	1943	16.6
1944	16.2	1944	20.5
1945	16.4	1945	16.8
1946	21.0	1946	13.5
1947	21.4	1947	13.2
1948	21.2	1948	12.4
1949	21.0	1949	13.8
1950 (Jan.–June estimate)	21.7	1950 (Jan.–June estimate)	13.7

Source: Statistical Office of the United Nations, Department of Economic Affairs, *National and Per Capita Incomes of Seventy Countries in 1949* (New York, 1950), pp. 6, 13, 17.

The estimated population of Metropolitan France on January 1, 1950 was 41,780,000.

EVOLUTION OF THE STRUCTURE OF THE POPULATION

(In Thousands)

Age Groups	*1851*	*1901*	*1921*	*1936*	*1950*
0–19 years	13,410	13,300	12,270	12,450	12,460
20–39 years	11,130	11,660	11,380	12,800	11,540
40–59 years	8,130	8,690	9,820	9,880	11,010
60 years and more	3,590	4,790	5,320	6,060	6,770
	36,260	38,440	38,790	41,190	41,780

Proportional Distribution

(Per Thousand)

Age Groups	*1851*	*1901*	*1921*	*1936*	*1950*
0–19 years	370	346	316	302	298
20–39 years	307	303	293	311	276
40–59 years	224	227	253	240	264
60 years and more	99	124	138	147	162
	1,000	1,000	1,000	1,000	1,000

Number of Adults (20–59 years) for each Old Person (60 years and more)

1851	*1901*	*1921*	*1936*	*1950*
5.4	4.3	4.0	3.7	3.3

Source: France, Ministère du Travail, *Revue française du Travail*, January–March, 1950, pp. 4–5.

The percentage of old persons (over 60) in France is 16.2, as compared with 9.9 in the United States, and 14.3 in Great Britain.

POPULATION OF CITIES OF OVER 100,000 IN FRANCE
(1946 Census)

Cities	*Population*	*Cities*	*Population*
Greater Paris *	5,483,166	Nancy	113,500
Marseilles	636,300	Reims	110,700
Lyons	460,700	Clermont-Ferrand	108,100
Toulouse	264,400	Limoges	107,900
Bordeaux	253,800	Rouen	107,700
Nice	211,200	Le Havre	106,900
Nantes	200,300	Nîmes	104,100
Lille	188,900	Grenoble	102,200
St. Étienne	178,000	Roubaix	101,000
Strasbourg	175,500	Dijon	100,700
Toulon	125,700	Le Mans	100,500
Rennes	113,800		

Source: France: Institut National de la Statistique et des Études Économiques, *Annuaire statistique*, 1946, p. 19.

TEMPERATURE AND PRECIPITATION

City	*Mean Temp. January*	*Mean Temp. July*	*Mean Annual Temp.*	*Annual Precipitation*
Paris	36.5° F.	65.5° F.	50.5° F.	20.8 in.
Lyons	36.3	70.2	53.1	32.0
Marseilles	43.3	72.1	56.8	21.5
Algiers	53.4	77.0	64.9	30.0
Tunis	49.6	79.3	64.2	17.9

* Includes the Department of the Seine and half the population of the Department of the Seine-et-Oise. Paris proper had a population of 2,725,-400.

THE FRENCH UNION

		Area, Sq. Miles		*Latest Available Census*	*Population (in 000's)*	
AFRICA						
French Equatorial Africa			958,256	July, 1936		3,423
Gabon	(Colony)	92,218		"	410	
Middle Congo	(Colony)	166,069		"	746	
Ubangi-Shari	(Colony)	238,767		"	834	
Chad	(Colony)	461,202		"	1,433	
Cameroons	(Trusteeship)		166,489	June, 1936		2,389
Algeria *			847,500	March, 1936		7,235
Morocco	(Protectorate)		153,870	March, 1947		7,900
Tunisia	(Protectorate)		48,300	Nov., 1946		3,231
French West Africa			1,815,768	July, 1936		14,614
Senegal	(Colony)	77,790		"	1,698	
French Guinea	(Colony)	96,886		"	2,011	
Ivory Coast	(Colony)	184,174		"	3,851	
Dahomey	(Colony)	43,232		"	1,352	
French Sudan	(Colony)	590,966		"	3,569	
Mauritania	(Colony)	323,310		"	386	
Niger	(Colony)	499,410		"	1,747	
Togoland	(Trusteeship)		21,893	June, 1945		919
French Somaliland	(Colony)		9,071	"		45
Madagascar and dependencies	(Colony)		241,094	1941		4,227
Réunion †			970	Oct., 1946		242

AMERICA						
St. Pierre and Miquelon	(Colony)		93	May, 1945		4
French Guiana and Inini †			34,740	March, 1946		29
Guadeloupe and dependencies †			688	April, 1946		278
Martinique †			385	May, 1946		262
ASIA						
French India	(Colony)		196	July, 1939		305
French Indo-China			280,849	July, 1936		23,030
Viet Nam ‡	(Associated State)	123,979		"	18,972	
Cambodia	(Associated State)	67,550		"	3,046	
Laos	(Associated State)	89,320		"	1,012	
OCEANIA						
French territories in the Pacific						
New Caledonia and dependencies	(Colony)		9,446	July, 1936		60
New Hebrides	(Anglo-French condominium)		5,700	1946		49
Pacific Islands, including Society Islands, Tuamotu Islands, Tubuai archipelagoes, etc.	(Colony)		1,520	June, 1946		56
TOTAL FRENCH UNION			4,596,828			68,298,000

Sources: Compiled from data published in France: Institut National de la Statistique et des Études Économiques, *Annuaire statistique*, 1946; Statistical Office of the United Nations, *Population and Vital Statistics Reports*, Statistical Papers, Series A, No. 4, 1949.

* The three northern departments of Algeria (Algiers, Oran, and Constantine) form an integral part of France. Southern Algeria is administered as a colony.

† Status changed to that of a department of France as of January 1, 1947.

‡ Includes Annam, Tonkin, and Cochin China.

GOVERNMENT AND POLITICS

NATIONAL ASSEMBLY

(Elected November 10, 1946)

Parties	*Number of Deputies*
Communist and Affiliated Groups	186
Mouvement Républicain Populaire (M.R.P.) and Affiliated Groups	166
Socialist (S.F.I.O.)	103
Rassemblement des Gauches and Affiliated Groups	70
Parti Républicain de la Liberté and Affiliated Groups	38
Independent Republican	29
Overseas Native Groups	16
Peasant Action and Affiliated Groups	7
Others	3
Total	618

COUNCIL OF THE REPUBLIC

(Elected November 1948)

	Seats
Rassemblement des Gauches	80
Socialist (S.F.I.O.)	62
Rassemblement du Peuple Français (Gaullists)	57
Independent Republican	38
M.R.P.	19
Communists	21
Peasant Party	16
Parti Républicain de la Liberté	12
Others	15
	320

DIPLOMATIC REPRESENTATION

France to the United States: Henri Bonnet, *Ambassador Extraordinary and Plenipotentiary.*

United States to France: David K. E. Bruce, *Ambassador Extraordinary and Plenipotentiary.*

UNIVERSITIES: ENROLLMENTS, July 31, 1948

Paris	53,158
Bordeaux	7,577
Lyons	7,455
Toulouse	7,347
Lille	6,882
Aix-Marseilles	6,234
Rennes	5,588
Strasbourg	5,354
Montpellier	5,287
Nancy	4,384
Algiers	4,448
Grenoble	3,967
Poitiers	3,872
Caen	2,745
Clermont-Ferrand	1,903
Dijon	1,559
Besançon	994
Total	128,754

SOCIAL ORIGIN OF FRENCH UNIVERSITY STUDENTS

Occupation of Parents	*Per Cent of Students (July 31, 1948)*
Liberal professions	18.0
Employers of labor in trade and industry	16.3
Civil Service and similar groups	27.3
Parents of independent means	11.8
Employees in trade and industry	9.6
Artisans	7.1
Industrial workers	1.1
Agricultural workers	0.5
Unclassified	7.8
	100.0

Source: The University of London Institute of Education, *The Year Book of Education, 1950* (London, 1950), p. 602.

THE FRENCH PRESS

		Circulation *
Paris Morning Newspapers		
Le Parisien Libéré	Independent	480,000
Le Figaro	Conservative	435,000
L'Aurore	Radical-Socialist	365,000
L'Humanité	Communist	233,000
Franc-Tireur	Socialist	190,000
Ce Matin	Conservative	164,000
Libération	Leftist	126,000
Le Populaire	Socialist	72,000
Combat	Independent Leftist	71,000
L'Aube	MRP	36,000
Paris Evening Newspapers		
France-Soir	Independent	690,000
Paris Presse-Intransigeant	Conservative	427,000
Ce Soir	Communist	213,000
Le Monde	Conservative	165,000
La Croix	Conservative, Catholic	162,000

		Circulation, 1948
Provincial Newspapers		
Ouest-France (Rennes)	MRP	450,000
Le Sud-Ouest (Bordeaux)	Independent	295,000
Le Progrès (Lyons)	Radical Socialist	290,000
La Voix du Nord (Lille)	Moderate	265,000
L'Est Républicain (Nancy)	Moderate	220,000
Les Allobroges (Grenoble)	Resistance	220,000
La Nouvelle République du Centre-Ouest	Radical Socialist	220,000
Paris-Normandie (Rouen)	Resistance	175,000
Le Dauphin Libre (Grenoble)		170,000
Le Provençal (Marseilles)	Socialist	160,000
Le Républicain Lorrain (Metz)	Resistance	160,000
Le Patriote du Sud-Ouest (Toulouse)	Communist	140,000
La République du Sud-Ouest		140,000
Les Dernières Nouvelles D'Alsace (Strasbourg)		135,000

Sources: Compiled from data contained in *Tirage moyen des Quotidens Parisiens*, a graph prepared by the French Embassy, Press and Information Division, New York, 1950; circulation, 1948, of leading provincial newspapers compiled from data published in *Editor and Publisher International Year Book Number*, 1949 (New York, January 31, 1949), pp. 377–378.

* Estimated for July 1950.

FRENCH PUBLISHERS, BOOKSTORES, AND BOOKS

The number of publishers in 1939 was 1,300; in 1949, 3,000
The number of bookstores in 1939 was 7,000; in 1949, 17,000
The number of books published in 1949 was 9,908, of which 851 were translations.

(This figure can be compared with 10,892 new books and new editions published in the United States in 1949.)

Sources: The French Embassy, Press and Information Division, "Courrier de France," October 1950, p. 5; France, *Perspectives*, No. 8, July 1950.

LIBRARIES

On January 1, 1951, there were in Paris, in addition to the world-renowned National, University, and other special libraries (Libraries of the French Institute, the Academy of Medicine, the Museum of Man, etc.), 85 Municipal Loan Libraries. There were 300 Municipal Libraries in the provinces as well as 47,000 Village School Libraries. Other library facilities included the departmental Central Loan Libraries and their traveling book vans.

Source: Jean Gallotti, "The Public Libraries of France," an article made available to the public by the Press and Information Division of the French Embassy in New York.

ECONOMIC STATISTICS

THE SHARE OF FRANCE IN THE WORLD ECONOMIC ACTIVITY

(A) Population (1936):	World	2,130 million
	France (Metropolitan and Overseas territories)	111 million
	Or 5.2 per cent of the world's population	

(B) Production:

	In percentage of world production		
	1913	*1929*	*1938*
World	100	100	100
U.S.A.	25.7	30	21.6
British Empire (including the United Kingdom)	22.0	17.3	17.8
Germany	9.7	7.3	10.7
U.S.S.R.	8.5	9.1	13.9
France (Metropolitan and Overseas territories)	5.9	5.7	5.4

(C) International Trade:

(1) *Imports*	In percentage of total world imports		
	1913	*1929*	*1938*
World	100	100	100
British Empire (including U.K.)	29.4	26.3	32.0
Germany	13.2	9.0	9.0
U.S.A.	9.1	12.2	8.0
France (Metro. and Overseas terr.)	9.9	8.5	7.6

(2) *Exports*	*1913*	*1929*	*1938*
World	100	100	100
British Empire (including U.K.)	28.4	26.3	27.1
U.S.A.	13.4	15.6	13.4
Germany	13.1	9.7	9.3
France (Metro. and Overseas terr.)	8.7	7.6	6.0

(D) Principal Resources of the Franc Area in Raw Materials

	1937–1938 average			
	Iron	*Bauxite*	*Pure Potash*	*Phos-phates*
	Per cent	Per cent	Per cent	Per cent
World production	100	100	100	100
France	16.0	21.6	15.8	31.3
U.S.A.	45.7	14.2	7.1	38.8
U.S.S.R.	16.4	7.3	7.5	22.7
Germany	5.5	3.1	54.5	—
Rank of France in the world	3	1	2	2
Percentage of domestically produced raw materials processed by French industry	46	40	—	25

(E) Transportation Network (1928):

	Total Length (in Miles)	Length (in Miles) per 1,000 Inhabitants	Length (in Miles) per 1,000 Sq. Miles of Area
I. *Railroads*			
U.S.A.	252,000	2.05	83
Germany	36,600	.587	196
France	25,800	.63	121
United Kingdom	18,600	.41	197
II. *Inland Waterway Channels* (available for transport)			
France	7,372		
United Kingdom	4,852		
Germany	4,593		
III. *Road Transport System*			
U.S.A.	2,898,000	23	957
France	378,600	9	1785
United Kingdom	151,600	3.3	1607
Germany	144,000	2.3	774

(F) The Productivity of Labor in France in Relation to Foreign Countries

	France	U.S.A.	England
National income per worker*	684	1,381	1,064
Net industrial production per worker (in dollars)	922	3,840	1,125
Daily output per miner in 1938 (in lbs.)	1,828	9,020	2,486

In 1938, the average age of the French stock of machine tools was approximately 25 years, as against 7 to 9 years in England, and 5 to 7 years in the United States.

* 1925–1934 average estimated in I.U. (international units) by Colin Clark in *Conditions of Economic Progress.*

(G) Use of Power in France, Great Britain, and the United States, 1938

	Total Number of h.p.h. Used c. 1938 (in billions)*	*Estimated Population (in thousands) Total*	*Employed*	*Number of h.p.h. Used Per Capita (in thousands)*	*Number of h.p.h Used Per Employed Persons (in thousands)*
France	153.3	41,950	20,400	3.6	7.5
Great Britain	436.6	47,500	21,800	9.2	20.0
U.S.A.	1,722.8	131,200	51,400	13.1	33.5

(H) Number of Persons Fed per Agricultural Worker

Year	*France*	*U.S.A.*
1895–99	4.3	7.6
1900–13	4.2	10.2
1925–30	4.3	12.2
1935–39	5.1	14.8

Largely because of insufficient mechanization, a single agricultural producer in France fed only 5 consumers, whereas in the United States he fed 15. For the economy as a whole, labor output in the United States (*c.* 1938) was three times greater than in France.

Source: France, Commissariat Général du Plan de Modernisation et D'Équipement, *Statistical Review of the Economic and Financial Situation of France at the Beginning of 1946* (Paris, 1946), pp. 6–7, 19–20.

* Horsepower hours.

SIZE OF FRENCH AGRICULTURAL HOLDINGS
(July 1947)

Size of Holdings	*Number of Holdings*		*Total Area of Farm Lands Included in These Holdings*	
0 to 2.47 acres	1,015,000	25%	1,789,750 acres	2%
2.47 to 24.7 acres	1,865,000	47%	23,600,850 acres	21%
24.7 to 123.5 acres	975,000	25%	55,575,000 acres	48%
123.5 to 247 acres	81,000	2%	15,128,750 acres	13%
Over 247 acres	32,000	1%	18,179,200 acres	16%

Source: Compiled from data published in *News From France*, February 1947, issued by the French Embassy, Press and Information Division, New York.

VALUE OF THE FRANC RELATIVE TO THE DOLLAR

1918	19.6 cents	1948	0.48 cent	
1920	6.0 "	1949 (before devaluation)	0.46 "	(official)
1926	2.5 "		0.30 "	(free)
1936	6.5 "	1949 (after devaluation)	0.28 "	
1938	2.8 "	1950	0.28 "	
1940	2.0 "	1951 (January)	0.28 "	
1945	1.7 "			
1946	0.8 "			
1947	0.8 "			

Source: Compiled from data published in Statistical Office of the United Nations, *Monthly Bulletin of Statistics*, January–December 1950.

COMPARATIVE DATA ON FRENCH BASIC INDUSTRIES AND AGRICULTURE

Industries	*Monthly Average* 1938	*1949*	*1st 9 Months of 1950*	*October 1950*
Coal (plus lignite), in 1,000 tons	3,964	4,420	4,324	4,603
Steel, in 1,000 tons	518	763	720.5	852
Iron ore, in 1,000 tons	2,755	2,619	2,409	2,796
Electricity, in million kilowatt-hours	1,548	2,380	2,508.6	2,825
Gas, in million cubic meters	141	204	196	210
Autos (passenger), in number of units	15,000	15,640	20,000	—
Potash, in 1,000 tons	277	439.7	481.5	543

Agriculture in tons	*Annual Average*		
	1930–39	*1949*	*1950*
Wheat	8,049,557	8,082,407	7,331,686
Corn	543,941	194,005	321,253
Potatoes	14,617,505	9,050,127	12,306,300
Sugar beets	9,117,065	9,611,011	13,000,000
Dried vegetables	250,758	131,645	193,677
Oil yielding crops	15,998	185,483	155,791
Wine, in 1,000 gallons	1,295,005	944,564	1,315,344

Source: *New York Times*, January 3, 1950.

LEVEL OF INDUSTRIAL PRODUCTION
(Base year, 1937 = 100)

1938	92	1946	73
1942	51	1947	87
1943	47	1948	102
1944	30	1949	112
1945	39	1950	112*

Source: Statistical Office of the United Nations, *Monthly Bulletin of Statistics*, October 1950, p. 29.

LEVEL OF OUTPUT PER MAN IN INDUSTRY
(1935–1938 = 100)

	1947	*1948*	*1949*
France	84	95	102

Source: Department of Economic Affairs of the United Nations, *Economic Survey of Europe in 1949* (Geneva, 1950), p. 6.

CONSUMPTION OF ENERGY FOR PRODUCTIVE PURPOSES
(In billions of kilowatt-hours electricity equivalent)

	1948	*1937*	*Per cent change, 1937–1948*
France	132.2	117.8	12.2
U.S.A.	1,562.7	911.0	71.5
United Kingdom	294.9	261.2	12.9
Italy	48.8	46.5	4.9

Source: The National Industrial Conference Board, *The Economic Almanac, 1950*, p. 548.

* Estimate, January–July.

IMPORTS AND EXPORTS

DISTRIBUTION OF FRENCH FOREIGN TRADE
(value in billions of francs)

Countries	*Imports* 1938	1948	1949	*Exports* 1938	1948	1949
United States	5.2	120	161	1.7	6	15
Germany	3.1	35	68	1.8	23	39
Australia	1.5	29	40	—	—	—
Great Britain	3.2	18	32	3.5	31	70
Belgian-Luxemburg Economic Union	3.1	25	32	4.1	31	45
Saudi Arabia	—	—	30	—	—	—
The Netherlands	1.1	16	22	1.3	18	36
Kuwait	—	—	20	—	—	—
Italy	0.5	11	17	0.5	2	4
Union of South Africa	0.4	7	16	—	—	—
Iraq	1.4	10	15	—	—	—
Switzerland	1.0	13	15	—	—	—
Sweden	0.6	9	14	0.5	6	13
Spain	0.2	4	12	0.4	0.8	7
New Zealand	0.3	7	12	—	—	—
Argentina	0.9	16	11	0.7	6	35

Source: French Embassy, Press and Information Division, *News from France,* June 15, 1950, p. 7.

FRENCH IMPORTS OF RAW MATERIALS FROM FOREIGN COUNTRIES

		1938	*1948*	*1949*
Coal	in thousands of tons	20,526	13,032	12,805
Crude oil	" " " "	6,978	7,620	11,807
Raw wool	" " " "	145	171	158
Raw cotton	" " " "	267	152	231
Raw silk	in tons	2,460	628	787

FRENCH TRADE WITH FOREIGN COUNTRIES

(weight in thousands of metric tons; value in millions of francs)

	1938		1948		1949	
	Weight	*Value*	*Weight*	*Value*	*Weight*	*Value*
Imports						
Fuels	30,143	8,736	25,710	119,795	31,004	183,930
Raw materials for industry: industrial origin	7,118	8,008	6,271	95,482	5,793	131,542
Raw materials for industry: agricultural origin	2,234	7,966	3,636	108,925	3,082	161,422
Raw materials for agriculture: industrial origin	461	331	457	5,539	438	6,749
Raw materials for agriculture: agricultural origin	374	376	487	8,088	316	6,960
Equipment: for industry	146	2,076	589	45,659	406	68,108
Equipment: for agriculture	8	114	50	7,547	36	7,907
Consumer goods: durable	37	1,331	32	6,426	21	6,882
Consumer goods: non-durable, for human consumption	6,586	3,551	4,853	71,413	4,919	90,340
Consumer goods: others	73	1,084	41	13,366	57	18,610
Total	47,180	33,573	42,126	482,240	46,072	682,450
Exports						
Fuels	1,721	447	4,967	20,664	8,237	40,360
Raw materials for industry: industrial origin	21,688	8,871	10,515	79,807	13,521	158,029
Raw materials for industry: agricultural origin	1,166	2,910	700	16,651	827	31,871
Raw materials for agriculture: industrial origin	410	76	945	4,875	1,470	11,348
Raw materials for agriculture: agricultural origin	341	325	142	4,279	414	9,579
Equipment: for industry	263	1,726	355	22,876	578	44,000
Equipment: for agriculture	13	47	32	1,889	40	3,169
Consumer goods: durable	116	1,560	173	23,906	228	41,387
Consumer goods: non-durable, for human consumption	1,055	2,773	647	25,704	1,399	51,289
Consumer goods: others	211	3,465	192	40,761	249	64,834
Total	26,984	22,200	18,668	241,412	26,963	455,866

Source: French Embassy, Press and Information Division, *News from France*, June 15, 1950, pp. 6, 8.

PRINCIPAL FRENCH IMPORTS FROM THE UNITED STATES
(first nine months of 1950)

Item	*Value in 1,000 francs*
Cotton	34,233,820
Machines, machine tools, and equipment	12,158,213
Grains	4,789,202
Rolling-mills and calendering machines	4,637,687
Equipment for aerial navigation	4,264,111
Chemical products	3,308,513
Boilers, motors, pumps, and compressors	3,246,691
Non-ferrous metal products	2,507,734
Electrical equipment (generators, transformers, etc.)	2,364,955
Lifting and handling equipment	2,121,896
Metal products, hot-rolled or forged, iron or steel	1,743,404
Solid mineral fuel	1,378,999
Petroleum oils, lubricants	1,288,543
Tractors	1,093,027

PRINCIPAL FRENCH EXPORTS TO THE UNITED STATES
(first nine months of 1950)

Item	*Value in 1,000 francs*
Laces	2,738,346
Semimanufactured steel products	1,219,494
Wines	1,084,045
Metal products, hot-rolled or forged, iron or steel	1,043,295
Manufactured textiles	963,155
Copper and copper alloys	684,893
Spirits	680,842
Rawhides	579,468
Wools and hairs	557,104
Tulle	549,181
Automobiles	502,571
Essential oils, resinoids, etc	516,389
Objets d'art	485,686
Precious gems	466,866

Source: Compiled from data published in France, Ministry of Finances and Economic Affairs, *Statistique mensuelle du Commerce extérieur de la France*, September 1950, pp. 369–372.

The total value of French imports from the United States during the first nine months of 1950 was 99,197,628,000 francs, while the total value of French exports to the United States in the same period was 22,851,325,000 francs.

BALANCE OF PAYMENTS
(in millions of current dollars at annual rate)

	1938	*1948*	*1949*
Metropolitan France			
Merchandise Transactions:			
Imports	870	2,510	2,035
Exports	640	1,082	1,567
Trade Balance	−230	−1,428	−468
Freight:			
Payments	—	318	247
Receipts	—	45	38
Net Freight	−14	−273	−209
Tourism:			
Payments	—	27	23
Receipts	—	97	144
Net Tourism	+101	+70	+121
Interest Payments on Public Debt		−77	−78
Net Payments for Foreign Workers	+130	−80	−55
Net Other Invisibles		+258	+150
Total Deficit on Current Account	−13	−1,530	−539
French Union			
Deficit on Current Account:			
Metropolitan France	−13	−1,530	−539
Overseas Territories	−60	−208	−167
Total, French Union	−73	−1,738	−706
Capital Payments:			
Loan Repayments	—	−37	−129
Other Capital Payments	—	−84	−381
Total Capital Payments	—	−121	−510
Total Payments Deficit		−1,859	−1,216
Financing of Payments Deficit:			
Use of Reserves	—	409	−23
Use of Foreign Loans and Miscellaneous Foreign Financing	—	632	170
ECA Aid, Total	—	818	1,069
Direct	—	754	855
Indirect	—	64	214
Total Financing of Payments Deficit		+1,859	+1,216

THE LEVEL OF FOOD CONSUMPTION IN TERMS OF NUTRIENTS

(in number of calories and grammes per person per day)

	Calories (numbers)			All proteins (grammes)			Fats from all sources (grammes)		
	1934–38	*1947/48*	*1948/49*	*1934–38*	*1947/48*	*1948/49*	*1934–38*	*1947/48*	*1948/49*
France	2,880	2,550	2,740	88	76	99	84	69	81
U.S.A.*	3,160	3,240	3,190	90	99	95	127	136	53

Source: Statistical Office of the United Nations, Department of Economic Affairs, *Economic Survey of Europe in 1949* (Geneva, 1950), p. 27.

* Prewar figures refer to 1935–1939.

INFLATION IN FRANCE

COST OF LIVING FOR AVERAGE LABORER IN PARIS REGION
(Index: September 1938 = 100)

Month	*Total*	*Food*	*Heat and Light*	*Rent*	*Clothing*	*Miscellaneous*
1938 September	100	100	100	100	100	100
1948 "	1250	1691	881	201	2503	1040
1949 "	1443	1760	1102	476	2561	1355
1950 April	1556	1937	1141	579	2627	1447

WAGES OF MALE WORKERS IN INDUSTRY AND COMMERCE IN PARIS
(Index: October 1938 = 100)

Month	*Hourly Wage Rates*	*Net Full-time Weekly Wages Plus Family Allowances for Average Laborer with Wife and Two Children*
1938 October	100	100
1948 April	734	1,137
1949 "	854	1,324
1950 "	928	1,363

THE EFFECT OF THE WAR ON FRANCE

MANPOWER LOSSES

Fighting force casualties:	
Killed, missing—1939–1940	123,466
Killed, missing—1940–1945 (including campaigns in Tunisia, Italy, France, and Germany)	32,580
Resistance	25,444
Losses among French drafted into German army (mostly Alsatians)	34,401
Prisoners who died in camps	41,062
Died after return to France	4,326
Total fighting force casualties	261,279
Civilian casualties:	
Deportee losses	222,000
Deaths from bombings	60,000
Executions	30,000
Deaths due to other causes	66,269
Total civilian casualties	378,269

The grand total military and civilian casualties were 639,548.

Source: Statement on French war losses by Pierre Jean Bellan, spokesman for the Veterans' Affairs Ministry, reported in the *Boston Traveler,* March 4, 1948; France, Direction de la Statistique Générale, *Premiers Résultats du Recensement générale, 10 Mars 1946* (Paris, 1947), p. 18.

DIRECT LOSSES OF CAPITAL EQUIPMENT IN FRANCE

(*a*) Financial Evaluation (in millions of 1938 francs)

	Destruction	*German Levies on Capital*	*Total*
(1) *AGRICULTURE*			
Farm buildings	26,635	—	26,635
Farm equipment	945	4,165	5,110
Livestock	5,040	11,445	16,485
Stored crops	2,905	9,555	12,460
Damage to soil	4,865	—	4,865
Damage to vineyards	1,120	—	1,120
Damage to woods and forests	1,470	—	1,470
Partial Total	42,980	25,165	68,145

	Destruction	*German Levies on Capital*	*Total*
(2) *INDUSTRY AND COMMERCE*			
Buildings and plants	14,630	4,900	19,530
Equipment	23,100	9,975	33,075
Raw materials	—	43,645	43,645
Stocks of manufactured and semimanufactured products	6,090	33,005	39,095
Partial Total	43,820	91,525	135,345
(3) *TRANSPORTATION AND COMMUNICATIONS*			
Public utility railways	14,175	54,600	68,775
Secondary railways and city transport facilities	518	112	630
Road communications	21,525	3,605	25,130
Inland waterways	3,342.5	787.5	4,130
Seaports	14,595	1,925	16,520
Merchant Marine	7,070	385	7,455
Telegraph, Telephone, and Postal Services	2,810.5	129.5	2,940
Radio transmission facilities	276.5	3.5	280
Civilian aviation	4,270	630	4,900
Partial Total	68,582.5	62,177.5	130,760
(4) *WAR MATÉRIEL*	16,625	52,500	69,125
(5) *REAL ESTATE AND PERSONALTY*			
Private buildings and dwellings	158,920	—	158,920
Public buildings	25,305	—	25,305
Household furniture	83,405	18,970	102,375
Additional expenditures for reconstruction	29,645	—	29,645
Partial Total	297,275	18,970	316,245
(6) *CASH, SECURITIES, OBJECTS OF ART*			
Gold	—	10,710	10,710
Currency, bonds and shares	—	7,000	7,000
Gems and valuables	—	3,080	3,080
Partial Total	—	20,790	20,790
OVERALL TOTAL	469,282.5	271,127.5	740,410

(*b*) Major Losses

(1) *TRANSPORT AND COMMUNICATIONS*

	Units	*Prewar Situation*	*Situation at Time of Liberation* Requisitioned	Destroyed	Total Losses	*Ratio of Losses %*
(a) Railroads						
Steam engines	Number	17,058	3,919	251	4,170	24.5
Freight cars	"	478,544	293,798	15,538	309,336	64.5
Passenger coaches	"	57,706	13,942	1,805	15,747	40.0
(b) Road Transport						
Business vehicles	Number	450,000	50,000	120,000	170,000	38.0
Pleasure vehicles	"	1,450,000	300,000	310,000	610,000	42.0
(c) Inland Waterways						
Ordinary barges	Number	12,025	1,188	9,375	10,563	87.0
Tankers	"	503	125	302	427	85.0
Tugs	"	609	259	195	454	75.0
(d) Merchant Marine	Gross					
Liners and Passenger's cargo vessels	Tonnage	1,177,722	56,034	486,457	542,491	45.0
Cargo vessels:	"					
General freight	"	916,214	283,474	538,295	821,769	87.0
Coalers	"	248,794	—	75,241	75,241	30.0
Tankers	"	306,118	—	76,686	76,686	25.0
Fruit ships		86,870	—	6,744	6,744	8.0

Source: France, Commissariat Général du Plan de Modernisation et d'Equipement, *Statistical Review of the Economic and Financial Situation of France at the Beginning of 1946*, pp. 25–26, French Embassy, Press and Information Division, *News from France*, November 15, 1950.

(2) *DESTRUCTION OF BUILDINGS* (in number)

Types	*Completely Destroyed*	*Partly Destroyed*	*Total*
Dwellings	291,000	938,000	1,229,000
Farm buildings	78,000	200,000	278,000
Industrial and commercial buildings	66,000	180,000	246,000
Public buildings	6,000	26,000	32,000
	441,000	1,344,000	1,785,000

In 1939, France had 9,975,000 buildings of which 9,777,000 were dwellings. Of the total number of buildings, 1,785,000 suffered damages due to war; 441,000 were completely destroyed and 1,344,000 partially destroyed. Approximately 18 per cent of French real property was damaged. French property losses during the Second World War ranked after those of the U.S.S.R., Germany, and Poland.

UNITED STATES AID TO FRANCE
(In millions of dollars)

	War Period (July 1, 1940– June 30, 1945)	*July– December 1945*	*1946*	*1947*	*1948*	*1949*	*Total*
U. S. Government Grants	2,581	79	1	12	620	807	4,100
U. S. Government Foreign Credits	–	–	1,295	590	184	53	2,122

FIRST TWO YEARS OF THE EUROPEAN RECOVERY PROGRAM
(April 3, 1948 to March 31, 1950)

Grants to France during the period totaled $1,838,800,000
Principal Commodities Received by France Under the Program

Petroleum and products	$217,000,000
Ocean freight	211,300,000
Cotton	209,000,000
Machinery and equipment	156,900,000
Non-ferrous metals and products	87,700,000

Bread grains	79,600,000
Fats and oils	63,200,000
Chemicals	46,400,000
Coarse grains	33,100,000
Aircraft and engines	26,400,000
Iron and steel products	25,800,000
Sugar	12,500,000

Total amount of counterpart funds deposed by France up to April 30, 1950—$1,568,400,000 (439.6 thousand million francs).

Counterpart funds approved for withdrawal—$1,444,900,000 (406.5 thousand million francs).

Utilization of the counterpart funds: (in millions of francs)

Agriculture	39,000
Coal mining	72,700
Electricity, gas, power	120,200
Railways	28,500
Merchant and fishing fleets	13,000
Manufacturing	26,200
Waterways and harbors	3,600
Roads and road bridges	1,000
Housing	13,100
Debt retirement	45,000
Other purposes and undistributed	44,200

Source, U. S. Department of Commerce, *Statistical Abstract of the United States, 1950* (Washington, 1950), pp. 832–834; *Keesing's Contemporary Archives, 1950*, pp. 10852–10853.

DEFENSE EXPENDITURES

In 1938, France spent 29.41 billion francs for defense. This constituted 47 per cent of the total national budget. In 1948, 353 billion francs, or 38.6 per cent of the total budget, was spent for defense. In 1950, the defense expenditure was 420 billion francs, 25 per cent of the total national budget.

Source: *The Economist* (London), May 15, 1948, p. 792; *Journal officiel de la République*, February 1, 1950.

Appendix II. Suggested Reading

On any modern state of the dimensions of France, the amount of material appearing annually is prodigious and baffling. A given specialist on France in the American government spends his or her waking hours in trying vainly to read everything that appears on just one angle of this complex development. The French are avid intellectuals and eager individualists; as a result, there has always been a lush growth of newspapers and periodicals, representing each nuance or point of view—and never has this been more true than during the extraordinary intellectual resurgence of the post-Liberation world. It is also unfortunately true that there is little in the way of general books to guide the reader through this morass of literature, and most of these are in French. British and Americans have in the past two decades written rather extensively on France, but little of this—at least in book form—deals with years since the end of the last war. We have felt, however, that it would not be particularly useful to most American readers to cite long lists of books in French, especially since many of these are not readily available. Hence, we have, with some exceptions, given only titles in English, and in general those which one would be likely to find in the library of an American city of say 150,000 population.

1. HISTORICAL BACKGROUND

No one who would understand contemporary France can neglect her history, and yet that history is too vast to be examined in more than rapid survey for the purposes of this book. Albert L. Guérard, in his brief, understanding, and attractively written *France, a Short History* (New York: Norton, 1946), provides a broad canvas. Somewhat longer books on the general history of France include the translation of Charles Seignobos' *Histoire sincère de la Nation française* with the title, *The Evolution of the French People*

(New York: Knopf, 1932), which brings the story down to World War I; the coöperative book in the "Nations of Today," edited by John Buchan, *France* (London: Hodder and Stoughton, 1923), which stresses the period after 1800; Paul Van Dyke, *The Story of France from Julius Caesar to Napoleon III* (New York: Scribner, 1929), which strongly emphasizes French "civilization"; and the convenient coöperative reference work written by British and French scholars and edited by Arthur Tilley, *Modern France, a Companion to French Studies* (Cambridge: The University Press, 1922). J. P. T. Bury has given us a brief and balanced account of the very modern development–*France, 1814–1940* (Philadelphia: University of Pennsylvania Press, 1949). On the Third Republic, there is the short and more analytical *Democracy in France* (London: Oxford University Press, 1946) by David Thomson, like Bury, an English scholar; or for those who prefer their history at length and on the high level of epigram, there is the brilliant but by no means facile *France under the Republic* (New York: Harper, 1940) by the encyclopedic, peripatetic and controversial Denis W. Brogan of the University of Cambridge.

2. THE LAND

To know the French scene, there is no real substitute for a visit, and preferably one at leisure. Raoul Blanchard, a distinguished French geographer, and one of his students, Millicent Todd, produced a brief and still usable *Geography of France* just after World War I (New York: Rand, McNally, 1919). That by H. Ormsby, *France, a Regional and Economic Geography* (New York: E. P. Dutton, 1938), is much more detailed; and for those who read French, there is a host of works from the pens of French geographers, long leaders in the field, with excellent maps and illustrations, not only of the great monuments but of regional architecture in its local physiographic setting. Jean Brunhes' two volumes on the *Géographie humaine de la France*, in Gabriel Hanotaux's *Histoire de la Nation française* (Paris: Plon-Nourrit, 1920–29), are good examples; they are copiously and beautifully illustrated.

3. THE PEOPLE

No two observers will ever agree on the subject of national characteristics. Perhaps the most sensitive assessment is by a German scholar, E. R. Curtius, *The Civilization of France* (New York: Macmillan, 1932), who has written with more understanding and objectivity than his ambivalently admiring and captious compatriot, Friedrich Sieberg, *Who Are these French?* (New York: Macmillan, 1932). Albert L. Guérard has written a balanced and interesting *French Civilization in the Nineteenth Century* (New York: Century, 1918), which is both historical and topical. The analysis by the Spanish scholar, Salvador de Madariaga, is often suggestive but will be too rigid for some—*Englishmen, Frenchmen, Spaniards* (London: Oxford University Press, 1929). André Siegfried is stimulating, as always, in his *France, a Study in Nationality* (New Haven: Yale University Press, 1930), but many of his views will now be considered old fashioned by the new generation of social scientists. The distinguished student of nationalism, Carlton J. H. Hayes, made a study in the twenties when many people viewed French nationalism as much more explosive than they did a decade later—*France: a Nation of Patriots* (New York: Columbia University Press, 1930).

4. GOVERNMENT

On the complicated and little understood French governmental scene, there are the rapid moving and anecdotal study by W. L. Middleton, *The French Political System* (London: E. Benn, 1932), the thoughtful account by Robert K. Gooch, "The Government and Politics of France" in James T. Shotwell, *Governments of Continental Europe* (New York: Macmillan, 1945), and the broader and more detailed study by Walter Rice Sharp, *The Government of the French Republic* (New York: Van Nostrand, 1938). More specialized, but highly informative, studies are those by Sharp, *The French Civil Service: Bureaucracy in Transition* (New York: Macmillan, 1931), and Gooch, *The French Parliamentary Committee System* (New York and London: Appleton-Century, 1935).

5. FRANCO-AMERICAN RELATIONS

A very large part of the material on the broad subject of the relations of France and the United States during the past two centuries is fragmentary. The study by Howard Mumford Jones, *America and French Culture* (Chapel Hill: University of North Carolina Press, 1927) is basic; that by André Tardieu, *France and America: Some Experiences in Coöperation* (Boston and New

York: Houghton Mifflin, 1927) is highly informative for the period of World War I. Elizabeth Brett White has canvassed a tremendous sweep of the press and periodical literature in her *American Opinion of France* (New York: Knopf, 1927). Standard works on American foreign policy are those by Thomas A. Bailey, *A Diplomatic History of the American People* (4th ed., New York: Appleton-Century-Crofts, 1950) and Samuel Flagg Bemis, *A Diplomatic History of the United States* (3rd ed., New York: Holt, 1950). The reader may consult also Archibald Cary Coolidge, *The United States as a World Power* (New York: Macmillan, 1908), which is older but full of wisdom, and the brief and stimulating interpretation, *The Evolution of American Foreign Policy* (New York: Oxford, 1948) by Dexter Perkins, whose more specialized works deal with the Monroe Doctrine. *The Giant of the Western World, America and Europe in a North-Atlantic Civilization* (New York: William Morrow and Co., 1930) by Francis Miller and Helen Hill is very suggestive.

6. DEFEAT, OCCUPATION, LIBERATION

On the years prior to the collapse of 1940, most of the literature is ephemeral and some of it is hysterical. A solid and balanced narrative of events is presented in the various books by the correspondent of the *Manchester Guardian*, Alexander Werth, a number of whose works have been brought together in a somewhat abbreviated form as *The Twilight of France, 1933–1940* (New York and London: Harper, 1942). The fundamental work in English on French foreign policy is that by Arnold Wolfers, *Britain and France between Two Wars, Conflicting Strategies of Peace since Versailles* (New York: Harcourt, Brace, 1940). Elizabeth R. Cameron has described the vestibule to appeasement—*Prologue to Appeasement, a Study in French Foreign Policy, 1933–1936* (Washington: American Council on Public Affairs, 1942). Charles A. Micaud has documented the extraordinary about-face in foreign policy of the French Right under the impact of the rise of the Communist "menace" at home and abroad—*The French Right and Nazi Germany, 1933–1939, a Study of Public Opinion* (Durham, N. C.: Duke University Press, 1943). John W. Wheeler-Bennett has written the basic book on the "great appeasement" and the five years preceding—*Munich, Prologue to Tragedy* (New York: Duell, Sloan and Pearce, 1948); there is at the end a very useful list of books for further reading on this period. The various volumes of Winston Churchill's *The Second World War* (Boston: Houghton Mifflin, 1948 ff.) place French events in the broader setting of European developments and include the great Britisher's comments on critical French problems. From the pen of the very able American journalist, Edmond Taylor, we have a penetrating view of the German conduct of the "phony" war in France in his *Strategy of Terror* (Boston: Houghton Mifflin, 1942). The pages of the French journalist, André Geraud ("Pertinax") are as somber and doom-filled as those of Tacitus–*The Gravediggers of France* (New York: Doubleday Doran, 1944); the narrative often needs checking with other sources. Theodore Draper has written a fast-moving and useful account of the military collapse, *The Six Weeks' War: France May 10–June 25, 1940* (New York: Viking, 1944), although this can only stand as a preliminary statement on a subject which will be investigated for years to come. Hamilton Fish Armstrong's account, *Chronology of Failure: the Last Days of the French Republic* (New York: Macmillan, 1940), is out of date, but gives a significant sense of the dramatic impact of these events on contemporaries.

Perhaps the most useful single account in English of the Vichy interlude and the post-Liberation months is Dorothy Pickles' brief book, *France between the Republics* (London and Redhill: Love and Malcomson, 1946). For conditions in occupied France, see Thomas D. Kernan, *France on Berlin Time* (Philadelphia and New York: Lippincott, 1941). The *locus classicus* for American policy is *Our Vichy Gamble* (New York: Knopf, 1947) by William L. Langer, who was given full access to the papers of the Department of State. Louis Gottschalk's is only one of many replies to Professor Langer's volume–"Our Vichy Fumble," *Journal of Modern History*, March 1948, pp. 47–56. The biographies and memoirs which throw light on our policy toward Vichy and de Gaulle are already numerous. Mr. Hull's full, invaluable, and querulous account–*The Memoirs of Cordell Hull* (2 vols., New York: Macmillan, 1948)–contrasts in tone with the memoirs of General Eisenhower–*Crusade in Europe* (New York: Doubleday, 1948); the latter is loath to criticize others and readily assumes blame himself, e.g.: "Bringing Peyrouton to Algeria as governor was a mistake . . ." (p. 131). In his *I Was There* (New York: McGraw-Hill, 1950), Fleet Admiral William D. Leahy writes an almost half-hearted defense of his important role in our Vichy policy. Secretary Stimson saw the de Gaulle issue before and after D-Day with great clarity–Henry L. Stimson and McGeorge Bundy, *On Active Service in Peace and War* (New York: Harper,

1947). Robert L. Sherwood throws interesting light on various phases of our wartime policy toward France—*Roosevelt and Hopkins, an Intimate History* (New York: Harper, 1948). For the naval side of the North African invasion, see the stirring account by Samuel Eliot Morison, *Operations in North African Waters, October 1942–June 1943* (Boston: Little Brown, 1947).

For the scattered materials on the Resistance, see Fred L. Hadsel, "Some Sources on the Resistance Movement in France during the Nazi Occupation," *Journal of Modern History*, December 1946, pp. 333–340. A. J. Liebling has gathered an important selection of Resistance writings, accompanied by his own inimitable interstitial pieces—*The Republic of Silence* (New York: Harcourt, Brace, 1947). A penetrating and important account of Communist activity during the war is that by a former Communist, Angelo Rossi, *A Communist Party in Action; an Account of the Organization and Operations in France* (New Haven: Yale University Press, 1949). For the flavor of the Resistance, see Guillain de Bénouville, *The Unknown Warriors, a Personal Account of the French Resistance* (New York: Simon and Schuster, 1949).

The documentation on General de Gaulle is scattered, inadequate, controversial, and mostly in French. The most useful biography is Philippe Barrès, *Charles de Gaulle* (New York: Brentano's, 1941), which obviously suffers from having been written early. The General's famous prewar book on the importance of a small, mechanized, professional force has been translated as *The Army of the Future* (Philadelphia and New York: Lippincott, 1941). There is an English collection of the wartime speeches, *The Speeches of General de Gaulle* (London and New York: Oxford, 1944).

7. CONTEMPORARY PROBLEMS

An excellent coöperative book of essays on a wide spectrum of contemporary and recent French problems, which the writer has read in manuscript, will have appeared before this book is published—Edward Mead Earle, editor, *Modern France, Problems of the Third and Fourth Republics* (Princeton: Princeton University Press, 1951). It will be followed at a somewhat later date by a second volume on France in the thirties and the forties, fruit of a seminar at the Institute of Advanced Study at Princeton in the autumn of 1950, attended by scholars from France, Britain, and the United States, and written by Edward Whiting Fox.

Economic Problems. The reader can examine the broad background of French economic development in the solid but somewhat old-fashioned book by the distinguished British economic historian, J. H. Clapham—*The Economic Development of France and Germany, 1815–1914* (4th ed., Cambridge: The University Press, 1936), or in *France, a History of National Economics, 1789–1939* (New York: Scribner, 1939) by Shepard B. Clough, who looks at economic problems in terms of government intervention to achieve national objectives. On the period of the past 35 years, the reader who has French will find two books in particular rewarding: Charles Rist and Gaetan Pirou, editors, *De la France d'avant guerre à la France d'aujourd'hui* (Paris: Librairie du Recueil Sirey, 1939), a coöperative work by leading French experts on a wide range of economic problems, 1914–1939; and Charles Bettelheim, *Bilan de l'économie française, 1919–1946* (Paris: Presses universitaires de France, 1947), which has numerous fresh insights. Less useful is the work by W. F. Ogburn and W. Jaffe: *The Economic Development of Post-war France* (New York: Columbia University Press, 1929). Neil Hunter has written interestingly and competently on French agriculture in a broad setting in *Peasantry and Crisis in France* (London: V. Gollancz, 1938). On the labor movement, see David J. Saposs; *The Labor Movement in Post-war France* (New York: Columbia University Press, 1931), and the excellent book by Henry W. Ehrmann, *French Labor from Popular Front to Liberation* (New York: Oxford University Press, 1947).

Materials on post-Liberation development in general are scattered for the most part in the press, periodicals, and government reports. On the Marshall Plan in its specific application to France, the reader can consult the convenient reports of the Economic Coöperation Administration for 1948—*European Recovery Program, France, 1948* (Paris: December 31, 1948) and *European Recovery Program, France, Country Study* (Washington: February 1949). These need to be supplemented by the valuable periodical reports of the Special Mission to France. On the broader aspects of the Marshall Plan, there is a considerable literature, from which the following may be suggested. Barbara Ward, the able commentator of the staff of the London *Economist*, has placed the Marshall Plan in the broad setting of the urgent problem of strengthening the western world in *The West at Bay* and *Policy for the West* (New York: Norton, 1948 and 1951, respectively). See also Howard S. Ellis *The Economics of Freedom, the Progress and Future of Aid to Europe* (New York: Harper, 1950) and Charles P. Kindleberger, *The Dollar Shortage* (Cambridge and New York: Technology Press of the Massachusetts Institute of Technology and Wiley, 1950). Seymour E. Harris has written one book on the Marshall Plan, *The European Recovery Program,* and edited a second coöperative work by a group of leading economists on problems reaching well beyond ERP, *Foreign Economic Policy for the United States* (both Cambridge: Harvard University Press, 1948). Edward S. Mason gives a balanced picture of his Barbara Weinstock lecture at the University of California, *Economics vs. Politics in International Relations, the European Recovery Program* (Berkeley: University of California, 1948). Mr. Mason was also deputy to Gordon Gray, hence had prime responsibility for the preparation of the so-called "Gray Report" on the Marshall Plan and connected problems–*Report to the President on Foreign Economic Policies* (Washington: U. S. Government Printing Office, November 10, 1950). The reader who wishes more detailed information can profitably consult the quarterly reports of the Economic Coöperation Administration. Various publications of the Organization for European Economic Coöperation and of the Economic Commission for Europe are also relevant.

The basic materials on the original "Monnet Plan" and its successor, The Long Term Program, have been issued by the Monnet office in Paris. See particularly the original plan–Commissariat Général du Plan de Modernisation et d'Equipement, *Rapport général sur le Premier Plan de Modernisation et d'Equipement* (Paris, November 1946). This has been followed by periodic reports of progress and a series of reports by special committees on different aspects of the economy, e.g., coke and gas industries, telecommunications, etc.

Political Problems. There is a whole literature in French–most of it ephemeral–on the post-Liberation political scene. Unfortunately, there is very little in English. Gordon Wright has written a balanced, penetrating, and often witty book, *The Reshaping of French Democracy* (New York: Reynal and Hitchcock, 1948), which analyzes the political evolution of France and the struggle to give the country a new constitution (Mr. Wright's "Bibliographical Note" will guide those who wish to go farther). Arthur M. Schlesinger, Jr., deals on a world plane with the question so fundamental to the building of a viable democracy in France, the evocation of a non-Communist Left–*The Vital Center, the Politics of Freedom* (Boston: Houghton Mifflin, 1949). H. Stuart Hughes presents a more skeptical view of "The Tottering Center" in a fresh interpretation of the nature of the twentieth century–*An Essay for Our Times* (New York: Knopf, 1950).

France Overseas. There is again relatively little in English on France overseas. The best general book is still that by an Australian scholar, Stephen Roberts, *History of French Colonial Policy, 1870–1925* (2 vols., London: P. S. King and Son, 1929). For the impact of the West on the colonial peoples of Southeast Asia, see especially the penetrating and finely chiseled statement by Cora DuBois, *Social Forces in Southeast Asia* (Minneapolis: University of Minnesota Press, 1949). Constant Southworth, in *The French Colonial Venture* (London: P. S. King and Son, 1931), attacks the problem: how worth while are colonies from an economic point of view? The French have written extensively on the empire, though at times in an apologetic vein. See especially the interesting collection of historical studies under the editorship of Gabriel Hanotaux and Alfred Martineau, *Histoire des colonies françaises et de l'Expansion de la France dans le monde* (6 vols., Paris: Plon, 1929–1933).

The International Scene. By definition this rubric must place France in a broad setting. Of the very numerous general books on international affairs which have appeared during the past half dozen years, see especially the two fundamental books by Sumner Welles, *The Time for Decision* (New York: Harper, 1944) and *Where Are We Heading?* (New York: Harper, 1946). Two books which deal with a wide sweep of international problems from an analytical point of view are Hans J. Morgenthau, *Politics among Nations* (New York: Knopf, 1949) and Robert Strausz-Hupé and Stefan T. Possony, *International Relations in the Age of the Conflict between Democracy and Dictatorship* (New York: McGraw-Hill, 1950). Both have substantial and useful bibliographies on each subject treated, and will enable the reader to find his way through the really massive, but very uneven, literature on this broad subject. John Foster Dulles, *War or Peace* (New York: Macmillan, 1950), is a penetrating analysis of the ills to which our present world is subject, but it is distinctly weaker on what to do about them beyond the necessary immediate building of military strength.

8. CURRENT DEVELOPMENTS

The New York Times, the *New York Herald-Tribune*, and *The Christian Science Monitor* all give serious and understanding attention to France, although the extent of coverage has declined in recent years with the reorientation of American interest. They are naturally no substitute for the much fuller coverage by the

French newspapers, of which the most useful for the American are *Le Monde* and *Figaro*, both conservative in tendency but offering a rich fare of thoughtful special articles.

Foreign Affairs, quarterly review published by The Council on Foreign Relations, offers serious articles by scholars and men of affairs and an indispensable critical bibliography of works on international affairs. The Foreign Policy Association publishes a series of *Foreign Policy Reports* which deal from time to time with French questions of key importance. *The Economist* (London) is almost indispensable for articles on France and the Continent, which are in no sense narrowly economic but range over the whole field of politics and international affairs. *The Atlantic Monthly*, *Harper's*, *The Yale Review*, *The Political Science Quarterly*, and *Current History* all publish articles on France from time to time, aimed more at the general reader than at the specialist. The Council on Foreign Relations publishes an annual volume, *The United States in World Affairs* (the most recent volume by Richard P. Stebbins), which reviews American policy for the year past. The Brookings Institution publishes a periodical *Summary of Developments in Major Problems of United States Foreign Policy*. *The Department of State Bulletin* (weekly) publishes speeches by leading American officials, key documents, and articles on questions of importance.

For those who use French, the key post-Liberation handbook is *L'Année Politique* (Paris: Éditions du Grand Siècle), edited annually by André Siegfried and others and analyzing the domestic French and foreign scene on a month-by-month basis.

INDEX

Accessibility, geographical, of France, 15
Acheson, Dean, 157
Adams, John, 83
Adams, John Quincy, 86; on Spoliation Claims, 87–88
Africa, French possessions in, 218–219
Agriculture, 17, 137–142; Long Term Program, 163–164; persons fed per agricultural worker, 296; size of holdings, 297; comparative data on industries and, 297–298; losses in World War II, 305
Algeciras convention, 95
Algeria, 218, 223; nationalist movement, 228
Algiers, "Manifesto of the Algerian People," 225
Alps, 12, 14
Alsace, 15, 18
Alsace-Lorraine, annexation of, 92
America Comes of Age (Siegfried), 102
American dream, 1–2
American Field Service, 96
American Revolution, French aid in, 77–81
Ampère, André Marie, 3
Anglophobia, French, 119
Annam. *See* Indochina
"À nous la Liberté," 41
Anticlericalism, 47, 48, 49, 184
Antimony, 16
Aquitaine, Basin of, 12
Area, of France and overseas empire, 11, 285, 288–289
Armistice, French, of 1940, 116–121
Armstrong, Hamilton Fish, quoted, 111
Army, remaking of, 255–256
Aron, Raymond, on Great Depression in France, 111
Arrondissement, 53
Artisans, 27–28
Assembly. *See* National Assembly
Atlantic Community, 10
Atlantic Pact powers. *See* North Atlantic Treaty
Atomic bomb, 260, 261, 265
Atomic power, European background of American achievement, 3
Axis of fertility, 20

Bailey, Thomas A., on Franco-American friendship, 91
Balance of payments, 157–158, 302
Balance of power, postwar concept of, 245–246
Bank of France, 213; nationalization of, 170
Bao Dai, and Viet Nam, 234, 238, 240, 242, 243; recognized by United States and Britain, 241
Barthou, Jean Louis, 114
Basques, 15
Bastille, fall of, 82
Bauxite, 16
Beaumarchais, Pierre Caron de, 78
Becquerel, A. H., 3
Bergson, Henri, 23
Bernard, Claude, 3

Bettelheim, Charles, on decline of French industry, 142–143
Bidault, Georges, 184, 190, 191
Birth rate, 22–25, 286
Bizerte, 120
Blanquists, 193
Bloc des Gauches, 179
Blum, Léon, 23, 24, 114, 196, 198; and Popular Front, 32, 57, 68, 111, 173, 194; on legislative and executive, 61; proposals for parliamentary reform, 66–67; loan negotiations with United States, 156; return from German prison camp, 195. *See also* Popular Front
Bonapartism, resurgence of, 58
Bonnet, 114, 181
Books published (1949), 293
Bookstores, 293
Bordeaux, 54; French government at, 117
Bourbon Monarchy, return of, 85
Bourgeoisie, 29–33; *haute bourgeoisie*, 33–35
Bretons, 15
Briand, Aristide, 55, 114, 189
British, self-discipline of, 40–41. *See also* Great Britain
Brittany, fishing industry, 13, 221; climate, 18
Budget, control of, under Third Republic, 65; effect of World War I on, 147
Buildings, destruction of, in World War II, 308
Bureaucracy, French and American, 56–57
Business, role of family in, 34; French attitude toward, 143–145

Cabinet, French. *See* Council of Ministers
Callender, Harold, on Monnet, 162
Calvinists, 46
Cambodia, independence guaranteed, 241–242
Cambodians, 233
Canning, George, 85–86
Canton, administrative division, 53
Cash, losses in World War II, 306. *See also* Money
Castellane, Boni de, 33–34
Castex, Admiral, on French overextension, 218
Catholicism, French, 37, 45–49; separation of Church and State, 48–49, 189–190. *See also* MRP
Caution, as French characteristic, 39–40
Ce Soir, Communist organ, 214
CFTC, Catholic trade union organization, 176–177, 189
CGE, activities of, 128–129
CGT, national confederation of trade unions, 28, 169, 172, 173–177; Communist domination, 196–197, 215–216
CGTU, 173–174
Chamber of Deputies, under Third Republic, 61, 62–65
Champlain Tercentenary, 94
Characteristics, of French, historical background, 36–37, 43; conservatism, 38; caution, 39–40; individualism, 40–41; energy, 41; courage, 41–42; influence of *lycée*, 43; logical attack, 43–44; American and French outlook on life, 44–45; religion, 45–49; nationalism, 49–50
Charles X, King of France, 86, 107
Charter of Amiens, 173
Charter of the Resistance, 168
Chemical industry, 16
Chinese, French compared with, 36; in Indochina, 231
Church, position of, 45–48
Church and State, separation of, 48–49, 189–190
Churchill, Winston, 118, 200; on proposed removal of French government to Africa, 121; on Western European Union, 265
Cité Universitaire, 209

Cities, growth of, 21–22; population, 287
Civic virtue, French lack of, 40
Clair, René, 41
Class structure, 25; peasants, 25–27; proletariat, 27–28; artisans, 27–28; middle class, 29–33; *haute bourgeoisie*, 33–35
Classe supérieure. See *Haute bourgeoisie*
Clemenceau, Georges, 97–98, 114
Cleveland, Grover, 93
Climate, 17–18; temperature and precipitation, 287
Clipperton Island, 221
Coal, 16; postwar production, 151–152; American shipments to France, 156
Coalitions, center, prior to World War II, 179–180. *See also* Third Force
Cobb, Irvin, 96
Cochin China, 233, 238; Republic recognized, 239
Coherence, geographic, 11–12; economic, political, and strategic, 12–14
Cohesion, French lack of, in 1940, 112–114
Collaboration, French, in World War II, 125–126
Colonial possessions, acquisition and extent, 217–222; policy in, 222–228; nationalist movement, 229–230; Communism in, 229; area and population, 288–289. *See also* Indochina
Comité Général d'Études. *See* CGE
Commerce. *See* Foreign trade
Commin, Pierre, 198
Committee of National Liberation, Algiers, 132, 134
Common Council for American Unity, on European Recovery Program, 159
Common interests, tradition and preservation of freedom, 1–2; French civilization in development of West, 2–4; economic, 4–5; security, 5–6
Commune, as administrative division, 52–53
Commune, Paris (1871), 92
Communications system, restoration of, 151; losses in World War II, 306, 307
Communism, contrasted with Socialism, 191–192; in French colonies, 229; in Southeast Asia, 240–241, 243
Communist Party, French, 28, 35, 41, 180, 194; in post-Liberation period, 68–72; underground activities, 113–114; in Resistance movement, 128; campaign of strikes, 157; and labor movement, 172–177; domination of CGT, 196–197; affinities with Gaullists, 199–200; organization, 207–211; nonparty support, 211–212; rural strength, 212–213; financial power, 213; press, 214; schools, 214; activities and fluctuations, 214–216; threat of, 216; plans for wartime underground, 256–257; defense against, in hypothetical war, 257–258
Compton, Dr. Karl, on American achievement in atomic power, 3
Concordat of 1801, 48
Confédération Française des Travailleurs Chrétiens. *See* CFTC
Confédération Générale du Travail. *See* CGT
Confédération Générale du Travail Unifié. *See* CGTU
Confucianism, in Indochina, 234
Congress of Tours, 194
Conseil supérieur de la magistrature, 71
Conservatism, French, 38
Constitution, of 1791, 59; of 1848, 59; of 1875, 58–59, 61; of 1946, 59, 61, 69–72
Containment, policy of, 260–261,

267–268; role of France in, 262–263
Continental System, Napoleon's, 84, 86
Coolidge, Archibald Cary, on French aid in Revolution and Louisiana Purchase, 84; on United States and war with Spain, 94
Coolidge, Calvin, on war debts, 102
Coöperation, French resistance to, 40–41
Council general, representative body of department, 53–54
Council of Europe, 250, 282
Council of Ministers, under Third Republic, 61
Council of the Republic, 67, 71, 72; party representation, 290
Courage, French, 41–42
Crèvecœur, Michel Guillaume de, 79
Cuba, 89
Curie, Pierre and Marie, 3
Curtius, Ernst, on French countryside, 138
Cuvier, Georges, 3
Czechoslovakia, French alliance with, 115; German absorption of, 116

Dakar, 219
Daladier, Édouard, 113, 114, 181
Darlan, Admiral, 122
Davis, Richard Harding, 96
Dawes mission, 104
Dean, Vera Micheles, quoted, 216
Death rate, 24, 286
Debt problem, after World War I, 102–105
Declaration of Principles (1946), 71
Declaration of Rights, of allied French Communists and Socialists, 70, 71
"Declaration of the Rights of Man and Citizen," 81
Defeat of 1940, 110–116
Defense expenditures, 309
DeGaulle, Charles, 112, 119, 190, 226, 255; influence of, 32, 124, 252–254; idea of proportional representation, 69; leads French Resistance, 71–72, 127, 128; faith in victory, 118; United States and, 132–134; estimate of, 134–136, 200–207; Rally of the French People, 157, 204–205; position on nationalization, 169–170; MRP and, 187–188; on French Communist Party, 208. *See also* Gaullists
Democracy, American dream as essence of, 1–2
Department, as administrative division, 53–54
De Wendel family, 34
Diplomacy, French role in, 256
Diplomatic representation, 290
Diversity, geographical and cultural, of France, 14–15
Dreyfus Affair, 48, 93–94, 109, 180, 183–184, 193
DuBois, Cora, on white man's burden, 232–233
Duhamel, Georges, 101

ECA. *See* Economic Coöperation Administration
École de la France d'Outremer, 226
École Nationale d'Administration, 256
École Normale Supérieure, 23
Economic Coöperation Administration, 1, 165
Economy, agriculture, 137–142; industry, 142–148; World War II, 148–150; post-Liberation problems, 150–154; American contributions to relief and recovery, 155–156, 308–309; operations of European Recovery Program, 156–160; Long Term Program, 160–161, 163–167; Monnet Plan, 161–162; nationalization, 167–172;

organized labor, 172–178; statistics, 293–298
Éditions de Minuit, 131
Eisenhower, Dwight D., 128, 133; on French sentiment in North Africa, 122
Eliot, Charles W., 95
Emigration, French, 285
Encyclicals, papal, 59, 188
Energy, French, 41
England. *See* Great Britain
Enlightenment, eighteenth-century, 47
Entente Cordiale, Anglo-French, of 1904, 95
Equilibrium in balance of payments, 157–158
ERP. *See* European Recovery Program
Estates General, 79, 81
Ethiopian crisis, 105
Europe. *See* Western Europe
European Economic Coöperation, 282
European Recovery Program, 271, 272, 281, 282; operations of, in France, 156–160; Communist opposition, 215–216; grants to France, 308–309
Evangelical Church, 46
Evarts, William M., 93
Export-Import Bank, loans to France, 156
Exports, statistics of, 294, 299–302. *See also* Foreign trade
Extremism, political, 199

Fairbank, John K., on American policy in Far East, 269
Family, role of, in French business, 34
Family allocations, system of, 24
Far East, French possessions in, 221; European exploitation of, 232–233; problem of American policy in, 269
Farming. *See* Agriculture
Fascist leagues, 113
Fashoda incident, 94
Faure, Félix, on presidential functions, 60
Feis, Herbert, cited, 31
Ferry, Jules, 48
FFI, organization and activities of, 128
Flanders Gateway, 14
FO. *See Force Ouvrière*
Foch, Marshal, on Rhineland, 247
Food, in occupied France, 130; level of consumption, 304
Forces Françaises de l'Intérieur. See FFI
Force Ouvrière, 175–176
Foreign policy, object of, 115; French, in 1940, 115–116; French, since Liberation, 246; American, problems of, 267–269; American, in France, 269–273
Foreign Service, American, lack of personnel, 266–267
Foreign trade, 143; with United States, 4, 301; in French recovery, 157–158; French share in, 294; distribution of, 294, 299; imports of raw materials, 299; commodity figures, 300; balance of payments, 302
Frachon, Benoît, 161
Franc, value relative to dollar, 297
France, geographical position, 8–10; size, 10–11; population, 11; economic, political, and strategic coherence, 11–14; geographical diversity, 14–15; cultural differences, 15; accessibility, 15; natural resources, 15–17; climate, 17–18; strength, 18–19; problems of American policy in, 269–273; facts about, 285–309; United States aid to, 308–309. *See also* Colonial possessions
Franco-American relations, traditional view of, 74–75; divergent national development, 75–76; colonial America and France, 76–77; France and American Revo-

lution, 77–81; French Revolution, 81–83; Napoleon, 83–85; aftermath of Napoleonic wars, 85–88; Revolutions of 1830, 1848, 1870, 88–89; Napoleon III and Mexico, 89–91; Third Republic, 91–95; coöperation in World War I, 95–98; disillusionment of twenties, 98–104; in 1930's, 105
Franco-Prussian War, 91–92
Franco-Russian alliance (1944), 247
Franc-Tireur, 198
Franklin, Benjamin, 78
Free Church, 46
Freedom, tradition and preservation of, 1–2
French Committee of National Liberation, 225
French Equatorial Africa, 218, 219, 226
French Guiana, 222
French North Africa, proposed removal of French government to, 116–121; nationalist movement, 228–230
French Revolution, 31, 37, 47, 51, 107; United States and, 78–79, 81–83
French Union, 226–228. *See also* Colonial possessions
French West Africa, 218, 225–226
Fuels, 16–17

Gallatin, Albert, 86, 87
Galliéni, Joseph Simon, 223
Gambetta, Léon, on Senate under Third Republic, 67
Gamelin, Maurice Gustave, 112, 114
Gasoline, 16–17
Gaullists, program of, 180; affinities with Communists, 199–200. *See also* De Gaulle, Charles
Genêt, Citizen, 82–83
Geography, changing concept of, 7–8; geographic coherence, 11–12. *See also* France
Germany, rising power of, 94–95; frontier problem after World War I, 98; preparations for World War II, 112; pact with Soviet Union (1939), 113, 212; absorption of Czechoslovakia, 116; occupation policy in France, 149; evolution of French attitude toward, 246–250, 275–276, 281; and Schuman Plan, 250–252; rearming of, 276; dispatch of additional American troops to, 278–279; Berlin air lift, 279
Gibraltar, 80
Giraud, Henri Honoré, 134
Giraudoux, Jean, 23
Gottschalk, Louis, on Lafayette, 80
Gould, Anna, 34
Government, changes in regime, 51–52; local, 52–54; central administration, 54–57; ministries, 55–56; French and American bureaucracy compared, 56–57; role of Premier, 57; Third Republic, 58–68; post-Liberation, 68–73; statistics, 290
Grand Committees, of Chamber of Deputies, 65
Grant, Ulysses S., 91
Great Britain, in colonial America, 76–77; intervention in Mexico, 90; Entente Cordiale of 1904, 95; negotiations with Soviet Union (1939), 116; attack on French fleet at Mers-el-Kebir, 119, 122; recognition of de Gaulle, 132, 133; Dominions, 217
Great Depression, in France, 110, 113
Guadeloupe, 221–222
Guarantee, Treaty of, 98, 100
Guesde, Jules, 192
Guesdists, 193

Haiphong, massacre at, 239
Hanoi, Viet Nam attack on, 239
Harding, Warren G., 99, 258

Haute bourgeoisie, 33–35
Hawaiian Islands, 89
Hayes, Rutherford B., 92
Herriot, Édouard, 105, 117, 182
High Command, weakness of, in France, 111–112
Hill, Helen, on American tourists in France, 100
History, French and American attitudes toward, 26–38
Hitler, Adolf, 95, 105; psychological offensive, 114; appeasement of, 116; interest in North Africa, 120
Ho Chi-minh, and Viet Nam, 237–241 *passim*
Hoffman, Paul, on Marshall aid, 159
Hoover, Herbert, 99
Hoover moratorium (1931), 104
Housing, shortage of, 153, 280
Hull, Cordell, on postwar French government, 132; opposition to de Gaulle, 133
Human nature, 35
Humanité, Communist Party organ, 113, 209, 212, 214
Hydroelectric power, 17. *See also* Power

Ideas, France as fabricator of, 3–4
Immigration, labor shortage and, 152
Imports, statistics of, 294, 299–302. *See also* Foreign Trade
Independent Republicans, 186
India, French ports in, 221
Individualism, French, 40–41
Indochina, 11, 220; Japanese occupation, 119, 236–237; geographical situation, 231; social setting, 233; problems of colonization, 233–234; rise of nationalism, 234–236; postwar situation, 237; Viet Nam Republic, 237–239; triumph of Bao Dai, 240–241; Communism in, 240–241, 243; Associated States of, 241–242; French military effort, 242–243, 244*n.*, 275; American policy in, 243–244
Industrial Revolution, 13, 15, 108; and growth of cities, 21–22; regional redistribution of population, 22
Industry, 142–148; chemical, 16; textile, 16; psychology of workers, 27–28; postwar production problems, 152–153; Long Term Program, 164–167; plants and methods, 164–165; comparative data on agriculture and, 297–298; level of production, 298; level of output per man, 298; wages, 303; losses in World War II, 306. *See also* Production
Infant mortality, 24
Inflation, after World War I, 147; after World War II, 150, 303
Inland waterways, 295; losses in World War II, 307
Interim Aid Act, 158
Investments, American, in France, 4
Iron, French resources, 11, 16
Isolationism, French and American, 6; influence of World War II, 7; post-Revolutionary, in United States, 81; American, after World War I, 99, 100, 105; American, current French reaction to, 273

Jackson, Andrew, and Spoliation Claims, 87–88
Japan, occupation of Southeast Asia, 236–237
Jaurès, Jean, 23, 196, 206
Jay, John, 80
Jefferson, Thomas, 21; Minister to France, 81
Jeunesse Ouvrière Catholique. *See* JOC
Jews, 46
JOC, Catholic youth movement, 177
Joliot-Curie, Frédéric, 3, 211
Joliot-Curie, Irène, 3

Jones, Howard Mumford, 3
Jones, John Paul, 94
Jouhaux, Léon, 175
Juárez, Benito, 91
Jusserand, Jules, 95

Katz, Milton, on American dream, 1–2
Kennan, George, 157; on avoidance of war, 262
Kent, Sherman, on "Declaration of the Rights of Man and Citizen," 81–82
Koenig, General, 128
Korean crisis, evaluation of, 273–274; effects of, in France, 274–276

Labor, structure and fluctuations of, 27–28, 172–178; postwar shortage, 152–153; French inexperience with unions, 278; need for more effective non-Communist movement, 280; productivity of, 295
Lacordaire, J. B. H., 188
Lafayette, Marquis de, 79–80, 86, 95; statue of, 94
Lafayette Squadron, 96
Lagrange, Joseph Louis, 3
La Lutte, 209
Lamarck, Jean Baptiste de, 3
Lamennais, Félicité Robert de, 188
Landes, David, on business in France, 144
Laos, independence guaranteed, 241–242
Laotians, 233
Laplace, Pierre Simon de, 3
La Terre, Communist weekly, 214
Lattre de Tassigny, General de, 244
Laval, Pierre, 21, 113, 114, 118; and Vichy regime, 121–122; trial of, 130
Lavoisier, Antoine Laurent, 3
Lay spirit, 46–48
Leadership, French lack of, in 1940, 114–115; French, in international field, 256
Leahy, William D., on Pétain, 123
League of Nations, 98, 99, 100, 105
League of the Young Republic, 188, 189
Lebanon, 219
Le Havre, destruction of port, 148–149
Lend-Lease, 104; operation of, in France, 156
Lesseps, Ferdinand de, 92, 93
Letourneau, Jean, 241
Levant, French possessions in, 219
Leverrier, Urbain Jean Joseph, 3
Libraries, 293
Liebling, A. J., on French Resistance, 126–127
Life, French and American outlook on, 44–45
Lippmann, Walter, cited on Atlantic Community, 10
Lloyd George, David, War Cabinet, 66
Logical attack, as French characteristic, 43–44
Long Term Program, of French recovery, 160–161, 163
Lorient, destruction of, 149
Lorraine, climate, 18
Loti, Pierre, 221
Louis XIV, age of, 2
Louis XVIII, 86, 107
Louis Napoleon. *See* Napoleon III
Louisiana Purchase, 83–84
Louis-Philippe, King of France, 87, 88, 107–108
Lowell, A. Lawrence, on Frenchman in politics, 62
Lowell, James Russell, on French, 92
Lutherans, 46
Luxembourg Gardens, 2
Lyautey, Louis Hubert, 223
Lycée, influence of, on French character, 43
Lyons, 54; growth of, 21

MacDonald, Ramsay, 99
MacMahon, Marshal, 60, 62
Madagascar, 219
Madariaga, Salvador de, on Frenchman and Britisher, 43
Maginot Line, 43, 105, 114
Malraux, André, on Gaullism, 202
Mandel, Georges, 117
"Manifesto of the Algerian People," 225
Manpower shortage, 145–146, 152
Mao, victories in China, 240; support of Viet Minh, 243
Maritain, Jacques, 190
Marjolin, Robert, 24; on objective of French economy, 162–163
Marseilles, 54; growth of, 21; destruction of port, 148
Marshall, George C., 157; on Marshall Plan, 5
Marshall Plan, 4–5. *See also* European Recovery Program
Martinique, 221–222
Marxism, 192–193
Mauriac, François, quoted, 26
Maximilian, Emperor of Mexico, 90
Mediterranean area, climate, 18
Mendès-France, 185
Merchant marine, losses in World War II, 307
Mers-el-Kebir, British attack on French fleet at, 119, 122
Methodist Church, 46
Mexico, French invasion, 89–91; joint intervention in, 90
Middle class, 29–33
Military policy, as arm of foreign policy, 115; French, in 1940, 115–116
Military tradition, French, 255
Miller, Francis, on American tourists in France, 100
Millerand, Alexandre, 60
Millerand case, 193
Mineral resources, 16–17
Ministries, functioning of, 55–56, 57
Miquelon, 221
Mistral, 18
Moch, Jules, 196, 257, 276
Mollet, Guy, 198
Molotoff, V. M., 209
Money, French preoccupation with, 31, 44–45. *See also* Cash
Monnet, Jean, 161–162; on Schuman Plan, 251
Monnet Plan, 141–142, 154, 161–162
Monopolies, government, in France, 169
Monroe, James, 86
Monroe Doctrine, 85–86, 91
Morale, French, problem of, 258, 277–278
Morand, Paul, on French and Chinese, 36
Morison, Samuel Eliot, cited, 118
Morize, André, cited, 141
Morocco, 218; Algeciras convention, 95; French planes in, 120; nationalist movement, 229
Moslems, in French colonial possessions, 228
Mouvement Républicain Populaire. See MRP
MRP, postwar Catholic party, 49, 69-72, 73, 168, 181, 186–191
Mus, Paul, 226
Mutual Defense Assistance Program, 263

Napoleon, 46, 53, 65, 107; Concordat of 1801, 47–48; American relations with, 83–85
Napoleon III, 88, 201; reign of, 58, 61, 108; *coup d'état* of 1851, 89; invasion of Mexico, 89–91
National Assembly, 58, 61; party representation, 290
National Communist Movement, 209. *See also* Communist Party
National Council of Resistance, 129, 190
National differences, 35
National Intelligencer, on revolutions in France, 89

National Security Council, on consequences of withdrawal to Western Hemisphere, 262
Nationalism, French, 49–50; movement for, in French colonial possessions, 228–231; in Far East, 232–234; in Indochina, 234–236; American, 268–269
Nationalization, postwar, in France, 167–172
Natural resources, 15–17, 143. *See also* Raw materials
Navy, French, in 1940, 118; Vichy government and, 122–123
Nazis, growing threat of, 105. *See also* Germany
Nenni group, 192
Neutralism, 6, 275
Neutrality, French, in hypothetical war, 255
Neutrality Proclamation, Washington's, 82
New Caledonia, 221, 226
New Hebrides, 221
Nord, Department of, 22
Normandy, seafaring tradition, 13
North Africa, invasion of, in World War II, 122–123
North Atlantic Council, 263, 264
North Atlantic Drift, 17–18
North Atlantic Treaty, 282; United States and, 263–265; France and, 264–266, 279–280

Objects of Art, losses in World War II, 306
Occupation, German, and French economy, 149
Oceania, French, 221
Oran, 120
Order, French preoccupation with, 31–32
Ozanam, Antoine Frédéric, 188

Pacifism, French, in 1940, 114
Panama Canal, 92, 93
Panama scandal, 51
Paris, predominant position of, 2–3, 54–55; geographical location, 13–14; climate, 18; growth of, 22
Paris Basin, 12, 14
Parkman, Francis, 76; on British and French in North America, 77
Parti des Fusillés, 215
Parti Républicain de la Liberté, 187
Party system, French, 61–62. *See also individual parties by name*
Pas-de-Calais, Department of, 22
Pasteur, Louis, 3, 40
Peace, outlook for, 261
Peasants, 25–27; Communist concern with, 212–213
People, population as whole, 20–21; rate of population growth, 21, 22–25; growth of cities, 21–22; Industrial Revolution and regional redistribution, 22; class structure, 25; peasants, 25–27; proletariat, 27–28; artisans, 28–29; middle class, 29–33; *haute bourgeoisie*, 33–35; influence of historical background, 36–37, 43; conservatism, 38; caution, 39–40; individualism, 40–41; energy, 41; courage, 41–42; influence of *lycée*, 43; logical attack, 43–44; American and French outlook on life, 44–45; religion, 45–49; nationalism, 49–50. *See also* Population
Perkins, Dexter, on Monroe Doctrine, 91; on American outlook, 94
Personality, losses in World War II, 306
Pertinax, on Gamelin, 112
Pétain, Henri Philippe, 118, 119, 190; on defeat of 1940, 114–115; and Vichy regime, 121–122, 123, 124, 127
Petroleum, 16–17
Petsche, Finance Minister in Pleven cabinet, 276
Philosophy of Command (de Gaulle), 200

Pius XI, Pope, 189
Pleven, René, 57, 186, 190; government, 188, 276
Poincaré, Jules Henri, 3
Poincaré, Raymond, 55, 60, 114, 147, 184
Poland, defeat of, in World War II, 112; French alliance with, 115; British and French guarantee of boundaries, 116
Policy, American, since independence, 75; French colonial, 222–228. *See also* Foreign policy
Politics, influence of, on industry, 146
Poole, DeWitt, conception of Right and Left, 199
Popular Democratic Party, 188–189
Popular Front, 32, 35, 68, 113, 169, 173, 174, 183, 194
Population, of French empire, 11; statistics, 285–287, 293. *See also* People
Portes, Madame de, 118
Ports, 13; destruction of, in World War II, 148–149
Possessions. *See* Colonial possessions
Possibilists, 193
Power, use of, 296
Pravda, 209
Precipitation, 287
Prefect, role of, in departmental government, 54
Premier, role of, 57; under Third Republic, 61, 62, 64
President, powers of, under Third Republic, 59–61; in post-liberation government, 71–72
Press, French underground, in World War II, 128; political affiliation and circulation, 292
Price controls, 268
Privateers, French, in West Indies, 83
PRL. *See* Republican Liberty Party
Production, postwar, 152–153; world, French share in, 293; industrial, level of, 298; consumption of energy, 298. *See also* Industry
Proletariat. *See* Working class
Proportionalism, in French electoral system, 69
Protestantism, French, 46
Proust, Marcel, 33
Publishers, 293
Pyrenees, 12, 14

Queuille, Henri, 204; government, 35, 153, 159, 276

Race, Nazi distortion of term, 35
Racial areas, 20–21. *See also* People
Racialism, in France and possessions, 222–223
Radical Socialist Party, 32; history and analysis of, 181–185. *See also* Socialist Party
Radioactivity, discovery of, 3
Railroads, 295; restoration of, 151; losses in World War II, 307
Rally of the French People, 156, 185; affinities with Communists, 199–200; fluctuations and progress, 204–205
Ramadier, 184
Rassemblement Démocratique Révolutionnaire. *See* RDR
Rassemblement des Gauches Républicaines, 185
Raw materials, postwar shortages, 152; statistics, 294, 299. *See also* Natural resources
RDR, 198
Real estate, losses in World War II, 306
Rearmament, of Western Europe, 254; French, 160, 275, 277, 280, 282; German, 276
Recovery. *See* European Recovery Program; Long Term Program; Monnet Plan; Schuman Plan
Reformed Church of France, 46
Reign of Terror, 82, 107
Relations. *See* Franco-American relations

Relief, American contributions to, 155–156. *See also* European Recovery Program
Religion, 45–49. *See also* Catholicism
Rent controls, 153–154
Reparations problem, after World War I, 103–104
Republican Liberty Party, 186
Republicanism, rise of, in France, 58. *See also* Third Republic
Resistance Charter, 129
Resistance Movement, 42–43, 125–131; UDSR, 185–186; Social Catholics in, 186, 190; role of Socialists in, 194–195. *See also* De Gaulle, Charles
Retail trade, 145
Review of Reviews, on corruption in French society, 93
Revolution of 1830, 107–108
Revolution of 1848, 108
Reynaud, Paul, Premier, 113, 114, 118,255
Rhineland, 98, 115, 247, 248
Rhône-Saône Depression, 12
Rivers, 12–13
Road transport system, 295; losses in World War II, 307
Rochambeau, Comte de, statue of, 94
Rodin, Auguste, 94
Rommel, Erwin, 120
Roosevelt, Franklin D., 258; on Lafayette, 79; opposition to de Gaulle, 133; garden hose metaphor, 155
Roosevelt, Theodore, 94, 95
Rothschild family, 34
Roubaix, growth of, 21–22
Roumania, British and French guarantee of boundaries, 116
RPF. *See* Rally of the French People
Ruggles, Richard, on gross investment, 166
Ruhr, 102, 247, 248
Russia, rise of, as power, 10; French alliance with, 93. *See also* Soviet Union

Saar, 98, 247–250
Sahara, 218
Saint Étienne, growth of, 22
St. Pierre, 221
Sangnier, Marc, 189
Saratoga, Battle of, 78
Sarraut, Albert, 224
Sartre, Jean-Paul, on French Resistance, 131
Saving, French preoccupation with, 30, 31, 40
Scènes de la Vie future (Duhamel), 101–102
Schlesinger, Arthur, Jr., cited, 175
Schneider family, 34
Schumacher, Kurt, on Schuman Plan, 251
Schuman, Robert, 191, 204, 276
Schuman Plan, 248, 250–252, 256, 276, 282
Sea, role of, in French history, 13
Section Française de l'Internationale Ouvrière. *See* SFIO
Securities, losses in World War II, 306
Security, French preoccupation with, 31, 39, 100, 102
Seine system, 13
Self-discipline, British, 40–41
Senate, under Third Republic, 67–68. *See also* Council of the Republic
Separation Law, Church and State, 48–49
Seven Years' War, 77
Seward, William H., 90
SFIO, 193
Sherwood, Robert, 93
Siegfried, André, 138; on French conservatism, 38; on French resistance to coöperation, 41; on religion and politics, 46; on Franco-American relations, 96; *America Comes of Age*, 102; on Radical Socialists, 182

Sillon movement, 189
Smoot-Hawley Act (1930), 104
Social Catholic Party. *See* MRP
Socialism, contrasted with Communism, 191–192
Socialist Party, 28, 127; in post-Liberation period, 69–72, 73; nationalization program, 169; *Force Ouvrière*, 175–176; in Third Force, 180; history and analysis of, 191–198. *See also* Radical Socialist Party
Société Indochinoise d'Électricité, 225 *n.*
Society. *See* Class structure
Sonora, State of, 89
South, position of, in Revolutions of 1848 and 1870, 88–89
Soviet Union, pact with Germany (1939), 113; French alliance with (1936), 115; British and French negotiations with (1939), 116; pact with Germany (1909), 212; threat to France, 246; Franco-Russian alliance (1944), 247; influence of, on present-day France, 254; danger of, 259–262. *See also* Russia
Spain, in American Revolution, 80; revolt of colonies, 85; intervention in Mexico, 90; Franco, recognition of, 124
Spanish-American War, 94, 95
Spoliation Claims, 86–88
Stassen, Harold, 191
Statue of Liberty, 93
Stavisky scandal, 51, 56
Stimson, Henry L., 133
Strasbourg Congress, 209
Suggested reading, 310–319
Sun Yat-sen, 235
Syria, 219; French forces in, 120

Tahiti, 89, 221
Tardieu, André, on French deputies, 63–64; on American relief in World War I, 96; High Commissioner to United States, 96
Tariffs, 143–144
Tax evasion, 40
Tax system, 280
Temperature, 287
Texas, independence of, 88
Textile industry, 16
Thiers, Adolphe, 33
Third Force, 73; membership and tenets, 180–181; Radical Socialists, 181–185; MRP, 181, 186–191; UDSR, 185–186; Independent Republicans, 186; Republican Liberty Party, 186; Socialist Party, 191–198
Third International, 193
Third Republic, 52, 108–109; Church in, 48; origin, 58; government of, 58–68; Constitution of 1875, 58–59, 61; presidential function, 59–61; role of Premier and Council of Ministers, 61, 62, 64; Chamber of Deputies, 61, 62–65; party system, 61–62; governmental instability, 62, 64; lack of budget control, 65; reform proposals, 65–67; Senate, 67–68; American relations with, 91–95; center coalitions, 179–180
Thompson, Richard W., 92
Thorez, Maurice, 209
Thorp, Willard, on postwar exports to France, 156
Titoism, 209
Tonkin, 233, 238, 243
Toulouse, 54
Tourists, American, in France after World War I, 99–100; French, in United States, 101–102; in French recovery, 158
Tours, 117
Trade. *See* Foreign trade
Transportation, 12–13, 295; losses in World War II, 306, 307
Treaty of 1783, 80–81
Truman, Harry S, on ending of Lend-Lease, 104
Tunisia, 218, 230; French forces in, 120

UDSR, 185–186
Underground, French. *See* Resistance movement
Unemployment, 111
Union Démocratique et Socialiste de la Résistance. *See* UDSR
Union Française, 226–228. *See also* Colonial possessions
Unions, French inexperience with, 278. *See also* Labor
United States, in postwar world, 258–260; foreign policy problems, 267–269; aid to France, 308–309
Unity, French lack of, in 1940, 112–114
Universities, enrollments, 291; social origin of students, 291

Valmy, Battle of, 82
Varenne, Alexandre, 226
Vercors, 131
Vergennes, Charles Gravier de, 77–78, 80
Vichy regime, 121–125; resistance to, 125–131
Viet Minh, 237, 239; Chinese support of, 243; defeat by French and Viet Nam forces, 244 *n.*
Viet Nam, 237–239; independence guaranteed, 241–242; defeat of Viet Minh forces, 244 *n.*
Viviani, René, on budget control, 65
Voltaire (François Aroue), on Canada, 77

Wages, control of, 177–178; problem of, 278; of male workers, 303
Waldeck-Rousseau, P.M.R., 180
War matériel, losses in World War II, 306
War of 1812, 84–85
War potential, French lack of, in 1940, 111
Washington, George, 78, 80; Proclamation of Neutrality, 82
Washington Conference of 1922, 102
Wealth, concentration of, 33
West, French civilization in development of, 2–4
West Indies, 82, 83; French possessions in, 221–222
Western Europe, critical position of, 260–262
Western Hemisphere, French possessions in, 221; consequences of withdrawal to, 262
Weygand, Maxime, 117
Weygand Line, 117
Wilson, Woodrow, 97–98, 99
Working class, 27–28; unrepresented in recent French governments, 197; wages, 278, 303
World War I, losses, 23–24; Franco-American coöperation, 95–98; effects on French industry, 146–148; French clergy in, 189
World War II, 105; effects of, on France, 24, 148–150, 305–309; historical setting in France, 106–110; debacle of 1940, 110–116; problem of French armistice, 116–121; United States and Vichy, 121–125; Resistance Movement in France, 125–131; United States and de Gaulle, 132–136; effects of, in United States, 155
Wright, Gordon, on Fourth Republic, 68; on Vichy regime, 125

XYZ affair, 83

Yalta Conference, 253
Yorktown Centenary, 93
Young mission, 104
Youth, French distrust of, 39

FRANCE
CITIES AND TOWNS
Over 500,000
100,000 to 500,000
50,000 to 100,000
Under 50,000
TERRAIN
Mountains
Plateaus and Hills
Plains
RAILROADS AND INDUSTRY
Main R. R.
Major Industrial Areas Of France
French Ironfields
French Coalfields
0 50 100 150 Miles
0 50 100 150 200 Kilometres
Thames R.
LONDON
SOUTHAMPTON
PLYMOUTH
Boulogne
ENGLISH CHANNEL
le Tréport
Dieppe
Cherbourg
GUERNSEY
CHANNEL ISLANDS
JERSEY
LE HAVRE
ROUEN
Caen
NORMANDY
Seine R.
Granville
St. Malo
Brest
BRITTANY
Versailles
Quimper
RENNES
Laval
Lorient
le Mans
Sarthe
Angers
St. Nazaire
NANTES
Loire R.
Saumur
Tours
Cher R.
GÂTINE HILLS
Poitiers
Indre R.
Niort
La Rochelle
Rochefort
LIMOUSIN PLATEAU
Creuse
BAY OF BISCAY
LIMOGES
MASSIF
Tulle
BORDEAUX
Dordogne R.
Garonne R.
Montauban
Adour R.
Bayonne
TOULOUSE
San Sebastian
GASCONY
PYRENEES
SPAIN
Ebro R.
ANDOR